VIARTIS

PEDRO CABRAL

James Roxburgh MacClymont
William Brooks Greenlee
Pero Vaz de Caminha

PUBLISHING DATA

TITLE : Pedro Cabral

AUTHORS : James Roxburgh MacClymont, William Brooks Greenlee, Pero Vaz de Caminha

EDITORS : Keith Bridgeman, Tahira Arsham

ISBN : 978-1-906421-01-4

PUBLISHER : Viartis (http://viartis.net/publishers)

PUBLICATION DATE : 2009

PLACE OF PUBLICATION : England

LANGUAGE : English

FORMAT : Paperback

EDITION : First

TOPICS : Biography

LIBRARY CLASSIFICATION (Dewey decimal classification) : 920

SHORT DESCRIPTION : The biography of Pedro Álvares Cabral (c1467-c1520), the Portuguese commander whose fleet completed one of the greatest voyages of discovery ever made.

LONG DESCRIPTION : The biography of Pedro Álvares Cabral (c1467-c1520), the Portuguese commander of a fleet of ships that made what was then the longest voyage in history, and that was one of the greatest voyages of discovery ever made. They were the first to sail across the South Atlantic, where they discovered Brazil. They were the first to sail from America to India. They discovered Madagascar, and were the first Europeans to travel to parts of East Africa and the Middle East by the southern route, via which they established trade with India. Included are all the first hand accounts of the journey, written by Pero Vaz de Caminha, Master John, and "the anonymous narrative", and all of the reports written on their return by King Manuel, Amerigo Vespucci, Bartolomeo Marchioni, Ca' Masser, and those that appeared in "The Venetian letters" and the "The Venetian diaries".

SIZE : 229 mm x 152 mm

PAGES : 233

COPYRIGHT : © 2009 Keith Bridgeman, Tahira Arsham

INTRODUCTION

Pedro Álvares Cabral was born in Portugal, probably in 1467. When Vasco da Gama returned from India in 1499, King Manuel I chose Pedro Cabral to sail a fleet of ships to establish trade with India.

Pedro Cabral's fleet was one of the largest fleets that had ever sailed the Atlantic. It set sail for India in 1500 on what turned out to be the longest voyage in history up to that time, and one of the greatest and most influential voyages of discovery ever made.

After passing Cape Verde Islands, Pedro Cabral's fleet took a south westerly course, which led to them inadvertently becoming the first ships to sail across the South Atlantic.

On shore they encountered strange people with bodies painted and tattooed, and decorated with coverings of brilliant feathers. Their appearance and customs were entirely unlike any that the Portuguese had seen before. Pedro Cabral had discovered Brazil, writing the first page in its history, and had opened up South America to further discoveries.

The continuation of their voyage led Pedro Cabral's men to be the first to sail from America to India. They discovered Madagascar, and were the first Europeans to travel to parts of East Africa and the Middle East by the southern route. Their epic voyage continued despite the considerable loss of lives and ships.

Included are all of the first hand accounts of the journey, written by Pero Vaz de Caminha, Master John, and "the anonymous narrative", and all of the reports written on their return by King Manuel, Amerigo Vespucci, Bartolomeo Marchioni, Ca' Masser, and those that appeared in "The Venetian letters" and the "The Venetian diaries".

This voyage was the beginning of trade between Europe and the East by the Atlantic route. This caused the eventual decline of the prosperity of those nations that had conducted trade with Asia via the existing routes. Few voyages or discoverers have been of greater importance to posterity. Yet there are few that have been less appreciated during their lifetime.

CONTENTS

CONTENTS

CHAPTER 1

THE ANCESTRY OF PEDRO CABRAL

According to a family tradition the Cabraes were descended from a certain Carano or Caranus, the first king of the Macedonians and the seventh in descent from Hercules. Carano had been instructed by the Delphic Oracle to place the metropolis of his new kingdom at the spot to which he would be guided by goats, and when he assaulted Edissa his army followed in the wake of a flock of goats just as the Bulgarians drove cattle before them when they took Adrianople. The king accordingly chose two goats for his cognisance and two goats passant purpure on a field argent subsequently became the arms of the Cabraes. Herodotus knows nothing of Carano and the goats. Another and a more probably true tradition is to the effect that this family is descended from a Castilian one - the Cabreiras - and the origin of the Coat of Arms is thus explained. A certain fidalgo who was commander of a fortress at Belmonte was with the garrison being starved into submission by investing forces. Two goats were still alive in the fortress. These were killed by order of the commander, cut into quarters and thrown to the enemy, whereupon the siege was raised as it was considered by the hostile commander that it was of no use to attempt to starve a garrison that could thus waste its provisions. It is also narrated that the son of the Castellan was taken prisoner and slain and that the horns and beards of the heraldic goats are sable as a token of mourning in consequence of this event. Examples of the coat of arms could be seen in the church of São Thiago at Belmonte and, almost wholly effaced, on a flat tombstone opposite the chapel of Our Lady of the Rosary in the north nave of the Old Cathedral of Coimbra and in the Sala das Armas of the Palace of Sintra. The last-named escutcheon was painted during the reign of Emmanuel. We are not to suppose that the navigator used these arms. That privilege would belong to his elder brother, João Fernandes Cabral.

The earliest Cabral known to history is Gil Alvares de Cabral who lived in the reigns of Affonso II (1211-1223) and Sancho II (1223-1248). He married his cousin Maria Gil de Cabral and had a son called Pedro Annes who may have been the Pedro Annes who was First Gentleman of the Bedchamber to Affonso III (1248-1279). A Pedre Annes Cabral is mentioned in a Contract or Agreement between Dom Affonso, Lord of Portalegre, a son of Affonso III and the Knights of the Order of Aviz respecting certain property that the prince had in São Vicente de Elvas. This document is dated September 1288, and was therefore signed in the reign of Diniz (1279-1325). Brandão is of opinion that this Pedre Annes was not the Pedro Annes who held the office of Reposteiro mór.

A son of Pedro Annes Cabral was named Ayres Cabral. His name appears in two documents that are preserved in the Archivo do Torre do Tombo. In one of these he claims the privileges of a place of asylum for Rial in the parish of São Martinho do Valle. The other document records the act of homage that Ayres Cabral rendered in respect of the Castle of Portalegre. It would appear that Ayres Cabral had originally held the Castle from Dom Affonso, a brother of Diniz, and that, with the consent of the prince, Ayres was to be relieved of his obligations towards him and was thenceforward to hold the Castle by virtue of an act of homage paid to the king. The document is dated 15th of December, 1325. Ayres Cabral married Catharina de Loureiro and had a son named Alvaro Gil Cabral.

Alvaro Gil Cabral was an ardent supporter of the claim of the Master of Aviz to the throne and took part in his election as João I (1385-1433) when the Cortes assembled at Coimbra for the purpose of electing a king. Alvaro Gil was alcaide mór or governor of the Castle of Guarda and refused to surrender it to the Castilian sovereign Juan I when he invaded Portugal, seeking to place upon the throne his wife Beatriz, daughter of the defunct king, Fernando. Her succession to the throne would have involved the union of the two kingdoms to which all patriotic Portuguese were vehemently opposed.

La Guarda, of which he was Governor, was founded in 1199 by Sancho I. It is situated in the northern division of the province of Beira, known as Beira Alta, in a mountainous district and its castle was regarded as one of the important fortresses of the kingdom. The bestowal of the alcaideria mór of La Guarda by Fernando in 1383 upon Alvaro Gil Cabral marks the commencement of the connection of the Cabral family with the province of Beira in public capacities - a connection that was to endure for many generations. João I was a grateful monarch who showered benefits upon his supporters and the good results of the support given by Alvaro Gil were speedily observable. The grants of land and of offices are so numerous that we cannot enter at length into the subject in a memoir that purports to be a biographical note on Pedraluarez Cabral, not a history of the Cabral family. I will therefore merely indicate the purport of those deeds that are reproduced in the work of Senhor Ayres de Sá, following a chronological order.

1. Appointment of Alvaro Gil Cabral as alcaide mór of the Castle of La Guarda in place of the Count Dom Henrique by Fernando, king of Portugal and Algarve. Lisbon, 22nd of June, 1383. Chancellaria de D. Fernando, Liv. 3°, fl. 77 v.

2. Grant of the Lands of Zurara to Alvaro Gil Cabral and his heirs by João I. Lisbon, 27th of March, 1384, Chancellaria de D. João I, Liv. 1°, fl. 4.

Azurara-da-Beira, or Zurara in archaic form, was situated about ten miles south-west of Vizeu in a district of which Mangoalde is the principal town.

3. Grant of 180 libras payable by the municipality of Valhelhas and 150 libras payable by the municipality of Manteigas by João I. Lisbon, l0th of May, 1384. Chancellaria de D. João I, Liv. 1°, fl. 10 v.

Manteigas was situated about twelve miles north of Covilhã on the Serra da Estrella, and was one of the most elevated localities in the Serra. Its name is said to be derived from the butter (manteiga) that it produced in abundance. Valhelhas was situated about eight miles north of Covilhã.

4. Grant to Alvaro Gil Cabral of the village of Folhada hard by Gouvêa with all royal dues there payable. Lisbon, 9th of August, 1384, Chancellaria de D. João I, Liv. 1°, fl. 50.

5. Grant of the lands of Tavares in the almoxarifado (district controlled

by one Receiver of Customs) of Lamego. Alemquer, 9th of November, 1384. Chancellaria de D. João I, Liv. 1°, fl. 74

Lamego was situated about seventy miles east of Oporto.

6. Grant by João I during his good pleasure of all dues paid by the town of La Guarda. Coimbra, 7th of April, 1385. Chancellaria de D. João I, Liv. 1°, fl. 135 v.

7. Grant to Alvaro Gil Cabral and his heirs of the estate of Santo André in the judicial district of Zurara. Coimbra, 12th of April, 1385. Chancellaria de D. João I, Liv. 1°, fl. 136 v.

8. Grant of the lands of Moimenta to Alvaro Gil Cabral confirming a previous Grant made by the King's Procurator, Ruy Pereira. Coimbra, 19th of April, 1385. Chancellaria de D. João I, Liv. 1°, fl. 136 v.

Moimenta was situated about twenty-eight miles south-east of Lamego and on the outskirts of the Serra de Carapita.

Genealogists are not agreed regarding the name of the wife of Alvaro Gil Cabral. In the Livro das Linhagens of Damião de Goes, continued by D. Antonio de Lima, his wife is called Maria Eanes de Loureiro. In a genealogical account of the Cabraes it is stated that a daughter of Diogo Affonso de Figueiredo and Constança Rodriguez Pereira was married to Alvaro Gil. Perhaps he was married twice. Among his children by the daughter of Diogo Affonso de Figueiredo were Luiz Alvares, Brites Alvares who married João Peixoto and Maria Alvares, who married Fernão Velho, and became the mother of Gonçalo Velho who was one of the discoverers of the Azores.

From the public gardens at Covilhã, there was an extensive prospect over an undulating champaign towards the Serra das Mesas on the west and north-west. The Zezere waters this tract on its way to join the Tagus at Abrantes. At the north-eastern extremity of the range and at the distance of about twelve miles stood a hill detached from it and crowned by the ruins of the ancient castle of Belmonte around which cluster historic memories; on the slope below the castle, towards the south-west, the village lies.

A document in the Torre do Tombo (Liv. 9° de inquirições de D. Diniz, fl. 35. Liv. de inquirições da Beira e Alem Douro, fl. 6. (Frei Gonçalo Velho por Ayres de Sá, vol. I. p. 15.) dealt with the jurisdiction in the area : "Borough of Belmonte. The depositions show that the deponents have heard it stated that Belmonte is within the limits of Covilhã and moreover that they have heard it stated that in the beginning only the place that is called Cento Celas was given to the See of Coimbra and the Bishops of Coimbra continually extended their boundaries at the expense of the king and of the Municipality of Covilhã that consisted of Belmonte and eight other villages and these pay a contribution of fourteen pounds to the king and those of the town render their service to the king along with those of the Municipality of Covilhã and the Bishop does not wish the people of the villages to go there and they all pay him respect and he has his own magistrates and collectors of fees there but when an appeal is made from Belmonte they take the appeal to Covilhã. Let this so continue until the king shall know more of this matter."

Belmonte Castle, as we will learn shortly, was built by a Bishop of Coimbra and there is documentary evidence to prove that it was in the possession of a Bishop of Coimbra in 1387, only ten years before it was granted in perpetuity to Luis Alvares Cabral and his heirs male. The document to which I allude gives us a curious insight into the customs of the times and also establishes the fact that Belmonte was an appanage of the See of Coimbra and I shall therefore translate a portion of it as follows :

"Dom Joham, by the grace of God King of Portugal and Algarve, to all to whom this letter shall come we make known that Dom Martinho, Bishop of Coimbra, [a member] of our Council, has informed us that his Castle of Belmonte has lost many inmates owing to this war and has prayed us to give asylum in it to twenty refugees that they may remain there and re-people that place and assist him in defending it and, seeing that he who thus prayed came to us and begged us to show him favour, we hold it good and we command that twenty men, - not more, - who have been fugitives for any offences and crimes whatsoever that they may have committed or with which they are charged and who will come thither in order to settle in and remain in the said Castle of Belmonte, shall receive asylum there and shall not be arrested in that place nor within its boundaries, provided always that the aforesaid offences and crimes do not amount to treachery or treason and that the said fugitives be not [natives] of that place or policy. Moreover we decree that the magistrates of the aforesaid Belmonte and the Council may give leave once each year and not oftener to the said refugees to go away in an orderly manner for two months or a little more in order to receive by our authority provisions and other things that they may require and shall give them for this purpose their letter, sealed with the seal of the said Council and if they go away holding the said licence or come and go within the said place [Belmonte] and its boundaries, we command all our officers of justice not to arrest them nor to do them any harm nor injury because of the aforesaid offences and crimes but this is not to hold good if, after being in the aforesaid place, they go out and perpetrate other offences and crimes than those which have been pardoned, in which case the said asylum shall not be available and in testimony hereof we ordain that these letters patent be given him [to the Bishop of Coimbra]. Given in the city of Braga on the fifteenth day of November by command of the King-Martym Gomçalluez executed this - in the Era [of Augustus] one thousand four hundred and twenty-five years [A.D.1387]."

We know not precisely how the lordship of Belmonte came to be transferred from the Bishops of Coimbra to the House of Cabral ? The Marquis de Ruvigny in his work, "The Nobilities of Europe", states that rights of primogeniture constituting Belmonte a "morgado" or entailed estate were granted in a document bearing the date 9th of May, 1397. It is not stated in whose favour the deed was granted but there is no doubt that Luis Alvares Cabral, the son of Alvaro Gil Cabral, was made first Lord of Belmonte of the family of Cabral by João I, for evidence to prove that Alvaro Gil died previously to the 6th of October, 1385, is contained in a grant of that date of Zurara, Valhelhas, Manteigas and Moimenta to Fernão Alvares Cabral in which the earlier grant to Luis Alvares is quoted and also in the renewed grant of Belmonte Castle to Fernão Cabral in which Fernão de Alvares Cabral and Luis Alvares Cabral are mentioned as the two previous grantees. The date of this document is 20th of September, 1466. That which is most remarkable concerning Luis Alvares is that he held the office of Comptroller of the Household (Veador) of Dom Henrique and was present with him at the taking of Ceuta in 1415 and thus brought the family of which he was a member into that close connection with the mercantile policy of the kings of Portugal of the House of Aviz that was to result in the appointment of Pedraluarez Cabral as commander of the second Indian fleet. Luis Alvares married, first, Constança Annes, of whom were born Fernão de Alvares, Izabel and Beatris. His second wife, of whom no offspring was born, was Leonor Dominguez. As the grant of the lands of Zurara-de-Beira and of the estate of Santo André was confirmed to Fernão de Alvarez Cabral by Dom Duarte in 1433 it is probable that Luis Alvarez Cabral died in that year.

The head of the family next after Luis Alvarez Cabral was the grandfather of Pedraluarez and was named Fernão Alvarez. We find his name in three deeds or royal grants. By virtue of an instrument dated 8th of December, 1433, Dom Duarte confirms the grant of Moimenta, in another deed of the same date the king confirms the grant of the lands of Zurara in Beira and Manteigas and of the quinta of Santo André and finally the grants of Zurara, Valhelhas, Manteigas and Moimenta are confirmed by Affonso V in a deed dated 20th of March, 1449. Fernão Alvarez was also Lord of Belmonte. He married Tareja or Thereza de Navaes, daughter of Ruy Freire de Andrade and granddaughter of Dom Nuno Freire, Master of the Order of Christ. She was the widow of Estevão Soares de Mello. Fernão, father of Pedralvarez Cabral, was their son. There was also a daughter or, according to some genealogists, a stepdaughter named Aldonça, who, although known as Aldonça Cabral, may have been a daughter of Estavao Soares de Mello.

When the expedition to Ceuta was organized in 1415, Prince Henry made Luis Alvarez Cabral Captain of one of the ships of the fleet. The position of Veador in immediate attendance upon the prince was thus temporarily vacant and the youthful Fernão Alvarez was selected by the prince to take his father's place and to accompany him in his galley to Ceuta. However, when the vessel was in the Straits of Gibraltar the young man fell seriously ill. Prince Henry proposed to disembark him at Tarifa in order to increase his chance of recovery but the sick man protested against removal from the prince's galley and was permitted to remain. After his recovery, that must have been speedy and after the capture of Ceuta, he went to that city and remained there for several years, during which time he distinguished himself on various occasions in combats against the Moors. He became the Guarda mór (Captain of the Body Guard) of Prince Henry and died (says Fernam Lopez) subsequently to the siege of Tangiers. As according to Fernam Lopez Fernão Alvarez was at the time of his death still in the service of Prince Henry and as Prince Henry died in 1460 the chronicler must allude to the first siege of Tangiers, which took place in 1437.

A list of documents relating to Fernão Cabral will convey an idea of the active life led by the father of the discoverer and eldest son of Fernão Alvarez Cabral.

1. Letters patent granting to Fernão Cabral the patronage of the Church of São Giaoo (? João) of Azurara upon his estate and requiring the Bishop of Vizeu to ratify presentations to that church made by Fernão Cabral or his heir. Santarem, 30th of April, 1462. Chancellaria de D. Affonso V, Liv. 1°, fl. 75 v.

2. Injunction to the Corregedor and subordinate judicial officers of Beira and Riba de Côa to accept the appointment of Fernão Cabral as Regedor da Justiça and to obey him and his Ouvidor as they would obey the King. Castello Branco, 2nd of November, 1464. Chancellaria de D. Affonso V, Liv. 8°, fl. 43.

3. Grant of annual allowance of 28,800 reis brancos to Fernão Cabral, being a sum equal to his moradia. Castello Branco, 8th of November, 1464. Chancellaria de D. Affonso V, Liv. 8°, fl. 43 v

4. Letters patent granted to Fernão Cabral by which all Corregedors and all other officers of justice are required to restrain all persons from making requisitions or possessing manors in the lands of Zurara, which are the property of the Crown. Castello Branco, 8th of November, 1464, Chancellaria de D. Affonso V., Liv. 8°, fl. 43 v.

5. Ratification of a Contract made between Fernão Cabral on the one part and Vasco Fernandez de Gouvêa and Lianor Gomçalvez on the other part regarding what was due to him on his marriage and regarding the shares of the property that fell to Vasco Fernandez and Lianor Gomçalves on the death of João de Gouvêa and the share that would fall to Vasco Fernandez on the death of his mother aforesaid. Castello Branco, l0th of November, 1464. Liv. 2° da Beira, fl. 33.

The Contract is approved by Affonso V. Fernão Cabral married Izabel de Gouvêa, daughter of João de Gouvêa who was alcaide mór of Castello Rodrigo and lord of Almendra and Valhelhas. Lianor Gomçalvez was his wife and Vasco Fernandez his son. Izabel de Gouvêa appears to have been a widow when she was married to Fernão Cabral, and to have been previously the wife of Vasco Fernandez de Sampayo. Castello Rodrigo was a frontier fortress near the Côa about twenty miles north-east of Troncoso. Almendra is about twenty-eight miles north-east of Troncoso, four miles east of the river Côa and is in the neighbourhood of three rivers, the Côa, the Aguiar and the Douro, that render the district a fertile one. Valhelhas is situated on the eastern slope of the Serra da Estrella in a valley watered by the Zezere. It was sold by Luis Alvarez Cabral together with Tavares and became either then or subsequently the property of the head of the Gouvêa family. I do not find any intimate connection between the Gouvêa family and the small town of the same name on an outlying portion of the Serra da Estrella any more than I find a connection between the Cabral family and Cabra, a village on the Douro, south-east of Vizeu. Govea was the name of a distinguished rector of the University of Coimbra who flourished under João III.

6. Authority to convey to Fernão Cabral, member of the King's Council, Regedor da Justiça of the Comarca of Beira, the sequestrated property of João Fernandes, resident in Freixo de Espada Cinta, who took some sheep to Castile without the King's authority. Oporto, 29th of January, 1466. Chancellaria de D. Affonso V, Liv. 14°, fl. 6 v.

7. Conveyance to Fernão Cabral of the Castle of Belmonte that he may hold the same 'as his father Fernão de Alvares Cabral and his grandfather Luis Alvares Cabral held it,' and appointment of Fernão

Cabral as alcaide mór of the said Castle. Evora, 20th of September, 1466. Chancellaria de Affonso V, Liv. 16°, fl. 144, v.

Senhor Ayres de Sá remarks that no confirmation is to be found of the statement that the Cabraes held the Castle of Belmonte without rendering homage in respect of it.

The Castle appears to have been built in the thirteenth century as appears from letters patent granted by Affonso III to Dom Egee of the following import :

"Let all who shall see these presents know that I Affonso, by the grace of God King of Portugal and Count of Boulogne, command and permit Dom Egee, Bishop of Coimbra, to make a Tower in Belmonte and to build his Castle of Belmonte and there to exercise his functions. In evidence whereof I have granted to him these my letters patent. Given at Guimaráes the third day of the Kalends of April. By order of the King given by Dom Egidio Martin, majordomo of the Royal Household." Dominico Petri drew this up in 1266.

The 'Dom Egee' of this charter became Archbishop of Santiago. His surname was Fafes and he was descended from a certain Count Dom Fafes Sarracins and Dona Ouroana Mendes de Bragança.

8. Grant of all the rents, quitrents and duties payable in the town of Belmonte to Fernão Cabral, fidalgo of the Royal Household, Regedor das Justiças of the Comarca of Beira and alcaide mór of the Castle of Belmonte and to his successors, being eldest legitimate male children. Evora, 24th of September, 1466. Chancellaria de D. Affonso V, Liv. 22°, fl. 30 v.

9. Letter granting to Fernão Cabral, fidalgo of the Royal Household, Regedor das Justiças of the Comarca of Beira and Riba de Côa, the privilege of grazing not more than twenty mares in the parks and pasture-grounds of any cities or towns. Lisbon, 20th of July, 1469. Chancellaria de D. Affonso V, Liv. 31°, fl. 98.

10. Grant of an annual allowance of 26,000 reis brancos to Fernão

Cabral, member of the King's Council, Regedor da Justiça in the Comarca of Beira, in consideration of the services he has rendered to the King. Lisbon, 1st of October, 1471. Chancellaria de D. Affonso V, Liv. 16°, fl. 144 v.

11. Letters patent of Dom Affonso V reserving Monte de Crestados within the bounds of Belmonte as a Royal Park and appointing Fernão Cabral Chief Ranger. Lisbon, 6th of October, 1471. Chancellaria de D. Affonso V, Liv. 16°, fl. 144 v.

12. Letter to Fernão Cabral requiring the magistrates of Colmeal and others to maintain the rights and privileges of Fernão Cabral in Colmeal, inherited by him on the death of Vasco Fernandez de Gouvêa, Torres Vedras, 19th of August, 1476. Chancellaria de D. Affonso V, Liv. 7°, fl. 43 v.

CHAPTER 2

THE EARLY LIFE OF PEDRO CABRAL

The father of Pedro Álvares Cabral, Fernão Cabral, married Izabel de Gouvêa in 1464. His wife had inherited valuable lands in her own right, some of which had previously belonged to the Cabral family. Izabel de Gouvêa died in 1483 and Fernão Cabral in 1493.

By his will, published at Belmonte the 6th of May 1494, his property was to be divided by lot among nine of the eleven children, two of the daughters having been provided for previously in their dowries.

João Fernandes Cabral, the eldest son, remained at Belmonte. João Fernandez Cabral married Joanna de Castro, daughter of Rodrigo de Castro, Lord of Valhelhas and Almendra. His second son Jorge had a distinguished career. He went to India, where, after many years of service, he was appointed Capitão mór of the Malacca seas in 1524 and he was Chief Captain of the Indian fleet that sailed in 1536, and Captain of the fortress of Bassein in 1545, where he was when, on the death of Garcia de Sá in 1549, he became Governor of India and held that office until the arrival of Dom Affonso de Noronha as Viceroy in the following year.

The other sons were Jorge Dias, Vasco Fernandez and Luis Alvarez, and the daughters were Violante, who was married to Luis da Cunha, Lord of Santar (? Santarem) and Barriero and Brites, who was married to Dom Pedro de Noronha, a son of Dom Pedro de Menezes, first Marquez de Villa Real and alcaide mór of Almeida.

In the seignorial residence and in the judicial atmosphere of Belmonte it is almost certain that Pedraluarez first breathed the air. Various attempts have been made to fix approximately the date of his birth. We find in Brockhaus's 'Konversations Lexicon' a statement to the effect that he was born about 1460. Senhor J. A. d'Oliveira Mascarenhas in his novelette, 'O Brazil,' has a note to the effect that Pedro Alvares was born at Belmonte in 1467. This date is in all probability approximately correct for it may be remembered that the Contract of Marriage between Fernão Cabral and Izabel de Gouvêa was ratified in 1464 and that Pedraluarez was the second son and perhaps the second child of this marriage.

There is perhaps no distinguished discoverer regarding whose life, apart from his discoveries, we know so little as we do regarding the life of Pedraluarez Cabral. Of the youth of Pedraluarez we know almost nothing. However, it is possible that he is the Pedrallvarez who drafted the grant from João II to Fernam Domimguez de Arco of the governorship of a certain island that he had discovered, the name of which is not mentioned. The document is dated Santarem, 30th of June, 1484. We know that in that year Pedraluarez and João Fernandez, his eldest brother, were 'moços fidalgos' and received moradias from João II.

At the court of João II Pedraluarez studied the humanities that were taught at that period. On the death of João II he continued at the Court of Dom Manuel with the position of fidalgo of his council, and secured the habit of the Order of Christ and an annuity.

There is no portrait of Cabral, but as the son of the "Giant of Beira" he may have inherited his father's physique. De Barros states that he was selected because "of the presence of his person". The portrait that usually represents Cabral was first published in Retratos e Elogios dos Varões e Donas (Lisbon, 1817). The editors, however, do not state from whence this was derived. In the monastery of the Jeronimos at Belem there are four medallions representing busts of early navigators that adorn four of the main columns. They have been supposed to represent Vasco da Gama and his brother Paulo, Nicoláu Coelho, and Pedro Álvares Cabral, but none of them shows any individuality.

Little else is known of Pedro Cabral's early life. There is no record of his having been at sea previous to the voyage that subsequently made him famous.

Pedro was the second son and was therefore not obliged to retain his father's name. So prior to that voyage he seems to have used the surname of his mother, and was known as Pedro Alvares or Pedralvarez de Gouvêa. Cabral is given this name in a letter dated the 12th of April, 1497, in which Dom Manuel confirms to Pedro Álvares de Gouveia and to his elder brother, João Fernandes Cabral, an annuity of 13,000 reis each, and containing a statement that they had thanked Dom João II, probably as master of the Order of Santiago.

CHAPTER 3

PEDRO CABRAL CHOSEN AS COMMANDER

Vasco da Gama had returned to Lisbon from India on the 29th of August, 1499, and was received with great honour. He was made Count of Vidigueira and given an irrevocable commission to act as the chief of any future fleet to India, should he so desire.

Alvard conceding to Dom Vasco da Gama the chief captaincy of all the ships departing for India during his lifetime, the king not being able to intervene in this matter, etc. :

"We, the King, make known to all to whom this our alvará may come, that in consideration of the very great and signal service that Dom Vasco da Gama of our council did to us and to our kingdoms in the discovery of India, for which reason we should give him all honour, increase and reward, and because of this, it pleases us that we grant him by this present alvará that of all the armadas that in his life we shall order made and shall make for the said parts of India, whether they be only for the trade in merchandise or whether it is necessary to make war with them, he may take and takes the chief captaincy of these, so that in the said armadas he has to go in person, and in them to serve us, and when he thus wishes to take the said captaincy, we may not place in them nor appoint another chief captain save him, because of his honour, and we confide in him that he will know very well our service; it pleases us that we grant and we in fact grant this reward and privilege as is said. Furthermore, we order to be given to him this our alvará by us signed, that we order shall be in every way kept and guarded, as in it is contained our reward, without impediment or any embargo that might be placed upon it. And it pleases us, and we wish that it be as valid as a letter by us signed and sealed with our seal, and passed by our Chancellery, in spite of our ordinance, even though it may not be passed by the officers of the Chancellery. Done."

To the Portuguese people Vasco da Gama's voyage was accomplished by the will of God, who had destined them for the control of the East, and, regardless of obstacles, they must continue. So preparations were made for the dispatch of a second fleet to Calicut the following March.

The second expedition was of a less purely commercial character than the first, for the Rajah of Calicut, if he should prove contumacious, was to be punished and irreconcileable Arabs to be brought into subjection. The desire of the Portuguese to hasten these preparations was partly to prevent the Arabs from arming for defence and still further inciting the Hindus against them.

However, Vasco da Gama was tired. The voyage had been long and difficult, and he wished leisure to recuperate. It was da Gama's wish and that of the king that the leader of the next expedition to the East should be a man of a different type, who might be able to change to friendship the hostility that the native rulers had shown towards the Portuguese during the previous voyage. Perhaps Vasco da Gama had in mind also that after a more successful voyage by Cabral he himself might again return to show the Zamorin the true position of his country. At this time da Gama and Cabral were friends, and da Gama is said to have suggested Cabral's name for this office.

There were other reasons that induced Dom Manuel to select Cabral as chief captain of the Indian fleet. He had undoubtedly known him well at court. The standing of the Cabral family, their unquestioned loyalty to the Crown, the personal appearance of Cabral, and the ability that he had shown at court and in the council were important factors. Two of his brothers, João Fernandes Cabral and Luiz Álvares Cabral, were members of the council of Dom Manuel in 1499, and may have had some influence in this selection before the return of da Gama. The fact that Cabral was a collateral descendant of Gonçalo Velho, the honoured navigator to the Azores, may also have added a sentimental reason. The conditions that existed at court in those days are not recorded, but we know that there was much intrigue and jealousy. Cabral may have belonged to a faction that aided his choice. The selection of the chief captain for this fleet required great care. Cabral, therefore, must have been a man who was not only acceptable to Vasco da Gama and to the king but who also had the confidence of the people of Portugal and the respect of those who went with him.

Pedro Álvares Cabral was two years older than Dom Manuel, and was thirty-two years of age when he was selected in 1499 as chief captain of the fleet that was to go to India the following year. The name used in his appointment as chief commander of the fleet for India was Pedralvarez de Gouveia.

The shipyards and arsenals were busy making ready one of the largest and certainly the most imposing fleets that had hitherto sailed the high seas of the Atlantic. The purpose of the voyage meant that the ships constituted an armada as well as a flotilla. So it is probable that some of the vessels were equipped with heavy armament such as bombardas and culverins. Provisions and supplies for twelve hundred men for a year and a half had to be provided, and a cargo with which to trade. The selection of the officers and crew was made with great care. There was no difficulty in securing them. They were to go with pay and not subject to the reward of the king as were those of Vasco da Gama. The captains were chosen to impress the rulers of India with the greatness of Portugal, and for this reason members of noble families commanded many of the ships. There went also Franciscan friars and clergy, some of whom were to remain in India. The cargo was in the charge of a factor with assistants, for a factory was to be permanently established at Calicut.

CHAPTER 4

SHIPS AND PERSONNEL

An inscription on the South America of the Cantino Chart alleges that Cabral had fourteen vessels in his fleet. It runs thus : "A vera cruz + chamada p. nome aquall achou pedraluares cabrall fidalgo da cassa del Rey de portugall & elle a descobrio indo por capita moor de quatorze naos que o dito Rey mandaua a caliqut en el caminho indo topou com esta terra aqual terra se cree ser terra firma em aqual a muyta gente de discricam & andam nu os omes & molheres como suas mais os paria[m] sam mais brancos que bacos tem os cabellos muyto corredios foy descoberta esta dita terra em aera de quinhentos."

Cabral's fleet consisted of both ships and caravels. There is no official document that tells how many belonged to each class, and the only authors who give us exact statements are Castanheda, who says that there were three round ships, and the rest were ships (probably meaning caravels), and Gaspar Corrêa, who states there were ten large ships of 200 to 300 tons and three small ones. In the account of the voyage written by a Portuguese pilot and published by Ramusio, Cabral is said to have commanded thirteen vessels. Barros also avers that the fleet comprised thirteen sail. Castanheda, who gives the best narrative of the voyage and usually refers to the vessels as caravels, was probably right. Corrêa had the classes reversed. This uncertainty in the description of the vessels is due to the inexact way in which ships were then designated. The Capitania, or flagship, and the ships of Simão de Miranda and Sancho de Tovar were undoubtedly naos redondos, or round ships. The remaining vessels were probably small ships and caravels, with possibly a few caravelas redondas that combined the two types. There is no description of any of the ships of Cabral's fleet. The illustration of the fleet shown in the Livro das Armadas da India was made long after the voyage, and was derived from references to the ships as given by the historians. It is therefore of little real value. The ships must have been similar to those in Vasco da Gama's fleet and to other vessels of the early sixteenth century.

The "round ships" were so called because when viewed from the front or rear they appeared round on account of their wide beam and bulging sails and to distinguish them from the "long ships" or galleys of the Venetians. These round ships were provided with castles fore and aft, which were used as living-quarters, and which were also of advantage for boarding in case of a naval engagement. They had three masts. The fore-masts and mainmasts were square-rigged, and the mizzen-mast had a lateen sail. There was also a square sprit-sail at the bow. No sails were employed above the top sails, but in fair weather bonnets were used. The caravels had three or four lateen-rigged masts and were often provided only with an aft castle. With the caravela redonda the foremast was square-rigged and the others lateen-rigged. This type had the advantage of being steadier than the caravels and of permitting the use of two castles. It is doubtful if any of the ships in the fleet exceeded 300 tons, and the smallest was not over 100 tons. The ships of Pedro Álvares Cabral and Simão de Miranda were the largest and may have had a capacity of 250 or 300 tons. Because Sancho de Tovar went as second in command, his ship of 200 tons would probably only be exceeded in size by these two. A comparison of the respective tonnages of the fleets of Vasco da Gama and Cabral shows that Cabral's fleet was about five times the size of da Gama's. Six of Cabral's vessels were lost at sea. From a financial standpoint, that of Sancho de Tovar was the most serious.

Some of the vessels of the second Indian fleet may have been merchantmen freighted by merchants or mercantile firms and permitted by the king to accompany the fleet under conditions such as are preserved for us by João de Barros who writes in his relation of the voyage of João da Nova to India in 1501 with four ships after that of Cabral's voyage in 1500 : "The captains of the other ships" (than that of Da Nova himself) "were Dioga Barbosa, servant of Dom Alvaro, brother of the Duke of Brangança for the ship was his and Francisco de Novaes, servant of the king and the other captain was Ferñao Vinet, a Florentine by nation, because the ship in which he sailed belonged to Bartolomeo Marchioni, who was also a Florentine, a resident in Lisbon and the richest the city had produced at that period. In order that those of this kingdom who were engaged in commerce might have a trade open to them, the king ordained that they should be permitted to freight vessels for those parts, some of which have sailed and others are laded and this method of bringing spices is still employed. And, seeing that upon those persons to whom the king granted this concession it was imposed as a condition in their contracts that they must present for the approval of the king the captains of the ships or barques that they freighted and whose appointments were to be confirmed by the king, they often proposed posed persons selected rather because they were well fitted for the business of the voyage and the charge laid upon them than because they were of noble blood." Evidence that one of the vessels that accompanied the fleet commanded by Pedro Cabral was freighted by a Lisbon merchant is contained in a letter from D. Cretico, Envoy from Venice to the King of Portugal, dated 27th of June, 1501 and written to an unnamed correspondent who is addressed as "Serenissime princeps." "This ship which has arrived," writes the Envoy, "is that of Bartholomio, the Florentine, with the cargo, that consists of about 350 cantaros of pepper, 120 cantaros of cinnamon, 50 to 60 cantaros of lac and 15 cantaros of benzoin".

There was no difficulty in securing men for Cabral's voyage. For this reason it was felt wise to determine their pay in advance. The king in consultation with Vasco da Gama, Pedraluarez Cabral and Jorge de Vasconcellos, superintendent of the royal store-houses, (Provedor dos almazens do Reyno) fixed the salaries and wages to be paid to the officers and men.

The Chief Captain was to receive ten thousand cruzados, five thousand of which were to be paid in advance. The captains were to receive one thousand cruzados for every hundred "toneis" of their ships and one thousand cruzados of the total amount was to be paid in advance. One year's wages, - one hundred and thirty cruzados, - were to be paid in advance to the married able-bodied seamen and sixty-five cruzados to the unmarried, six months' wages, - sixty-five cruzados, - were to be paid in advance to the ordinary seamen, if married and thirty-two cruzados and a half to those who were not married.

Gaspar Corrêa tells us that "What was decided was that the chief captain of the armada should have for the voyage 10,000 cruzados and 500 quintals of pepper, paid for from his salary of 10,000 cruzados at the price at which the king might purchase it, on which he should not pay taxes, except the tenth to God for the monastery of Nossa Senhora de Belem; and to the masters and pilots 500 cruzados for the voyage and thirty quintals of pepper and four chests free; and to the captains of the ships 1,000 cruzados for each 100 tons, and six chests free, and 50 quintals of pepper for the voyage; and to the mariners 10 cruzados per month and ten quintals of pepper for the voyage and a chest free; and to every two ordinary seamen, the same as one mariner; and to every three pages, the same as to one ordinary seaman; and to the mates and boatswains, as to a mariner and a half; and to the official men, that is, in each ship two caulkers, two carpenters and two rope makers, a steward, a bleeding barber, and two priests, the third of that of two mariners; and to the men at arms, five cruzados per month and three quintals of pepper for the voyage; and in each ship went a chief gunner and two bombardiers; to the chief gunner 200 cruzados and 10 quintals of pepper for the voyage and two chests free; and to the bombardiers the same as to mariners; and to each man at arms his free chest. And all the quintals of pepper loaded with their money with only the tenth to God; and the payment of this pepper to be made to them by the king in money, according to the price he might sell it for with a deduction, if any, because the pepper dried on the voyage, a soldo to a liura; and payment in advance to the men at arms, and one year in advance to those married, and to bachelors half, and the same to all officials of the ships, and to the chief captain, 5,000 cruzados, and to each captain 1,000 cruzados, and to the men at arms six months each, and in their chests white clothing."

The chief officers and pilots occupied the aft castle. On Cabral's ship provision was also made for the meetings of the council and for entertainment. The chief factor with his principal aids evidently went with Cabral and they too would be quartered there. The crew, each provided with a bed roll and a chest, slept below decks. In the waist of the ship, cannon could be placed on either side, and in the centre was a large hatchway into which the ship's boats were lowered. The caravels probably had a bombard at the bow. Sails were manipulated with winches or capstans, that were also used for handling the cargo. At the stern was hung the farol, an iron cage in which firewood was burned at night. The sombre pitch-covered hulls were relieved by the bright colours with which the superstructures were painted. The flagship determined the speed and the changes in the course of the fleet; the others followed. The food for the crew consisted of biscuit, dried or salted meat and fish, rice, sardines, dried vegetables and fruits, particularly figs. Oil, honey, sugar, salt, and mustard were provided. Wine was evidently furnished to the crew, because large quantities of it were carried on other fleets. The officers naturally fared better. Caminha states in his letter that chickens and sheep were carried on the ships. The crew suffered greatly from scurvy, and oranges were obtained as a remedy whenever possible. In addition to large quantities of provisions and supplies the fleet had cargo for trade. Two of the caravels, those of Bartolomeu and Diogo Dias, were destined for the coast of Sofala. These carried copper and small wares, such as looking-glasses, bells, and coloured beads, which the Portuguese, in their trade on the Guinea coast, had learned were desired by the natives. More valuable cargo may also have been taken for trade with the Arabs. The main fleet took copper, in bars or worked, vermilion, cinnabar, mercury, amber, coral of various grades, and cloths, particularly fine woollens, satins, and velvets in bright colours. The latter were chiefly used by the rich for decorations, since the people of the East were satisfied with their scanty cotton garments. Silks could be obtained to better advantage from China and embroideries from Cambay. For their purchases in the East the Portuguese also carried gold. This was in currency. As this was desired because of its intrinsic value, coins of nations other than Portugal were also taken. Those of Venice were particularly esteemed, because they were better known. These coins were called "trade money" and were those which had not been greatly debased. Most of the money was carried in the flagship, since the factors made purchases for the king, and every care must be taken that his interests be protected. The representatives of the Italian merchants and Ayres Correia with his staff were probably also provided independently, as they evidently traded on their own account, with a percentage deducted for the Crown.

The Captains

On comparing the names of the captains of the ships as we find them in the "Asia" of Barros with the names mentioned by Correa we find that Correa has ten of the thirteen names mentioned by Barros and four that are not amongst the thirteen. The number of captains is thus raised from thirteen to seventeen. According to Barros, Simão de Miranda sailed in a different vessel from the Chief Captain. The captains whom Barros mentions by name are the following : Pedraluarez Cabral; Sancho de Tovar, son of Martin Fernandez de Tovar; Simão de Miranda, son of Diogo de Azevedo; Aires Gomez da Silva, son of Pero da Silva; Vasco de Taide; Pedro de Ataíde, whose sobriquet was "Inferno"; Nicolao Coelho; Bartholomeu Dias; Pero Dias; Nuno Leitão; Gaspar de Lemos; Luis Pirez and Simão de Pina. The additional names to be found in the "Lendas da India" are those of Bras Matoso, Pedro de Figueiró, Diogo Dias and André Gonçalves. Three small vessels (navios pequenos) were commanded by Luis Pirez, Gaspar de Lemos and André Gonçalves.

The story, of the voyage as it is told by Barros and Correa will not permit us to omit any of the Captains whose names they record and the only possible reconciliation of the two narratives lies in the adoption of all the names as genuine. We must believe therefore that seventeen, or, if we include the ship belonging to Bartholomeu Florentym, eighteen vessels constituted the fleet that was led by Cabral.

The following is known of those captains :

Sancho de Tovar, or Toar, sent with the fleet as second in command with powers to succeed Cabral in case of the latter's death. He was a Castilian fidalgo, who, after killing the judge who had condemned his father to death for following the side of Afonso V against Ferdinand and Isabella, fled to Portugal. His appointment as a member of the fleet was evidently due to his loyalty to the Portuguese Crown. The choice, however, does not seem to have been a happy one. His ship, probably the El Rei, of 200 tons, ran ashore near Malindi and was lost with its cargo of spices. Tovar later took command of the caravel of Nicoláu Coelho and visited Sofala. He did not sail again to India.

Simão de Miranda, a nobleman and son-in-law of Ayres Correia. His name is placed third in lists of captains by all authorities except Castanheda. His ship was probably about the size of the flagship. Because it accompanied the flagship and was sent on no special missions, this ship and its commander are mentioned only incidentally by the historians. It may have contained merchandise belonging to Ayres Correia and other Portuguese officials that did not belong to the Crown. It evidently took on cargo at Calicut. Miranda died in 1512, when captain of Sofala.

Aires Gomes da Silva, a nobleman of highest rank. His caravel was lost during the storm in the South Atlantic.

Vasco de Ataíde, a nobleman. According to Caminha and in the first edition of Castanheda he commanded the ship that lost company near the Cape Verde Islands. Other authors state that this was commanded by Luis Pires. Neither reached India, so the question is not of importance. Since Caminha saw the captains often while in Brazil, his statement cannot be questioned. The author of the Anonymous Narrative, a contemporary document, states that Vasco de Ataíde did not return to Lisbon. Castanheda, and following him de Barros and de Goes, claim that he did, although later Castanheda says that six ships were lost, which evidently included this one. According to Corrêa his vessel was a poor sailor and had difficulty in keeping up with the rest of the fleet. There is also a divergence of opinion as to whether the ship was lost during a storm. Caminha, our best authority, says that it was during clear weather.

Pedro de Ataíde, a nobleman and probably related to Vasco de Ataíde. Vasco da Gama married Catarina de Ataíde after his return from India, and this may have influenced the selection of the two Ataídes as captains. It was the caravel of Pedro, the São Pedro, which was sent to secure the elephant for the Zamorin. His ship was loaded at Cranganore. On the return voyage it became separated, but rejoined the flagship at Beseguiche. Pedro de Ataíde went again to India with Vasco da Gama in the São Pedro. He accompanied the fleet of Sodré to the Straits and returning with Francisco de Almeida was shipwrecked and died at Mozambique. De Barros and de Goes give him the nickname of "Inferno".

Nicoláu Coelho, an experienced captain who had gone with da Gama as commander of the Berrio and took an active part in that voyage. He returned to Lisbon before da Gama. Nicoláu Coelho was a fidalgo of great valour to whom El-Rey, Dom Manuel, gave the captaincy of a ship to go in company with the great Vasco da Gama to discover India, in which he acted with great distinction and prudence; and when he returned, he arrived first at Cascaes before Vasco da Gama. Through him the king learned of all that happened in that discovery. He again sailed to India with Cabral, possibly in the same caravel. On the return voyage he replaced Nuno Leitão da Cunha as the commander of the Anunciada and reached home nearly a month before the rest of the fleet. He went to India a third time in 1503 under Francisco de Albuquerque and on the return voyage was shipwrecked and died with that commander in January 1504.

Bartolomeu Dias, also known by the name of de Novaes, a fidalgo and an able navigator. After returning from his memorable voyage around the Cape, he continued his interest in this voyage. He supervised the construction of da Gama's ships and gave him much advice. He had three brothers, Pero, Alvaro, and Diogo. Pero accompanied him on his first expedition, and Diogo was a captain of Cabral's fleet. Bartolomeu Dias was lost during the storm shortly after the fleet left Brazil.

Diogo Dias, a brother of Bartolomeu, who had gone with da Gama as a writer on the São Gabriel. On Cabral's voyage he was the captain of the caravel which, having become separated from the fleet in the South Atlantic, sailed too far east and discovered Madagascar. Caminha speaks of him in his letter as a jovial man who was well liked by his companions.

Nuno Leitão da Cunha, whom de Barros calls a cavaleiro. He commanded the Anunciada, which was financed by Marchioni and other Italians. This was one of the smallest though the fastest of the caravels. It was this captain who saved the life of Antonio Correia, the son of Ayres Correia, at Calicut. Da Cunha filled an important position at Lisbon after his return.

Gaspar de Lemos, a fidalgo about whom little is known. He commanded the supply-ship that returned from Brazil carrying letters to the king. This was the vessel that could best be spared from the fleet.

Nothing is known of its return voyage. No place names are recorded on subsequent maps to indicate that it skirted the coast to the north for the purpose of further discovery. The credit for the discovery of this coast probably belongs to Vespucci, who after landing at Cape Saint Roque followed it to the south. De Lemos probably proceeded direct to Lisbon, in accordance with Cabral's instructions.

Luis Pires, who may have been the captain of the caravel financed by the Count of Porta Alegra. Nothing is known of his life, and his ship capsized during the storm.

Simão de Pina, a nobleman who was related to the chronicler Ruy de Pina. He commanded a caravel that was lost during the storm.

The Factors

Three factors were identified with Cabral's fleet, Ayres Correia, the chief factor, Afonso Furtado, who was factor of the two caravels destined for Sofala, and Gonçalo Gil Barbosa, who went out as a writer but was left in charge of the factory at Cochin. There evidently were other assistant factors, some of whom were lost on the voyage, because according to the Instructions one factor was to go with each ship. It is probable that the Italian merchants had one of their own on the Anunciada. Corrêa names Gonçalo Gomes Ferreira as a factor who was left at Cananore, but he is not mentioned by other historians. The duties of the factors were to make commercial treaties, to conduct trade with the natives, and to take charge of the cargo. The writers were under their supervision and to them their duties were sometimes delegated. While under the authority of the chief captain, the factors were largely independent and were governed by a special section of the Instructions. Their salary is not given by Corrêa and it seems probable that other arrangements were made for them, either in the form of commissions or permission to trade on their own account.

Ayres Correia was evidently an experienced merchant in Lisbon with a knowledge of Eastern commodities. According to Castanheda it was from him that the store-ship of two hundred tons in the fleet of da Gama was purchased. As chief factor he was an important member of the council but looked to Cabral as his superior officer. In addition to all matters connected with trade, he had in his charge the making of commercial treaties. On this account he may be considered almost on an equal footing with the chief captain. He spoke Arabic fluently and probably had previously traded in Morocco. Correia has been blamed for the massacre in Calicut. This was due largely to lack of knowledge of Malayalam and to over-reliance on the word of the Arab traders. He died fighting on the shore. His son, Antonio, a boy of twelve, who was saved, later became one of the most famous captains in the East.

Afonso Furtado is given by Castanheda as the factor who was to be left at Sofala. De Barros and de Goes state that he was to be left there as a writer. He probably filled both offices. Bartolomeu Dias and Diogo Dias, with whom Furtado was to remain in Sofala, were to stay on the East African coast and carried cargo for that purpose. On this account Furtado was sent ashore at Kilwa, the capital of the coast of Sofala. He may have succeeded Ayres Correia after his death.

Gonçalo Gil Barbosa was a brother of Diogo Barbosa, who was in the service of the Duke of Bragança and in that of Dom Alvaro, who sent a ship with Cabral's fleet, but which was lost in the South Atlantic. It was probably through Dom Alvaro that Gonçalo Gil Barbosa was able to secure the position of writer under Ayres Correia. Diogo Barbosa had a son, Duarte Barbosa, the author of the Book of Duarte Barbosa, who it has been claimed accompanied his uncle and remained with him at Cochin. Gonçalo Gil Barbosa was acting as factor at Cochin and was left there when Cabral's fleet hurriedly departed for its return voyage. When da Gama reached India on his second voyage, Barbosa was transferred to Cananore to take charge of a permanent factory that was established there. Corrêa gives him the name of Gil Fernandez. He seems to have learned Malayalam while at Cochin and was thus of great value in the development of commercial relations both there and at Cananore.

The Writers

The writer (escrivão) or clerk kept the records and accounts and made the reports for the factors. We do not know how many accompanied the fleet, but probably at least one for each ship. From the fact that two were left at Cochin there seem to have been more than those whose names have been recorded. Pero Vaz de Caminha, Gonçalo Gil Barbosa, and João de Sá may have ranked above the others, and may because of this have had the duty of writing the account of the voyage. We have previously mentioned the two former.

João de Sá had gone with da Gama on his first voyage as a clerk on the São Raphael. He was held in high esteem by da Gama and when da Gama left for Terceira with his dying brother, Paulo, he was given the command of the São Gabriel. His name is among those who went with Pedro de Ataíde to capture the ship from Cochin. De Sá was later treasurer of the India House.

Other writers mentioned are Lourenço Moreno and Sebastião Alvares, who were left at Cochin, and Diego de Azevedo and Francisco Anriquez, who, Corrêa says, were selected for Calicut and Cananore. Corrêa gives Fernão Dinis in place of Sebastião Alvares.

The Pilots

Each of the ships seems to have had a pilot, though the office of pilot and master may have been combined in some of the smaller vessels. Six ships sailed independent courses during parts of the voyage. Only the flagship and that of Simão de Miranda remained continuously together.

The pilots were evidently under one or more chief pilots who remained on Cabral's ship. With the chief pilots were associated the native pilots for the East African coast and the Indian Ocean.

Caminha gives the names of two pilots, Afonso Lopez and Pero Escolar, but none is mentioned by other writers. Afonso Lopez is referred to by Caminba as 'our pilot', which may indicate that he was one of those with Cabral on the flagship.

Pero Escolar did good service with da Gama and was rewarded by the king on his return. He, too, may have been on Cabral's ship. Pero

Escolar continued to act as pilot in succeeding fleets. In November 1509 he was at Cochin in this capacity, and in 1515 he was the pilot of the ship Conceyçam.

Brito Rebello believes that João de Lisboa, one of the most notable pilots at this time, also went with Cabral's fleet. It is not possible to state definitely that João de Lisboa went with Cabral, but it may be assumed that with Nicoláu Coelho would go one who was with him on the first voyage as Pero d'Alemquer, who went with Dias, followed in that of Gama.

Besides the pilots there also went in the fleet an astronomer, After the fleet left Brazil, Master John is not heard of again and so he may have continued on one of the smaller vessels that was lost.

The Interpreters

Only two official interpreters are mentioned as being with the fleet, Gaspar da Gama and Gonçalo Madeira of Tangiers, who Castanheda says was left at Cochin. There were others, however, who spoke Arabic. Ayres Correia seems to have had the best knowledge of that language. He probably knew the dialect spoken in Morocco and may have had some difficulty in speaking correctly the language used by the Arabs in India. In the relations of the Portuguese with the Indians, Arab interpreters were necessary. Because of the lack of Portuguese interpreters, many misunderstandings arose at Calicut. The native fishermen whom da Gama had brought to Portugal had been taught Portuguese, but these, because of their low caste, were nearly useless. While Gaspar da Gama is called an interpreter, he does not seem to have been of much assistance in that capacity during Cabral's voyage, and does not appear to have been ashore at Calicut at the time of the massacre. He was apparently treated with some distrust in spite of his conversion and marriage in Portugal as told by Ca' Masser.

Other Members of the Fleet

Sancho de Tovar, as has been said, was the captain who went to succeed Cabral in case of his being incapacitated. Apparently there were other noblemen who went with similar instructions to replace other captains, or who filled subordinate positions. Several of these are mentioned. Among them were Dom João Tello, who is referred to by Caminha, and the Spaniard, Pedro Lopez de Padilla, who is named in the letter of Dom Manuel written in 1501.

Men of minor importance who have not been mentioned elsewhere are Vasco da Silveira (de Barros), Fernão Peixato and João Rois, who were saved by Coje Benquim at Calicut (Castanheda), Fernão Perez Pantaja (Corrêa), who accompanied Duarte Pacheco, and Vasco da Silveira on the caravel that attacked the ship from Cochin, and Francisco Correa (Osorio) and Diogo de Azevedo (Corrêa), who were sent by Cabral to the Zamorin. Gonçalo Peixato is also named as one who escaped after the attack at Calicut (Osorio).

The natives who went with the fleet were Baltasar and four Indian fishermen, whom Vasco da Gama had taken from Calicut by force, Moorish pilots who Corrêa says had returned with da Gama, and an ambassador from the King of Malindi.

On the homeward voyage there came the two Christians, Priest Joseph and Priest Mathias, two natives from Cochin, an ambassador from the King of Cananore, possibly the converted Indian yogi, Miguel, though this is not sure, and a hostage from Sofala.

Friars and Priests

Vasco da Gama had reported that the people of India were Christians though not using the rites of Rome. For their instruction in the Catholic Faith, Franciscan fathers, well educated in the doctrines of the Church and strict observers of its rites, were sent in Cabral's fleet. These have been identified as follows : Frei Henrique, of Coimbra, guardian, Frei Gaspar, Frei Francisco da Cruz, Frei Simão de Guimarães, Frei Luis do Salvador. All of these were preachers and theologians. There went in addition Frei Maffeu as organist, Frei Pedro Neto, a chorister, and Frei João da Vitoria, a lay brother. Frei Henrique had formerly been a judge of the Casa da Supplicação. He took the Franciscan habit in the convent of Alemquer and became celebrated for his learning and eloquence.

Frei Henrique officiated at the first religious services in Brazil. The Franciscan brothers were on shore at Calicut when the factory was attacked, endeavouring to attend to their religious duties although they did not understand the native language. Three were lost during the massacre, and Frei Henrique, who was wounded, narrowly escaped. He returned to Portugal. He was Bishop of Ceuta in 1505, confessor to Dom Manuel, and Inquisitor. In the last position he presided at the first burning of a Jew in Portugal, at Lisbon. Frei Henrique died at Olivença in 1532. No record remains of the religious efforts of these fathers during the voyage, except the mention of the conversion of the yogi christened Miguel. There were also in the fleet eight priests, in the charge of a vicar, whose names are not known. The vicar as representing a bishop had jurisdiction in his behalf.

CHAPTER 5

INSTRUCTIONS FOR THE OUTWARD VOYAGE

Instructions to obey Pedro Cabral's command

Instruction's were given by Dom Manuel to obey the command of Pedro Cabral during the voyage. The source of this document was Torre do Tombo - Chancellaria de D. Manuel, L°. 13, fl. 10. (Frei Gonçalo Velho, I. pp. 283-285.)

"We, Dom Manuel, & c., make known to you, captains, fidalgos, knights, esquires, shipmasters and pilots, able-bodied and ordinary seamen, officers and all other persons who go and whom we send in the fleet and armada that is to sail to India, that we, because of the great confidence that we have in Pedraluarez de Guouueia, fidalgo of our Household and because we know that in this matter and in every other matter that will lay upon him he will well understand how to serve us and will give a very good account of himself and his commission, we therefore give to him and entrust him with the captaincy-in-chief of all the aforesaid fleet and armada and we hereby notify you to this effect and we command all generally and each one in particular to comply with all that shall be demanded of you by him and required of you in our name and to do in every particular that which he orders you to do and to obey his commands in the same manner and as perfectly and with the same diligence and great care that we ourselves would expect of you and to do this as if it was told to you and commanded you by ourselves in person for so we hold it good and for our service and those who comply and who act in this manner will render us a great service in this matter and those who act in the contrary manner (that we hope will not occur) will do us a great disservice and we will inflict upon them chastisement commensurate with their evil deserts. Moreover in order that the affairs of our service may be attended to and carried out as they ought to be in a fleet and armada such as this is and in order that any who commit offences and crimes against our service now or in any circumstances that arise may be punished, we give to him by these presents all our whole authority and prerogative that he shall make use of in all cases and entirely until his death and all his decisions and commands shall be obeyed and no appeal of any kind will be permitted from his decisions; this power and authority however shall not be understood to apply to the Captains of large and small ships who go with him nor to the fidalgos and others whom we send in the aforesaid fleet and armada when they commit crimes for which they ought to be punished, for legal processes shall be instituted in such cases and they shall be reported to us in order that we may know them and [the offenders] will be punished and chastised according to their condition and in testimony of all that is contained herein we order these letters patent to be executed and they are signed and sealed with our seal and we command the same to be done wholly without fault. Given in our city of Lisbon on the fifteenth day of February - Antonio Carneiro executed this - in the year of our Lord Jesus Christ fifteen hundred."

Instructions to pay Pedro Cabral

Instructions were given by Dom Manuel to pay Pedro Cabral for his command of the fleet. The source of the document was Torre do Tombo - Chancellaria de D. Manuel, liv. 27°, fl. 70. (Trabalhos Nauticos, II. pp. 108-109.)

"Dom Manuel, by the grace of God King of Portugal and of the Algarves on this side of the sea and on the other side in Africa, Sovereign Lord of Guinea, to all to whom these our letters shall come we make known that Pedro Alluarez de Gouuea, fidalgo of our household, has at this time told us that he and Joham Fernamdez Cabral his brother received from my lord the king, whose soul may God save, an annual allowance during his good pleasure of twenty-six thousand reals in virtue of his instrument that he commanded to be given to him as appeared by the extract from it made word for word by Gil Fernamdez, Secretary of the Chancery of Dom Jorge, my much esteemed and beloved nephew, out of the books of the Chancellor's Office of the period in which the aforesaid annual allowance was granted by the king, for he [Dom Jorge] has in his possession those [books] of the period aforesaid and [he told us] that they had lost the original letters of the said king regarding the said allowance and were unable to find them in order to have them confirmed by us at this time and he has made request that inasmuch as the said letters have been lost we would be pleased to grant to each our letters patent concerning the amount of the allowance of twenty-six thousand reals that would fall to each so that each might receive payment of the aforesaid sums of money in such place as would please them according to our ordinance. And inasmuch as his petition seemeth to us to be just and as we have regard to his services and deserts, desiring to show him favour and thanks, we hold it to be right and it is our good pleasure that the aforesaid Pedro Alluarez de Gouuea have and receive from us each year, beginning as on the first day of January last of this year, fourteen hundred and ninety-seven and thenceforward as long as it shall be our good pleasure, the said thirteen thousand reals due to him as the half of the said twenty-six thousand reals that both received conjointly, as has been said, wherefore we command that other letters granting the other half, namely thirteen thousand reals, be given to the said Joham Fernandez so that each may receive payment separately and therefore we order the Comptrollers of our revenue to delete from our books of the revenue the said twenty-six thousand reals that the aforesaid two persons conjointly registered in them and we order them to register only the said thirteen thousand reals to the said Pedro Alluarez with a declaration that they are the moiety of the said twenty-six thousand reals that both received as has been stated and that they lost the other instrument of the said king that was given and we order [the Comptrollers] to give to each our letter granting thirteen thousand reals, being the moiety due to each, so that if at any time the other instrument should appear it may be torn in pieces and there may not be because of it payment made twice of the aforesaid sums; of which thirteen thousand reals he will receive a certificate of payment each year from our revenue [office], wherever they may be paid to him and for his own security and also for our better recollection we command that this letter be given him signed by us and sealed with our pendant seal. Given in our city of Evora this twelfth day of April - Pedro Lomeljm executed this - in the year fourteen hundred and ninetyseven."

Memorandum attributed to Vasco da Gama

There is a memorandum supposed to have been furnished by Vasco da

Gama, regarding the conduct of the fleet at sea before reaching the Cape of Good Hope.

Since Vasco da Gama had sailed to the Cape of Good Hope by the direct route, his advice to Cabral, who was to follow a similar course, would have been of assistance. Such advice was evidently secured and incorporated in Cabral's instructions.

Varnhagen, in his search for early documents in the Archives of Portugal, discovered the most important portion of Cabral's instructions. A short time later he found one leaf of a memorandum, apparently by Vasco da Gama, at a sale of old papers. This, he inserted in facsimile in the first edition of his Historia geral do Brasil. He there claimed that the document had been sent to the Torre do Tombo for preservation. However, there is no record that this was ever received, nor can it be found there. In spite of this cloud on its authenticity, the memorandum may still be accepted with some degree of confidence, for the instructions for later voyages resemble portions of it almost exactly.

It does not seem to have been written by Vasco da Gama but more probably, as Dr. Antonio Baião suggests, by the Secretary of State, Alcaçova Carneiro, during an interview with Vasco da Gama.

These notes were evidently those incorporated in the official instructions that Cabral probably issued to the captains of the various ships.

Vasco da Gama was impressed with the necessity for preventing the loss of convoy by the ships, since he probably had some difficulty in this respect during his voyage.

The methods he suggested were not new. Whenever ships went together out of sight of land, similar methods must have been used, but these evidently varied, and the recommendations of Vasco da Gama were those to be adopted for this voyage.

This memorandum is important, for it shows that Vasco da Gama not only suggested that the fleet should proceed in a southerly direction from the Cape Verde Islands and then east to the Cape, but he also advised, if the winds were favourable, that it should continue to the south-west from those islands, a course that Pedro Cabral followed. Inasmuch as these directions were entirely for navigation, there are no indications that a divergence westward was intended for any other purpose.

The memorandum consisted of more than one page, as is indicated by the fact that the sentence at the end is incomplete. The text is written in the centre of the page with notes on either side. It is crossed with lines showing that the information had been used and embodied in a more carefully worded document.

The translation given is from the text in the História da Colonização Portuguesa do Brasil, vol. i, pp. Xvi-xix :

"This is the way that it appears to Vasco da Gama that Pedroalvarez should follow on his voyage, if it please Our Lord.

In the first place, before he departs from here, to make very good ordinance so that the ships will not be lost some from the others, in this manner : namely, whenever they are obliged to change their course, the chief captain shall make two fires, and all shall respond to him, each with two similar fires. And after they thus respond to him they shall all turn. And he shall thus have given them the signals : that one fire will be to proceed, and three to draw the bonnet and four to lower sails. And none shall turn or lower sails or draw bonnet unless the chief captain shall first make the aforesaid fires, and all have replied. And after sails shall thus have been lowered, none will be hoisted until after the chief captain makes three fires, and all have replied [A]. And if any is missing they shall not hoist sail but only go with lowered sails until the coming of day, so that the ships cannot be carried so far that they are unable to see one another by day. And any ship that has its rigging down will make many fires to summon other ships so that it may be put in order.

After in good time they depart from here, they will make their course straight to the island of Samtiago, and if at the time that they arrive there, they have sufficient water for four months, they need not stop at the said island, nor make any delay, but when they have the wind behind them make their way towards the south [B, C]. And if they must vary their course let it be in the south-west direction. And as soon as they meet with a light wind they should take a circular course until they put the Cape of Good Hope directly east. And from then on they are to navigate as the weather serves them, and they gain more, because when they are in the said parallel, with the aid of Our Lord, they will not lack weather with which they may round the aforesaid cape. And in this manner it appears to him that the navigation will be shortest and the ships more secure from worms, and in this way even the food will be kept better and the people will be healthier.

And if it happens, and may it please God that it will not, that any of these ships become separated from the captain, then it must sail as well as it can to make the Cape and go to the watering place of Sam Bras. And if it gets here before the captain it should anchor in a good position and wait for him, because it is necessary for the chief captain to go there to take on water so that henceforth he may have nothing to do with the land, but keep away from it until Mozambique for the health of his men, and because he has nothing to do on it. [D, E, F.]

And if it be the case that the chief captain comes first to this watering place, before the ship or ships that are lost from him...

[The following notes, that appear on either side of the text, are indicated where they seem most appropriate.]

A (left). Save that if one of the ships cannot stand the sail as well as the captain's ship, and the strength of the wind requires him to draw it.

B (right). If the ships on leaving this city, before they pass the Canaries, should encounter a storm so that they have to return, they shall do everything possible so that all may return to this city. And if any one of them cannot do so, every effort should be made to reach Setuuel [Setubal]. And wherever it may be, it will at once make known here where it is, so as to receive orders as to what it should do.

C (left). They will return before the island of Sam Nicalao in case this is necessary [; or] because of sickness at the island of Samtiago.

D (left). If these ships departing from this coast should become separated from each other in a storm, so that some make for one port and others for another, the manner in which they are to join each other : and if the signs of guidance are not made by some one of the ships and it cannot be seen you will, with all the rest, make your way straight to the watering place of Sam Bras.

E (right). And there, while you take on water, the aforesaid ship will be able to overtake you. And if it does not overtake you, you will depart when you are ready, and will leave there for it such signs that it may know upon arriving there that you have gone on, and will follow you.

F (left). And signs should be set up, where routes are to be taken for the ships that lose each other, and this will be done with the very good experience of all the pilots."

CHAPTER 6

THE DISCOVERY OF BRAZIL

On the 8th of March 1500 the fleet of thirteen vessels was assembled in the Tagus, some three miles below Lisbon, near the small hermitage of Restello, where the monastery of the Jeronimos now stands.

Before their departure, pontifical mass was said with great solemnity. The king was there, and gave his last instructions orally to the young commander and presented him with a banner carrying the royal arms. The ships were decked with many coloured flags. Musicians with their bagpipes, fifes, drums, and horns added to the liveliness. The people, both those who were to sail and those on shore, were dressed as for a fête. All Lisbon had come to see them off and to wish them good fortune, for this was the first commercial fleet to sail for India. The way had been found, and it was this voyage that was to bring back a rich reward in jewels and spices and pave the way for even greater wealth to follow.

On the following day, Monday the 9th of March 1500, the fleet left the mouth of the Tagus and departed from the Bay of Cascaes. All sails were set, and on them was displayed the red cross of the Order of Christ, for Cabral's fleet also went to bring the true Faith to the people of India. The conversion of the heathen was not only the desire of Dom Manuel, but it was an obligation imposed by the Pope. The bulls of 1493, granted by Alexander VI as the head of the Church, had given spheres of influence over non-Christian countries with the implied duty of bringing them under the guidance of Rome. This was shown in the bull addressed to Dom Manuel in June 1497. In it the Pope granted the request of the king and permitted him to possess the lands conquered from the infidels, provided no other Christian kings had rights to them, and prohibited all other rulers from molesting him. At the end he requested him to endeavour to establish the dominion of the Christian religion in the lands that he might conquer. This may explain the religious tone of the king's letter to the Zamorin of Calicut.

The voyage thus begun was to be the longest in history up to this time.

The fleet sailed with the steady north-east trade wind and a favourable current over a course well known to the pilots, who had followed it many times to the coast of Guinea. On the following Saturday, the 14th March, they passed in sight of the Canary Islands and on Sunday the 22nd they reached São Nicolau of the Cape Verde Islands. No stop was made here, since it was not felt that supplies were needed. At daybreak the next morning the ship of Vasco de Ataíde was missing. The fleet searched for it for two days, but it was not found. Caminha, our most reliable authority, states that the weather was clear, although other authorities have claimed that there was a storm. This ship probably did not return to Lisbon, but the contemporary writers are at variance on this point. The fleet then continued its course, taking advantage of the north-east trade winds, and, in the hope of rounding the doldrums and the south-east trades, steered somewhat to the west of south. As the ships proceeded, the currents carried them farther west.

We do not know the exact course followed, but apparently the equator was crossed at about the thirtieth meridian. The fleet then resumed its route to the south-south-west and followed the coast of Brazil at a distance because of better sailing conditions until Tuesday the 21st of April, when signs of land were encountered. The fleet continued its course, and Mount Pascoal on the coast of Brazil was sighted the next day.

Soon after land was discovered, the fleet cast anchor. On Thursday the 23rd of April, the smaller vessels went directly towards shore and a landing was made. Many of the natives were seen on the beach as soon as the boat neared the land. This was probably the first time the Portuguese had set foot on American soil within their sphere. The new land was named Terra da Vera Cruz.

On the shore they encountered strange people with bodies painted and tattooed, and decorated with coverings of brilliant feathers. They had dark complexions and long straight hair. Their appearance and customs were entirely unlike any that the Portuguese had seen before. Those who had landed immediately returned to the Chief Captain and reported that the port appeared to be a safe anchorage. When the fleet had cast anchor the boat again went ashore in order to obtain closer acquaintance with the inhabitants. These, however, did not await the near approach of the newcomers but fled and could not be prevailed upon to return either by means of signs or of gifts thrown upon the ground. A third attempt to approach them was equally resultless. It had been the intention of the Chief Captain to land on the following day at this place but during the night the wind freshened to a gale - to the violence of which the ships were exposed and it was necessary to weigh anchor and to seek a more sheltered anchorage. Late in the afternoon of the day after arrival in American waters the fleet arrived at a large bay that the Chief Captain entered, sounding with the lead. Here was found a safe haven sheltered from the gale and good holding-ground. We cannot suppose that the progress made on the day on which land was sighted or on the following day exceeded the average of one hundred and twenty-four miles maintained between Lisbon and Santiago. One hundred miles might, I think, be reasonably assumed to be accomplished each day and such a rate of progress would result in the attainment of the vicinity of All Saints' Bay on the day after arrival. It is, moreover, very improbable that a bay that affords such good shelter and space for a large fleet to anchor in would be passed by. These considerations lead me to believe that All Saints' Bay (Bahia dos Todos Santos) was the Porto Seguro of Cabral. At the second anchorage Nicolao Coelho was sent on shore and attempted to have speech with the inhabitants. These were of more confiding disposition than those who had been encountered at the first anchorage. They awaited the approach of the strangers and replied to the signs made to them. In complexion they were similar to those previously seen. Correa styles them a white people and adds that their noses resembled those of Javans. They were armed with bows of great length and arrows having arrow-heads of cane. Some sailors who went a few miles inland found that their villages consisted of wooden houses thatched with grass. They slept in nets suspended by the extremities (that we now call hammocks) and a few of them wore garments or cloaks made of cotton twist (fio d'algodão) to which brightly coloured feathers were attached. If this bay was Bahia dos Todos Santos it is probable that the inhabitants thus described were either of the Tupuia or of the Tupinamba tribe. Osorio relates that the Chief Captain had a stone monument or "padrão" erected similar to those that Vasco da Gama had set up.

The fleet remained here until the 2nd of May, trading with the natives and replenishing its supply of water and wood. No effort was made to explore the coast, and it was not learned whether it was an island or the mainland.

Pedro Cabral and the council of captains held it to be their duty to inform Dom Manuel speedily of the discovery that they had made. Pedro Cabral sent back to Portugal a supply-ship under the command of Gaspar de Lemos. In it there were several natives of the country as was customary at that period and also specimens of their handiwork such as feather cloaks and hammocks. Parrots and brazil-wood were also sent to Portugal. This supply-ship probably returned directly to Lisbon and did not follow the coast, as claimed by the Portuguese historian Gaspar Corrêa. There is no record of the date of its arrival in Portugal.

The supply-ship carried letters to inform the king of the new discovery. Two of these letters have been preserved, one written by Pero Vaz de Caminha, who tells of what occurred while they were on shore, and another, which is of a more scientific nature, by Master John, an astronomer.

CHAPTER 7

PERO VAZ DE CAMINHA'S ACCOUNT OF THE DISCOVERY

Pero Vaz de Caminha had accepted the position of writer in the fleet under Cabral's command. He sailed in Cabral's flagship with other writers. One of the two letters sent by Pedro Cabral to the King of Portugal relating their discovery of Brazil was written by him on 1st May 1500. It is the first document describing the discovery of Brazil, and has sometimes been called the first page in the history of Brazil. It was kept in the Torre do Tombo, and classified as Corpo Chronologico, gaveta 8, maco 2, no. 8.

****

"Senhor : Although the chief captain of this your fleet, and also the other captains, are writing to Your Highness the news of the finding of this your new land which was now found in this navigation, I shall not refrain from also giving my account of this to Your Highness, as best I can, although I know less than all of the others how to relate and tell it well. Nevertheless, may Your Highness take my ignorance for good intention, and believe that I shall not set down here anything more than I saw and thought, either to beautify or to make it less attractive. I shall not give account here to Your Highness of the ship's company and its daily runs, because I shall not know how to do it, and the pilots must have this in their charge.

And therefore, Senhor, I begin what I have to relate and say that the departure from Belem, as Your Highness knows, was on Monday, the 9th of March, and on Saturday, the 14th of the said month, between eight and nine o'clock, we found ourselves among the Canary Islands, nearest to Grand Canary; and there we remained all that day in a calm, in sight of them, at a distance of about three or four leagues. On Sunday, the 22nd of the said month, at ten o'clock, a little more or less, we came in sight of the Cape Verde Islands, that is to say, of the island of Sam Nicolao, according to the assertion of Pero Escolar, the pilot. On the following night, on Monday at daybreak, Vasco d'Atayde with his ship was lost from the fleet without there being there heavy weather or contrary winds to account for it. The captain used all diligence to find him, seeking everywhere, but he did not appear again. And so we followed our route over this sea until Tuesday of the octave of Easter, which was the 21st of April, when we came upon some signs of land, being then distant from the said island, as the pilots said, some six hundred and sixty or six hundred and seventy leagues; these signs were a great quantity of long weeds, which mariners call botelho, and others as well which they also call rabo de asno. And on the following Wednesday, in the morning, we met with birds which they call fura buchos. On this day at the vesper hours we caught sight of land, that is, first of a large mountain, very high and round, and of other lower lands to the south of it, and of flat land, with great groves of trees. To this high mountain the captain gave the name of Monte Pascoal, and to the land, Terra da Vera Cruz. He ordered the lead to be thrown. They found twenty-five fathoms; and at sunset, some six leagues from the land, we cast anchor in nineteen fathoms, a clean anchorage. There we remained all that night, and on Thursday morning we made sail and steered straight to the land, with the small ships going in front, in 17, 16, 15, 14, 13, 12, 10, and 9 fathoms, until half a league from the shore, where we all cast anchor in front of the mouth of a river. And we arrived at this anchorage at ten o'clock, more or less. And from there we caught sight of men who were going along the shore, some seven or eight, as those on the small ships said, because they arrived there first. We there launched the boats and skiffs, and immediately all the captains of the ships came to this ship of the chief captain, and there they talked. And the captain sent Nicolao Coelho on shore in a boat to see that river. And as soon as he began to go thither men assembled on the shore, by twos and threes, so that when the boat reached the mouth of the river eighteen or twenty men were already there. They were dark, and entirely naked, without anything to cover their shame. They carried in their hands bows with their arrows. All came boldly towards the boat, and Nicolao Coelho made a sign to them that they should lay down their bows, and they laid them down. He could not have any speech with them there, nor understanding that might be profitable, because of the breaking of the sea on the shore. He gave them only a red cap and a cap of linen, which he was wearing on his head, and a black hat. And one of them gave him a hat of long bird feathers with a little tuft of red and grey feathers like those of a parrot. And another gave him a large string of very small white beads which look like seed pearls; these articles I believe the captain is sending to Your Highness. And with this he returned to the ships because it was late and he could have no further speech with them on account of the sea. On the following night it blew so hard from the south-east with showers that it made the ships drift, especially the flagship.

And on Friday morning, at eight o'clock, a little more or less, on the advice of the pilots, the captain ordered the anchors to be raised and to set sail. And we went northward along the coast with the boats and skiffs tied to the poop, to see whether we could find some shelter and good anchorage where we might lie, to take on water and wood, not because we were in need of them then, but to provide ourselves here. And when we set sail there were already some sixty or seventy men on the shore, sitting near the river, who had gathered there little by little. We continued along the coast and the captain ordered the small vessels to go in closer to the land, and to strike sail if they found a secure anchorage for the ships. And when we were some ten leagues along the coast from where we had raised anchor, the small vessels found a reef within which was a harbour, very good and secure with a very wide entrance. And they went in and lowered their sails. And gradually the ships arrived after them, and a little before sunset they also struck sail about a league from the reef, and anchored in eleven fathoms. And by the captain's order our pilot, Affonso Lopez, who was in one of those small vessels and was an alert and dextrous man for this, straightway entered the skiff to take soundings in the harbour. And he captured two well-built natives who were in a canoe. One of them was carrying a bow and six or seven arrows and many others went about on the shore with bows and arrows and they did not use them. Then, since it was already night, he took the two men to the flagship, where they were received with much pleasure and festivity.

In appearance they are dark, somewhat reddish, with good faces and good noses, well shaped. They go naked, without any covering; neither do they pay more attention to concealing or exposing their shame than they do to showing their faces, and in this respect they are very innocent. Both had their lower lips bored and in them were placed pieces of white bone, the length of a handbreadth, and the thickness of a cotton spindle and as sharp as an awl at the end. They put them through the inner part of the lip, and that part that remains between the lip and the teeth is shaped like a rook in chess. And they carry it there enclosed in such a manner that it does not hurt them, nor does it embarrass them in speaking, eating, or drinking. Their hair is smooth, and they were shorn, with the hair cut higher than above a comb of good size, and shaved to above the ears. And one of them was wearing below the opening, from temple to temple towards the back, a sort of wig of yellow birds' feathers, which must have been the length of a couto, very thick and very tight, and it covered the back of the head and the ears. This was glued to his hair, feather by feather, with a material as soft as wax, but it was not wax. Thus the head-dress was very round and very close and very equal, so that it was not necessary to remove it when they washed.

When they came on board, the captain, well dressed, with a very large collar of gold around his neck, was seated in a chair, with a carpet at his feet as a platform. And Sancho de Tovar and Simam de Miranda and Nicolao Coelho and Aires Correa and the rest of us who were in the ship with him were seated on the floor on this carpet. Torches were lighted and they entered, and made no sign of courtesy or of speaking to the captain or to any one, but one of them caught sight of the captain's collar, and began to point with his hand towards the land and then to the collar, as though he were telling us that there was gold in the land. And he also saw a silver candlestick, and in the same manner he made a sign towards the land and then towards the candlestick, as though there were silver also. They showed them a grey parrot that the captain brought here; they at once took it into their hands and pointed towards the land, as though they were found there. They showed them a sheep, but they paid no attention to it. They showed them a hen; they were almost afraid of it, and did not want to touch it; and afterwards they took it as though frightened. Then food was given them; bread and boiled fish, comfits, little cakes, honey, and dried figs. They would eat scarcely anything of that, and if they did taste some things they threw them out. Wine was brought them in a cup; they put a little to their mouths, and did not like it at all, nor did they want any more. Water was brought them in a jar; they took a mouthful of it, and did not drink it; they only washed their mouths and spat it out. One of them saw some white rosary beads; he made a motion that they should give them to him, and he played much with them, and put them around his neck; and then he took them off and wrapped them around his arm. He made a sign towards the land and then to the beads and to the collar of the captain, as if to say that they would give gold for that. We interpreted this so, because we wished to, but if he meant that he would take the beads and also the collar, we did not wish to understand because we did not intend to give it to him. And afterwards he returned the beads to the one who gave them to him. And then they stretched themselves out on their backs on the carpet to sleep without taking any care to cover their privy parts, which were not circumcised, and the hair on them was well shaved and arranged. The captain ordered pillows to be put under the head of each one, and he with the head-dress took sufficient pains not to disarrange it. A mantle was thrown over them, and they permitted it and lay at rest and slept.

On Saturday morning the captain ordered sails to be set and we went to seek the entrance, which was very wide and deep, six or seven fathoms, and all the ships entered within and anchored in five or six fathoms; this anchorage inside is so large and so beautiful and so secure that more than two hundred large and small ships could lie within it. And as soon as the ships were in place and anchored all the captains came to this ship of the chief captain, and from here the captain ordered Nicolao Coelho and Bartolameu Dias to go on shore, and they took those two men, and let them go with their bows and arrows. To each of them he ordered new shirts and red hats and two rosaries of white bone beads to be given and they carried them on their arms, with rattles and bells. And he sent with them to remain there a young convict, named Affonso Ribeiro, the servant of Dom Joham Tello, to stay with them, and learn their manner of living and customs; and he ordered me to go with Nicolao Coelho. We went at once straight for the shore. At that place there assembled at once some two hundred men, all naked, and with bows and arrows in their hands. Those whom we were bringing made signs to them that they should draw back and put down their bows, and they put them down, and did not draw back much. It is enough to say that they put down their bows. And then those whom we brought, and the young convict with them, got out. As soon as they were out they did not stop again, nor did one wait for the other; rather they ran, each as fast as he could. And they and many others with them passed a river which flows here with sweet and abundant water that came up as far as their waists. And thus they went running on the other side of the river between some clumps of palms, where were others, and there they stopped. And there, too, the young convict went with a man who, immediately upon his leaving the boat, befriended him, and took him thither. And then they brought him back to us, and with him came the others whom we had brought. These were now naked and without caps. And then many began to arrive, and entered into the boats from the seashore, until no more could get in. And they carried water gourds and took some kegs that we brought and filled them with water and carried them to the boats. They did not actually enter the boat, but from near by, threw them in by hand and we took them, and they asked us to give them something.

Nicolao Coelho had brought bells and bracelets and to some he gave a bell and to others a bracelet, so that with that inducement they almost wished to help us. They gave us some of those bows and arrows for hats and linen caps, and for whatever we were willing to give them. From thence the other two youths departed and we never saw them again.

Many of them, or perhaps the greater number of those who were there, wore those beaks of bone in their lips, and some, who were without them, had their lips pierced, and in the holes they carried wooden plugs that looked like stoppers of bottles. And some of them carried three of those beaks, namely, one in the middle and two at the ends. And others were there whose bodies were quartered in colour, that is, half of them in their own colour, and half in a bluish-black dye, and others quartered in checkered pattern. There were among them three or four girls, very young and very pretty, with very dark hair, long over the shoulders, and their privy parts so high, so closed, and so free from hair that we felt no shame in looking at them very well. Then for the time there was no more speech or understanding with them, because their barbarity was so great that no one could either be understood or heard. We made signs for them to leave, and they did so, and went to the other side of the river. And three or four of our men left the boats and filled I do not know how many kegs of water that we carried, and we returned to the ships. And upon seeing us thus, they made signs for us to return. We returned and they sent the convict and did not wish him to stay there with them. He carried a small basin and two or three red caps to give to their chief, if there was one. They did not care to take anything from him and thus they sent him back with everything, and then Bertolameu Dias made him return again to give those things to them, and he returned and gave them in our presence, to the one who had first befriended him. And then he came away and we took him with us. The man who befriended him was now well on in years, and was well decked with ornaments and covered with feathers stuck to his body, so that he looked pierced with arrows like Saint Sebastian. Others wore caps of yellow feathers, others of red, others of green; and one of the girls was all painted from head to foot with that paint, and she was so well built and so rounded and her lack of shame was so charming, that many women of our land seeing such attractions, would be ashamed that theirs were not like hers. None of them were circumcised, but all were as we were. And, thereupon, we returned, and they went away.

In the afternoon the chief captain set out in his boat with all of us and with the other captains of the ships in their boats to amuse ourselves in the bay near the shore. But no one went on land, because the captain did not wish it, although there was no one there; only he and all landed on a large island in the bay, which is very empty at low tide, but on all sides it is surrounded by water so that no one can go to it without a boat or by swimming. There he and the rest of us had a good time for an hour and a half, and the mariners fished there, going out with a net, and they caught a few small fish. And then, since it was already night, we returned to the ships.

On Low Sunday in the morning the captain determined to go to that island to hear mass and a sermon, and he ordered all the captains to assemble in the boats and to go with him; and so it was done. He ordered a large tent to be set up on the island and within it a very well-provided altar to be placed, and there with all the rest of us he had mass said, which the father, Frei Amrique, intoned and all the other fathers and priests who were there accompanied him with the same voice. That mass, in my opinion, was heard by all with much pleasure and devotion. The captain had there with him the banner of Christ, with which he left Belem, and it was kept raised on the Gospel side. After the mass was finished, the father removed his vestments, and sat down in a high chair, and we all threw ourselves down on that sand, and he preached a solemn and profitable sermon on the history of the Gospel, and at the end of it he dealt with our coming and with the discovery of this land, and referred to the sign of the Cross in obedience to which we came; which was very fitting, and which inspired much devotion.

While we were at mass and at the sermon, about the same number of people were on the shore as yesterday with their bows and arrows, who were amusing themselves and watching us; and they sat down, and when the mass was finished and we were seated for the sermon, many of them arose and blew a horn or trumpet and began to leap and to dance for a while, and some of them placed themselves in two or three almadias that they had there. These are not made like those I have already seen; they are simply three logs fastened together, and four or five, or all who wanted to, entered them, scarcely moving away at all from the land, but only far enough to keep their footing. After the sermon was finished the captain and all the rest proceeded to the boats with our banner displayed and we embarked, and thus we all went towards the land, to pass along it where they were, Bertolameu Dias going ahead in his skiff, at the captain's order, with a piece of timber from an almadia that the sea had carried to them, to give it to them. And all of us were about a stone's throw behind him. When they saw the skiff of Bertolameu Dias, all of them came at once to the water, going into it as far as they could. A sign was made to them to put down their bows, and many of them went at once to put them down on shore and others did not put them down. There was one there who spoke much to the others, telling them to go away, but they did not, in my opinion, have respect or fear of him. This one who was telling them to move carried his bow and arrows, and was painted with red paint on his breasts and shoulder blades and hips, thighs, and legs, all the way down, and the unpainted places such as the stomach and belly were of their own colour, and the paint was so red that the water did not wash away or remove it, but rather when he came out of the water he was redder. One of our men left the skiff of Bertolameu Dias and went among them, without their thinking for a moment of doing him harm; on the contrary, they gave him gourds of water and beckoned to those on the skiff to come on land. Thereupon Bertolameu Dias returned to the captain, and we came to the ships to eat, playing trumpets and pipes without troubling them further. And they again sat down on the shore and thus they remained for a while. On this island where we went to hear mass and the sermon the water ebbs a great deal and uncovers much sand and much gravel. While we were there some went to look for shell fish, but did not find them; they found some thick and short shrimps. Among them was a very large and very fat shrimp such as I had never seen before. They also found shells of cockles and mussels, but did not discover any whole piece. And as soon as we had eaten, all the captains came to this ship at the command of the chief captain and he went to one side with them and I was there too, and he asked all of us whether it seemed well to us to send news of the finding of this land to Your Highness by the supply ship, so that you might order it to be better reconnoitred, and learn more about it than we could now learn because we were going on our way. And among the many speeches that were made regarding the matter, it was said by all or by the greater number, that it would be very well to do so; and to this they agreed. And as soon as the decision was made, he asked further whether it would be well to take here by force two of these men to send to Your Highness and to leave here in their place two convicts. In this matter they agreed that it was not necessary to take men by force, since it was the general custom that those taken away by force to another place said that everything about which they are asked was there; and that these two convicts whom we should leave would give better and far better information about the land than would be given by those carried away by us, because they are people, whom no one understands nor would they learn quickly enough to be able to tell it as well as those others when Your Highness sends here, and that consequently we should not attempt to take any one away from here by force nor cause any scandal, but in order to tame and pacify them all the more, we should simply leave here the two convicts when we departed. And thus it was determined, since it appeared better to all.

When this was finished the captain ordered us to go to land in our boats in order to ascertain as well as possible what the river was like, and also to divert ourselves. We all went ashore in our boats, armed, and the banner with us. The natives went there along the shore to the mouth of the river, where we were going, and before we arrived, in accordance with the instructions they had received before, they all laid down their bows and made signs for us to land. And as soon as the boats had put their bows on shore, they all went immediately to the other side of the river, which is not wider than the throw of a short staff; and as soon as we disembarked some of our men crossed the river at once and went among them, and some waited and others withdrew, but the result was that we were all intermingled. They gave us some of their bows with their arrows in exchange for hats and linen caps and for anything else which we gave them. So many of our men went to the other side and mingled with them that they withdrew and went away and some went above to where others were. And then the captain had himself carried on the shoulders of two men and crossed the river and made every one return. The people who were there could not have been more than the usual number, and when the captain made all return, some of them came to him, not to recognize him for their lord, for it does not seem to me that they understand or have knowledge of this, but because our people were already passing to this side of the river. There they talked and brought many bows and beads of the kind already mentioned, and trafficked in anything in such manner that many bows, arrows, and beads were brought from there to the ships. And then the captain returned to this side of the river, and many men came to its bank. There you might have seen gallants painted with black and red, and with quarterings both on their bodies and on their legs, which certainly was pleasing in appearance. There were also among them four or five young women just as naked, who were not displeasing to the eye, among whom was one with her thigh from the knee to the hip and buttock all painted with that black paint and all the rest in her own colour; another had both knees and calves and ankles so painted, and her privy parts so nude and exposed with such innocence that there was not there any shame. There was also another young woman carrying an infant boy or girl tied at her breasts by a cloth of some sort so that only its little legs showed. But the legs of the mother and the rest of her were not concealed by any cloth.

And afterwards the captain moved up along the river, which flows continuously even with the shore, and there an old man was waiting who carried in his hand the oar of an almadia. When the captain reached him he spoke in our presence, without any one understanding him, nor did he understand us with reference to the things he was asked about, particularly gold, for we wished to know whether they had any in this land. This old man had his lip so bored that a large thumb could be thrust through the hole, and in the opening he carried a worthless green stone, which closed it on the outside. And the captain made him take it out; and I do not know what devil spoke to him, but he went with it to put it in the captain's mouth. We laughed a little at this and then the captain got tired and left him; and one of our men gave him an old hat for the stone, not because it was worth anything but to show. And afterwards the captain got it, I believe to send it with the other things to Your Highness. We went along there looking at the river, which has much and very good water. Along it are many palms, not very high, in which there are many good sprouts. We gathered and ate many of them. Then the captain turned towards the mouth of the river where we had disembarked, and on the other side of the river were many of them, dancing and diverting themselves before one another, without taking each other by the hand, and they did it well. Then Diogo Dias, who was revenue officer of Sacavem, crossed the river. He is an agreeable and pleasure-loving man, and he took with him one of our bagpipe players and his bagpipe, and began to dance among them, taking them by the hands, and they were delighted and laughed and accompanied him very well to the sound of the pipe. After they had danced he went along the level ground, making many light turns and a remarkable leap which astonished them, and they laughed and enjoyed themselves greatly. And although he reassured and flattered them a great deal with this, they soon became sullen like wild men and went away upstream. And then the captain crossed over the river with all of us, and we went along the shore, the boats going along close to land, and we came to a large lake of sweet water which is near the seashore, because all that shore is marshy above and the water flows out in many places. And after we had crossed the river some seven or eight of the natives joined our sailors who were retiring to the boats. And they took from there a shark which Bertolameu Dias killed and brought to them and threw on the shore. It suffices to say that up to this time, although they were somewhat tamed, a moment afterwards they became frightened like sparrows at a feeding-place. And no one dared to speak strongly to them for fear they might be more frightened; and everything was done to their liking in order to tame them thoroughly. To the old man with whom the captain spoke he gave a red cap; and in spite of all the talking that he did with him, and the cap which he gave him, as soon as he left and began to cross the river, he immediately became more cautious and would not return again to this side of it. The other two whom the captain had on the ships, and to whom he gave what has already been mentioned, did not appear again, from which I infer that they are bestial people and of very little knowledge; and for this reason they are so timid. Yet withal they are well cared for and very clean, and in this it seems to me that they are rather like birds or wild animals, to which the air gives better feathers and better hair than to tame ones. And their bodies are so clean and so fat and so beautiful that they could not be more so; and this causes me to presume that they have no houses or dwellings in which to gather, and the air in which they are brought up makes them so. Nor indeed have we up to this time seen any houses or anything that looks like them. The captain ordered the convict, Affonso Ribeiro, to go with them again, which he did. And he went there a good distance, and in the afternoon he returned, for they had made him come and were not willing to keep him there; and they had given him bows and arrows and had not taken from him anything that was his. On the contrary, he said, one of them had taken from him some yellow beads that he was wearing and fled with them; and he complained and the others at once went after him and returned to give them back to him. And then they ordered him to go back. He said that he had not seen there among them anything but some thatched huts of green branches, and made very large, like those of Entre Doiro e Minho. And thus we returned to the ships to sleep when it was already almost night.

On Monday after eating we all disembarked to take in water. Then many came there, but not so many as at the other times, and now they were carrying very few bows and they kept a little apart from us, and afterwards little by little mingled with us. And they embraced us and had a good time; and some of them soon slunk away. They gave there some bows for sheets of paper and for some worthless old cap, or for anything else. And in such a manner it came about that a good twenty or thirty of our people went with them to where many others of them were, with girls and women, and brought back many bows and caps of bird feathers, some green and some yellow, samples of which I believe the captain will send to Your Highness. And according to what those said who went there they made merry with them. On that day we saw them closer and more as we wished, for all of us were almost intermingled. And there some of them had those colours in quarters, others in halves, and others in such colours as in the tapestry of Arras, and all with their lips pierced, and many with the bones in them, and some of them without bones. Some of them were carrying prickly green nut shells from trees, that in colour resembled chestnuts, excepting that they were very much smaller. And these were full of small red grains that, when crushed between the fingers, made a very red paint with which they were painted. And the more they wetted themselves the redder they became. They are all shaved to above the ears, likewise their eyebrows and eyelashes. All of them have their foreheads from temple to temple painted with a black paint, that looks like a black ribbon the breadth of two fingers.

And the captain ordered that convict, Affonso Ribeiro, and two other convicts to go there among them, and likewise Diogo Dias, because he was a cheerful man, with whom they played. And he ordered the convicts to remain there that night. They all went there and mingled with them, and as they said later, they went a good league and a half to a village of houses in which there must have been nine or ten dwellings, each of which they said was as long as the captain's ship. And they were of wood with sides of boards and covered with straw, of reasonable height, and all had one single room without any divisions. They had within many posts, and from post to post a net is tied by the ends to each post, high up, where they sleep. And underneath they made their fires to warm themselves. And each house had two small doors, one at one end, and another at the other. And they said that thirty or forty persons dwelt in each house, and that thus they found them. And that they gave them to eat of the food that they had, namely, much manioc and other roots that are in the land, that they eat.

And, as it was late, they presently made all of us return and did not wish any one to remain there; and also, as they said, they wished to come with us. They traded there, for bells and for other trifles of little value that we were carrying, very large and beautiful red parrots, and two little green ones and caps of green feathers and a cloth of feathers of many colours, woven in a very beautiful fashion. All of these things Your Highness will see, because the captain will send them to you, as he says. And thereupon they came back and we returned to the ships.

On Tuesday, after eating, we landed to set a watch over the wood and to wash clothes. Some sixty or seventy men without bows or anything else were there on the shore when we reached it. As soon as we arrived they at once came to us without being frightened, and afterward many more came. There must have been a good two hundred, all without bows, and they all mingled so much with us that some of them helped us to load wood and put it in the boats, and they vied with us and derived much pleasure therefrom. And while we were taking on the wood two carpenters made a large cross from one piece of wood that was cut yesterday for this. Many of them came there to be with the carpenters; and I believe that they did this more to see the iron tools with which they were making it than to see the cross, because they have nothing of iron. And they cut their wood and boards with stones shaped like wedges put into a piece of wood, very well tied between two sticks, and in such a manner that they are strong, according to what the men said who were at their houses yesterday, for they saw them there. By now they kept us so much company as almost to disturb us in what we had to do. And the captain ordered the two convicts and Diogo Dias to go to the village, and to other villages if they should hear of them, and on no account to come to sleep on the ships, even if they should order them to; and so they went. While we were in this grove cutting wood, some parrots flew across these trees, some of them green, and others grey, large and small, so that it seems to me that there must be many in this land, but I did not see more than about nine or ten. We did not then see other birds except some pombas seixas, and they seemed to me considerably larger than those of Portugal. Some said that they saw turtle-doves, but I did not see any; but since the groves are so numerous and so large and of such infinite variety, I do not doubt that in the interior there are many birds. And towards night we returned to the ships with our wood. I believe, Senhor, that heretofore I have not given account to Your Highness of the form of their bows and arrows. The bows are black and long and the arrows long, and their tips of pointed reeds, as Your Highness will see from some which I believe the captain will send to you.

On Wednesday we did not go on shore, because the captain spent the whole day in the supply ship emptying it, and had transported to the ship what each one could carry. Many of the natives came to the shore, as we saw from the ships. There must have been some three hundred, according to what Sancho de Tovar said, who was there. Diogo Dias and Affonso Ribeiro, the convict, whom the captain sent yesterday to sleep there at any cost, returned when it was already night because they did not want them to sleep there, and they found green parrots and other birds that were black, almost like magpies, except that they had white beaks and short tails. And when Sancho de Tovar returned to the ship, some of them wished to go with him; but he did not want any except two proper youths. He ordered them to be well fed and cared for that night, and they ate all the food that was given them, and he ordered a bed with sheets to be made for them, as he said, and they slept and were comfortable that night. And so nothing more happened that day to write about.

On Thursday, the last of April, we ate early in the morning and went on shore for more wood and water, and when the captain was about to leave his ship Sancho de Tovar arrived with his two guests, and because he had not yet eaten, cloths were laid for him and food was brought, and he ate. We seated the guests in their chairs, and they ate very well of all which was given them, especially of cold boiled ham and rice. They did not give them wine, because Sancho de Tovar said that they did not drink it well. After the meal was over we all entered the boat and they with us. A sailor gave one of them a large tusk of a wild boar, well turned up. And as soon as he took it he at once put it in his lip; and because it did not fit there, they gave him a small piece of red wax. And this he applied to the back of his ornament to hold it and put it into his lip with the point turned upward, and he was as pleased with it as though he had a great jewel. And as soon as we disembarked he at once went off with it, and did not appear there again. When we landed there were probably eight or ten of the natives about, and little by little others began to come. And it seems to me that that day there came to the shore four hundred or four hundred and fifty men. Some of them carried bows and arrows and gave all for caps and for anything that we gave them. They ate with us of what we gave them. Some of them drank wine and others could not drink it, but it seems to me that if they accustomed themselves to it, they would drink it with great willingness. All were so well disposed and so well built and smart with their paints that they made a good show. They loaded as much of that wood as they could, very willingly, and carried it to the boats, and were quieter and more at ease among us than we were among them. The captain went with some of us for a short distance through this grove to a large stream of much water, which in our opinion was the same as the one that runs down to the shore, from which we took water. There we stayed for a while, drinking and amusing ourselves beside the river in this grove, that is so large and so thick and of such abundant foliage that one cannot describe it. In it there are many palms, from which we gathered many good sprouts. When we disembarked, the captain said that it would be well to go directly to the cross, which was leaning against a tree near the river, to be set up the next day, which was Friday, and that we should all kneel down and kiss it so that they might see the respect that we had for it. And thus we did. And we motioned to those ten or twelve who were there that they should do the same, and at once they all went to kiss it. They seem to me people of such innocence that, if one could understand them and they us, they would soon be Christians, because they do not have or understand any belief, as it appears. And therefore, if the convicts who are to remain here will learn their language well and understand them, I do not doubt that they will become Christians, in accordance with the pious intent of Your Highness, and that they will believe in our Holy Faith, to which may it please Our Lord to bring them. For it is certain this people is good and of pure simplicity, and there can easily be stamped upon them whatever belief we wish to give them; and furthermore, Our Lord gave them fine bodies and good faces as to good men; and He who brought us here, I believe, did not do so without purpose. And consequently, Your Highness, since you so much desire to increase the Holy Catholic Faith, ought to look after their salvation, and it will please God that, with little effort, this will be accomplished.

They do not till the soil or breed stock, nor is there ox or cow, or goat, or sheep, or hen, or any other domestic animal that is accustomed to live with men; nor do they eat anything except these manioc, of which there is much, and of the seeds and the fruits which the earth and the trees produce. Nevertheless, with this they are stronger and better fed than we are with all the wheat and vegetables that we eat.

While they were there that day, they continually skipped and danced with us to the sound of one of our tambours, in such a manner that they are much more our friends than we theirs. If one signed to them whether they wished to come to the ships, they at once made ready to do so, in such wise that had we wished to invite them all, they would all have come. However, we only took four or five this night to the ships, namely : the chief captain took two, and Simão de Miranda, one, whom he already had for his page, and Aires Gomes, another, also as a page. One of those whom the captain took was one of his guests whom we had brought him the first night when we arrived; today he came dressed in his shirt and with him his brother. These were this night very well entertained, both with food and with a bed with mattresses and sheets to tame them better.

And today, which is Friday, the first day of May, we went on land with our banner in the morning and disembarked up the river towards the south, where it seemed to us that it would be better to plant the cross, so that it might be better seen. And there the captain indicated where the hole should be made to plant it, and while they were making it, he with all the rest of us went to where the cross was down the river. We brought it from there with the friars and priests going ahead singing in the manner of a procession. There were already some of the natives there, about seventy or eighty, and when they saw us coming, some of them went to place themselves under it in order to help us. We crossed the river along the shore and went to place it where it was to be, which is probably a distance of two cross-bow shots from the river. While we were busy with this there came a good one hundred and fifty or more. After the cross was planted with the arms and device of Your Highness that we first nailed to it, we set up an altar at the foot of it. There the father, Frei Amrique, said mass, at which those already mentioned chanted and officiated. There were there with us some fifty or sixty natives, all kneeling as we were, and when it came to the Gospel and we all rose to our feet with hands lifted, they rose with us and lifted their hands, remaining thus until it was over. And then they again sat down as we did. And at the elevation of the Host when we knelt, they placed themselves as we were, with hands uplifted, and so quietly that I assure Your Highness that they gave us much edification. They stayed there with us until communion was over, and after the communion the friars and priests and the captain and some of the rest of us partook of communion. Some of them, because the sun was hot, arose while we were receiving communion and others remained as they were and stayed. One of them, a man of fifty or fifty-five years, stayed there with those who remained. While we were all thus he collected those who had remained and even called others. He went about among them and talked to them, pointing with his finger to the altar, and afterwards he lifted his finger towards Heaven as though he were telling them something good, and thus we understood it. After the mass was over the father took off his outer vestment and remained in his alb, and then he mounted a chair near the altar, and there he preached to us of the Gospel and of the apostles whose day this is, treating at the end of the sermon of this your holy and virtuous undertaking, which caused us more edification. Those who still remained for the sermon were looking at him, as we were doing. And the one of whom I speak called some to come there; some came and others departed. And when the sermon was over, Nicolao Coelho brought many tin crosses with crucifixes, which he still had from another voyage, and we thought it well to put one around the neck of each; for which purpose the father, Frei Amrique, seated himself at the foot of the cross, and there, one by one, he put around the neck of each his own tied to a string, first making him kiss it and raise his hands. Many came for this, and we did likewise to all. They must have been about forty or fifty. And after this was finished it was already a good hour after midday; we went to the ships to eat, and the captain took with him that same one who had pointed out to the others the altar and the sky, and his brother with him, to whom he did much honour. And he gave him a Moorish shirt, and to the other one a shirt such as the rest of us wore. And as it appears to me and to every one, these people in order to be wholly Christian lack nothing except to understand us, for whatever they saw us do, they did likewise; wherefore it appeared to all that they have no idolatry and no worship. And I well believe that, if Your Highness should send here some one who would go about more at leisure among them, that all will be turned to the desire of Your Highness. And if some one should come for this purpose, a priest should not fail to come also at once to baptize them, for by that time they will already have a greater knowledge of our faith through the two convicts who are remaining here among them. Both of these also partook of communion today. Among all those who came today there was only one young woman who stayed continuously at the mass, and she was given a cloth with which to cover herself, and we put it about her; but as she sat down she did not think to spread it much to cover herself. Thus, Senhor, the innocence of this people is such, that that of Adam could not have been greater in respect to shame. Now Your Highness may see whether people who live in such innocence will be converted or not if they are taught what pertains to their salvation. When this was over we went thus in their presence to kiss the cross, took leave of them, and came to eat.

I believe, Senhor, that with these two convicts who remain here, there stay also two seamen who tonight left this ship, fleeing to shore in a skiff. They have not come back and we believe that they remain here, because tomorrow, God willing, we take our departure from here.

It seems to me, Senhor, that this land from the promontory we see farthest south to another promontory that is to the north, of which we caught sight from this harbour, is so great that it will have some twenty or twenty-five leagues of coastline. Along the shore in some places it has great banks, some of them red, some white, and the land above is quite flat and covered with great forests. From point to point the entire shore is very flat and very beautiful. As for the interior, it appeared to us from the sea very large, for, as far as eye could reach, we could see only land and forests, a land that seemed very extensive to us. Up to now we are unable to learn that there is gold or silver in it, or anything of metal or iron; nor have we seen any, but the land itself has a very good climate, as cold and temperate as that of Entre Doiro e Minho, because in the present season we found it like that. Its waters are quite endless. So pleasing is it that if one cares to profit by it, everything will grow in it because of its waters. But the best profit that can be derived from it, it seems to me, will be to save this people, and this should be the chief seed that Your Highness should sow there. And if there were nothing more than to have here a stopping-place for this voyage to

Calicut, that would suffice, to say nothing of an opportunity to fulfil and do that which Your Highness so much desires, namely, the increase of our Holy Faith.

And in this manner, Senhor, I give here to Your Highness an account of what I saw in this land of yours, and if I have been somewhat lengthy you will pardon me, for the desire I had to tell you everything made me set it down thus in detail. And, Senhor, since it is certain that in this charge laid upon me as in any other thing which may be for your service, Your Highness will be very faithfully served by me, I ask of you that in order to do me a special favour you order my son-in-law, Jorge Do Soiro, to return from the island of Sam Thomé. This I shall take as a very great favour to me.

I kiss Your Highness's hands. From this Porto Seguro of your island of Vera Cruz today, Friday, the first day of May of 1500.

PERO VAAZ DE CAMINHA"

CHAPTER 8

LETTER OF MASTER JOHN TO KING MANUEL

Master John was a Galician. As personal physician and surgeon of Dom Manuel, his duties involved those of an astrologer, and because of this he held the position of astronomer on the fleet. He was on one of the smaller ships. The chief duty of Master John seems to have been to study the constellations of the southern hemisphere. On 1st May 1500, before Cabral's fleet left Brazil, Master John wrote a letter to the King Manuel, the king of Portugal, in which he details their position.

****

"SEÑOR : I, the bachelor Master John, physician and surgeon of Your Highness, kiss your hands. Señor : because Arias Correa as well as all the others have written to Your Highness at length concerning all that happened here, I shall write only regarding two points. Señor : yesterday, Monday, which was the 27th of April, we went on shore, I and the pilot of the chief captain and the pilot of Sancho de Tovar; and we took the height of the sun at midday; and we found 56 degrees, and the shadow was north. By this, according to the rules of the astrolabe, we judged that we were 17 degrees distant from the equinoctial and consequently had the height of the Antarctic pole in 17 degrees, as is manifest in the sphere. And this is what concerns one point. Whence Your Highness will know that all the pilots go beyond me to such an extent that Pero Escolar exceeds me by 150 leagues, and some more and some less; but which one tells the truth cannot be ascertained until in good time we arrive at the Cape of Good Hope, and there we shall known who goes more correctly, they with the chart, or I with the chart and the astrolabe. As regards the situation of this land, Señor, Your Highness should order a mappa mundi to be brought which Pero Vaaz Bisagudo has, and on it Your Highness will be able to see the location of this land. That mappa mundi, however, does not show whether this land is inhabited or not. It is an old mappa mundi, and there Your Highness will also find la Mina marked. Yesterday we almost understood by signs that this was an island, and that there were four, and that from another island almadias come here to fight with them, and they take them captive.

In regard, Señor, to the other point. Your Highness will know that I have done whatever work I could concerning the stars, but not much, because of a very bad leg which I have, for a wound larger than the palm of my hand has developed from a scratch; and also because this ship is very small and very heavily laden, so that there is no room for anything. I inform Your Highness only how the stars are located, but in which degree each one is, I have not been able to learn; rather it seems impossible to me to take the height of any star on the sea, for I labour much at it and, however little the ship rolls, one errs by four or five degrees, so that it cannot be done except on land. And I say almost the same thing about the India tables, for it cannot be taken with them save with very much work; for if Your Highness knew how they all disagreed in the inches, you would laugh at this more than at the astrolabe, because from Lisbon to the Canaries they disagreed with one another by many inches, for some said three and four inches more than others. And the same was true from the Canaries to the islands of Cape Verde; and this although all took precautions that the observation should be at the same hour, so that they judged rather how many inches there were by the length of the journey which it seemed to them they had gone, than the journey by means of the inches. Returning to the point, Señor, these guards are never hidden; rather do they always go round above the horizon, and even this is doubtful, for I do not know which of the two lowest ones is the Antarctic pole. And these stars, principally those of the cross, are large, almost as those of Ursa Major; and the star of the Antarctic pole, or south, is small, like that of the north, and very clear, and the star that is above the entire cross is very small.

In order not to trouble Your Highness, I do not wish to write further, except that I am asking Our Lord Jesus Christ to increase the life and estate of Your Highness as Your Highness desires. Done in Vera Cruz, the first day of May of 1500. At sea it is better to direct oneself by the height of the sun than by any star, and better with the astrolabe than with the quadrant or with any other instrument.

From the servant of Your Highness and your loyal servitor, Johanes artium et medicine bachalarius.

To the King our Lord."

CHAPTER 9

THEORIES FOR CABRAL'S WESTWARD DIVERSION

During the voyage of Cabral's fleet to India the course was diverted to the westward of a southerly course after leaving the Cape Verde Islands, and because of this diversion the mainland of South America was reached. While this course may have seemed justified at the time for better navigation and was probably advised by Vasco da Gama, no reason for it is given in any of the contemporary accounts of the voyage or by any of the reliable historians of the period, with the exception of João de Barros, who simply states that the fleet went westward to avoid the Guinea calms. Many of the subsequent voyages to India followed this route, some because a landing was desired on the coast of Brazil to secure wood and water and additional supplies, and others because this course, though longer, had the advantage of better sailing conditions and because the destination could be reached more quickly.

In the three centuries that followed the discovery of America the science of navigation developed steadily, but the narratives of voyages were considered chiefly as matter of record or of popular interest. Ramusio, Hakluyt, and others assembled the accounts of these voyages and incorporated them in their celebrated collections. It was not until towards the beginning of the nineteenth century that a serious study of these documents and narratives was undertaken. Two factors contributed to the better knowledge of early voyages and navigation. One was a renewed interest in the voyages of discovery, particularly in those to America, and the discovery and critical examination of documents and maps relating to them; the other was the scientific discovery of the great ocean currents chiefly through the studies of the English geographer George Rennell, and of Alexander von Humboldt. It was at this time that Muñoz found the valuable documents relating to the early Spanish voyages to America that were later published by Navarrete, and that the accounts of the voyages of Vespucci and others were first questioned and controversies started that have continued to the present day. During this period, attention was given to the voyage of Cabral, and the question arose as to why his course took him westward. Humboldt answers this in his Examen Critique with the positive statement that this occurred because the currents caused the fleet to deviate towards the west of its intended course. The authority of Humboldt and his brilliance as a scientist and critic caused this solution to remain unquestioned in the popular mind until comparatively recent years, but it was not entirely satisfactory. The importance of the voyage of Cabral in the history of Brazil brought about a discussion of this problem by several historians of that country in 1854 under the patronage of Dom Pedro II. This produced a series of studies that were published in the Revista do Instituto Histórico e Geográphico Brasileiro; yet the answer was not found. The question as to why Cabral went to the westward and so discovered Brazil has resulted in the formation of two schools, one of which claims that the voyage was made intentionally owing to previous knowledge of this shore, and the other that Brazil was discovered by chance. The former theory supposes that the land was revisited during this voyage, the latter that a real discovery was made. The uncertainty as to the motives for Cabral's westward diversion still exists, and has been accentuated by prominence given to a statement by a contemporary cosmographer, Duarte Pacheco Pereira, who claimed in his Esmeraldo de situ orbis that the King of Portugal had sent him to discover land to the west in the year 1498, two years prior to the landfall of Cabral.

The various theories for the westward diversion of the fleet commanded by Cabral are examined as follows :

I Fortuitous

(a) That the fleet lost its bearings in the vicinity of the Cape Verde Islands, and went westward.

One of the earliest theories advanced was that the fleet had lost its way while searching for the ship of Vasco de Ataíde. This theory was suggested in an ambiguous way by Antonio Galvão, who here repeats a popular tradition but without historical basis. As a matter of fact there went with the fleet the best navigators of that period, who were able to locate the approximate positions of the ships on their charts at any time, except for the influence of the ocean currents, which were not then known to exist.

(b) That it drifted westward because of the ocean currents.

Humboldt, in his critical studies of the early voyages to America, believed that he had solved the question from a scientific standpoint. Benjamin Franklin had discovered the Gulf Stream, and George Rennell the Agulhas Current. These had led to further investigations that showed that there also existed westward currents in the Atlantic, in the course followed by Cabral's fleet. While realizing the superiority of the Portuguese navigators, Humboldt pointed out that as they did not then have means for determining longitude at sea, these currents caused the diversion. Humboldt was acquainted with the contemporary documents, with the letter written by Dom Manuel in 1501, with that of Caminha, and with the Portuguese histories, and he agreed with them that Cabral reached the Brazilian coast by chance. He says, "Pedro Alvarez Cabral, whom Manuel sent on the track of Vasco da Gama to the Indies, wishing to avoid the calms of the Gulf of Guinea (de Barros).....landed unexpectedly on the shores of Brazil..... The intimate knowledge that we have today of the multiplicity of these currents or pelagic streams of different temperatures that traverse the great longitudinal valley of the Atlantic offers an easy explanation for the extraordinary drift towards the west that the little squadron of Cabral experienced." The desire on the part of Cabral's pilots to attempt to round the Guinea calms by taking a westward course seems plausible, and the westward drift of the ocean to the north and south of the "doldrums" is uncontestable. While both of these explanations may have had an influence on the diversion they do not explain entirely the route followed by Cabral.

II Intentional because of prior discovery.

(a) To revisit land previously known, supposed to be indicated on a map made by Andrea Bianco prior to 1448.

In the year 1894, Yule Oldham announced that he had discovered on a chart made by Andrea Bianco in 1448 indications of an extensive land of a shape roughly similar to that of South America, located to the south-west of the Cape Verde Islands. On this was a legend in two lines that he read, "Authentic island is distant 1,500 miles to the west." This map was also examined in the Marciana Library by Sig. Carlo Errera, who corroborated, in the following year, the finding of Yule Oldham, but read the distance 500 miles instead of 1,500. The question was further discussed by J.Batalha-Reis in 1897, who concluded that "somebody had certainly seen an island and perhaps landed on it", located south-west of Cape Verde, probably at a distance of 1,500 miles. There is no reference elsewhere, however, to this discovery having been made. Andrea Bianco helped Fra Mauro in the drawing of his celebrated map of the known world in 1457, and although Fra Mauro was most exact in placing on this map all available information that was known in his day, this land to the west is not shown. From the time of Aristotle and Ptolemy land was supposed to occupy at least half of the globe. While on later maps this exaggerated land area was usually represented by a hypothetical Antarctic continent, it might easily on this map have been shown as land to the west. The theory of this early discovery does not seem to have been proven, and there is no indication that Cabral had any knowledge of it.

(b) To revisit land to the westward, supposed to be shown on a map of "Bisagudo" referred to in the letter of Master John.

In the letter that Master John sent back to Dom Manuel from Brazil in 1500 he states, "Your Highness should order a mappa mundi to be brought which Pero Vaaz Bisagudo has, and on it Your Highness will be able to see the location of this land. That mappa mundi, however, does not show whether this land is inhabited or not. It is an old mappa mundi, and there Your Highness will also find la Mina marked." This map was thus known in Portugal at the time of Cabral's departure. He calls it a mappa antiga, which is but a relative term. Cartographers had made charts of the Atlantic on which several mythical islands in the Atlantic were indicated. It may have been to one of these that Master John referred. It has been suggested that such a map, and perhaps this one, had been used during the discussions prior to the signing of the Treaty of Tordesillas in 1494. A map of this sort would naturally show the Portuguese factory at Mina, on the Guinea coast, which was then important for the shipment of gold, ivory, and slaves. Batalha-Reis identifies the owner of this map as Pero Vaz de Cunha, called the Bisagudo, who was sent in 1488 by John II to build a fortress in the

Senegal. There is no reference to this map of Bisagudo except in this letter, and it is difficult to believe, in the absence of other evidence, that the map referred to indicated a prior discovery of Brazil.

(c) To claim officially for Portugal this land, which was believed to have been visited by Duarte Pacheco Pereira in 1498, as interpreted from passages in his Esmeraldo de Situ Orbis.

One of the most celebrated men in Portugal during this period was Duarte Pacheco Pereira. He was born in Lisbon about the middle of the fifteenth century, of a good family. He went to sea early and during the fourteen years of the reign of John II he was one of the captains in his confidence. With Diego de Azambuja, Bartolomeu Dias, Diogo Cão, and others he explored the coast of Africa. He was a witness to and signed for Portugal the Treaty of Tordesillas in the capacity of a cosmographer. Pereira probably did not go to India with Cabral. In 1505 he began to write a book for the king that was to serve as a pilot of the African coast. This was probably completed between that date and 1520, a period during which he remained on shore. To this book he gave the title Esmeraldo de Situ Orbis. The latter portion of the title had been used by Pomponius Mela for his famous work. In chapter ii of the first book he states that Dom Manuel had sent him to America in 1498 for the purpose of discovery. This statement, which has given rise to the theory that Brazil was discovered at that time and thus prior to the voyage of Cabral, is as follows :

"And in addition to what is said, experience, which is the mother of things, enlightens us and withdraws us from all doubt; and consequently, Happy Prince, we have known and seen, how in the third year of your reign of the year of Our Lord of 1498, whither Your Highness sent us to discover the western part, passing beyond the greatness of the ocean sea, where is found and navigated so great a terra firma, with many and large islands adjacent to it, which extends to seventy degrees of latitude from the equinoctial line against the Arctic pole, and although it may be somewhat distant, it is greatly peopled; and on the other side of the same equinoctial circle it goes beyond to twenty-eight and one-half degrees of latitude against the antarctic pole and it expands so much its greatness and extends to such great distance that of one part or of the other was not seen or known the end and finish of it; by which, according to the order that it carries, it is certain that it goes in a circle by all the roundness; so that we have learned that from the shores and coast of the sea of these kingdoms of Portugal, and from the promontory of Finis-terre and from whatever other place of Europe, and of Africa and of Asia, traversing beyond all the ocean directly to the West, where the west is according to the order of nautical art, a distance of thirty-six degrees which would be six hundred and forty-eight leagues of journey, counting eighteen leagues to a degree, and there are some places still farther away, this land is found in the navigation by the ships of Your Highness, and, by your order and licence, by those of your vassals and citizens; and going along this aforementioned coast from the same equinoctial circle beyond, for twenty-eight degrees of latitude against the antarctic pole, there is found in it much and fine brazil with many other things with which the ships come greatly loaded to these kingdoms.'

In chapter iii he also says : ".....and other ancient cosmographers who went to the same land for many years and other persons who have known that this is true information, have divided it in three notable parts. And in the third part, which Your Highness sent to discover beyond the ocean, as it was an unknown thing to them, they do not speak of."

Pereira does not here state that he went to Brazil in 1498, although he mentions the discovery of the coast of Brazil and refers to its having been explored for a distance of 28½° south. It must be remembered that the Esmeraldo was written subsequent to 1505, when the Brazilian coast was well known through the third voyage of Vespucci.

The voyages to America for the year 1498 are somewhat obscure. Harrisse mentions those of Vespucci, Cabot, Thirkill, Coronel, and Columbus. It is possible that there were others and that this voyage of the Portuguese to America was clandestine and that there are no records. The best known voyage to America in 1498 was the third voyage of Columbus. This sailed from San Lucar on the 30th of May of that year. Becoming frightened in the equatorial calms, or wishing to return to Hispañola more quickly, Columbus steered northward and after discovering the north coast of South America reached that island. He did not return immediately, but a fleet of five vessels left for Spain soon after his arrival, so that there was ample time for word to reach Lisbon before Cabral sailed. This voyage raises several questions. It was partly financed with money set aside by Ferdinand and Isabella for the celebration of the wedding of Dom Manuel. It sailed from the Portuguese islands of Cape Verde towards the equator and it proceeded over seas hitherto unexplored, where islands or mainland within the Portuguese sphere might be found. It is possible that it was a joint expedition sent by Spain and Portugal for the location of the line of demarcation. This determination as provided for in the treaty had been deferred from time to time. If the voyage had been made to the west for this purpose, Pereira, a cosmographer who had signed the Treaty of Tordesillas for Portugal, would naturally have been chosen to accompany it. Had Pereira gone on any of the known voyages of 1498 he would not have visited Brazil. These references in the Esmeraldo do not seem to have any relation to the voyage of Cabral.

(d) To substantiate the claim that land had been found there during the reign of João II.

When Columbus presented the plan for his voyage to João II it was refused by the junta of cosmographers, not because of doubt that Cathay could be reached by navigating to the west but because it was felt that India and its spices could be attained by the African sea route with greater certainty and the way was shorter. João II and his advisers probably knew more than Columbus about the Atlantic. They had learned all that was known of indications of land to the west from those to whom they had granted permission for its discovery. They also had able navigators who could make this voyage without acceding to such exorbitant demands as those made by Columbus.

Unfortunately, few records of the early navigation now remain. This is partly due to the neglect in their preservation in the Torre do Tombo, to their having been withdrawn for official use and not returned because of the changing location of the court, but chiefly because of a policy of secrecy which it was felt necessary to maintain. Not only have almost all the early records disappeared but also many of the chronicles. Even the writings of the historians of the sixteenth century were under such strict supervision that they cannot always be trusted. The policy of secrecy had existed since the first voyages of Prince Henry. It was due to two causes : first, to prevent other nations from learning of the discoveries and, second, because the voyages and trade were considered a royal monopoly and could be engaged in only at the will of the king, who usually received part of the profits. Except for the navigation of the Norsemen to Greenland and of the Spaniards to the Canary Islands, the Portuguese had claimed all but the coastal navigation of the Atlantic. It became not only the hope but the belief of João II that islands and probably mainland existed to the west. We have indications of this in the concession given to Fernão, Domingues do Arco of Madeira in 1484, who evidently intended to explore in that direction. It is evidenced also in a similar project approved in 1486 in favour of Fernão Dulmo of Terceira, and of Dulmo and João Afonso do Estreito in 1487. There are further indications that other voyages were planned, but there is no record that any discoveries were made in America. When the line of demarcation was fixed by the bulls of 1493 João used every effort to have this extended further west. While he sought chiefly to secure sea room for his ships to India he also sought an added area to the west where he believed or knew that land was to be found. There is no evidence that such a land had been discovered by the Portuguese beyond the Atlantic during João's reign, and those who make this claim do so with the belief that the documents that existed to prove it have disappeared.

If the Brazilian coast had been previously visited, or was even believed to exist, it is reasonable to suppose that a small fleet similar to that which was later sent with Amerigo Vespucci would have gone there not only to claim officially that portion within the Portuguese sphere, but also to continue the discovery along the shore to the north, where mainland had been touched by Columbus in 1498, and to go south to ascertain if land existed there as well.

The belief that Cabral's fleet was diverted to the westward to revisit Brazil while on its voyage to India is open to several objections.

Cabral did not immediately take possession for the king, and no effort was made for further discovery. On the contrary, the ceremony during which the royal arms were raised took place during a mass that was said just before the fleet departed, and it was not felt necessary for either the ship of Gaspar de Lemos or the main fleet to ascertain whether this new shore was an island or mainland. It is hard to understand why it was decided to send a ship back to Portugal to advise the king of this discovery if the fleet had been diverted to revisit a land already known to exist. It is also strange that, if this shore had been previously visited, there was no knowledge among the members of Cabral's fleet of the natives and of the parrots that they were so interested in finding there.

There is no contemporary account of his voyage either by a Portuguese or an Italian author that does not state that Cabral made this discovery. There is, furthermore, no historian until recent years who has questioned it. Duarte Pacheco Pereira himself, while he does not mention Cabral in this connection, does not definitely state that he visited the Brazilian coast.

Dom Manuel had no reason for maintaining secrecy regarding this or any prior voyage, particularly at a time when the thrones of Portugal and Castile were almost united.

Pero Vaz de Caminha states that Cabral's fleet found it, and he says further, "and God who brought us here did not do so without reason". Caminha would not have written this to the king had he believed that this land had previously been visited.

While Master John does not mention the discovery of Brazil, the wording of his letter gives no indication that he believed that it had previously been visited. He says, "Yesterday we almost understood by signs that this was an island and that there were four."

The land was named Vera Cruz by Cabral. This name was changed to Santa Cruz by the king. Had the land been visited earlier, a name would already have been chosen for it and the king would not merely have modified that given to it by Cabral.

The Cantino map of 1502, which may be considered the copy of one which was official, states that this coast was discovered by the Portuguese in 1500.

Perhaps the strongest proof is that the King of Portugal himself wrote a letter in 1501 to his cousin and mother-in-law, Queen Isabella, and to his father-in-law, King Ferdinand, with both of whom he was on very friendly terms, in which he states that this land had been discovered by Cabral.

In view of this contemporary evidence and of the fact that no documents have been discovered that were not known at that time, it would seem that more conclusive proof must be produced by those who challenge the discovery of Brazil by Cabral.

III Intentional, for discovery

(a) To ascertain what land, if any, existed within the Portuguese sphere to the east of the line of demarcation established by the Treaty of Tordesillas, 370 leagues to the west of the Cape Verde Islands.

At the commencement of the reign of Dom Manuel the best astronomers, mathematicians, and navigators in Europe were in Portugal. Many of the scientists were Jews who had been driven from Spain. They found asylum at Lisbon, where they were glad to aid the Portuguese kin because they were bitterly resentful of the treatment that their race had received from Ferdinand and Isabella. There were also in Portugal Florentine merchants who, through their commercial and banking relations, knew of the aspirations of the Spanish to obtain wealth in their newly found islands to the west. The results of the voyage of Columbus, during which the north coast of South America had been reached and pearls had been found, were undoubtedly known in Lisbon at the time of the departure of Cabral's fleet. The Portuguese were also aware that other voyages were being made by the Spaniards to this coast. They, in all probability, had obtained maps and sailing directions of the Spanish voyages to America and had undoubtedly during the eight years that followed the first voyage of Columbus sent representatives on some of them. It was opportune at this particular time to ascertain whether land existed within the Portuguese sphere, and to anticipate any Spanish voyages to lands that might be theirs. While Cabral's fleet was destined for India, there was a possibility of combining in this voyage a westward divergence from the Cape Verde Islands for this purpose. By following the route commenced by Columbus in his third voyage, it might proceed farther to the west than had Vasco da Gama in his voyage to the Cape. By this route some of the Portuguese sphere to the west might thus become known. The junta of cosmographers who planned Cabral's voyage might well have felt that by taking advantage of the north-east trade winds and, if possible, by rounding the calms, this divergence for discovery could be made without delaying the arrival in India. This might also be a safer and more practical route.

The belief that Cabral's fleet went to the south-west with the hope of discovery has added weight since in the same year Gaspar Corte-Real went to the north-west on a similar mission. The presence in the fleet of the astronomer, Master John, might thus be accounted for.

(b) To determine if the South American continent ended in this parallel, so that a course could thus be taken to India.

The theory that Cabral's fleet was diverted westward to reach India in that direction has nothing to commend it. There are no indications of such an intent and neither at this time nor later was there any desire on the part of Portugal to encroach, from this direction, on the Spanish rights as defined in the Treaty of Tordesillas.

IV Intentional, for reasons of navigation.

(a) To endeavour to round the Guinea calms, as asserted by de Barros.

The theory suggested by de Barros, which is the only one advanced by any authoritative writer during the sixteenth century, was that the fleet steered to the westward to endeavour to round the equatorial calms. These bend to the south-east before reaching the African coast south of Guinea. The Portuguese voyages to Mina were favoured by the strong Guinea current on their outward voyage, but on their return they were opposed by it. They thus had experience with this calm belt, that hemmed in their course to the south and made further voyages along the coast more difficult. Vasco da Gama had crossed it at some distance from the African coast. Columbus on his third voyage, after steering to the south-west from the Cape Verde Islands, had entered it and describes the terrific heat and discomfort of the tropical seas in words that must have been exaggerated. While Cabral's fleet would wish to avoid these calms, it is doubtful whether this was the only reason for the diversion.

(b) To take advantage of the favourable north-east trade winds and thus take a somewhat longer course westward for better navigation to the Cape, with the hope, perhaps, of discovering a western end of the equatorial calms, and rounding the south-east trades.

There were several ships in the fleet. These had a length of about three times their beam. They were clumsy and carried large sails that could not easily be adjusted to the wind. Since the fleet had to be kept together its speed was determined by the poorest sailor. The route for this reason seems to have been taken with the north-west trade winds after leaving the island of São Nicolau, following the suggestion of da Gama and the experience of Columbus. When the region of the equatorial calms was reached the course was taken to the south. Beyond these calms the prevailing wind was from the south-east, the direction that they were to take to the Cape. It was evidently not felt desirable to sail against this wind with the ships but to continue the course somewhat to the west for better sailing in the hope that light favourable winds might be found to carry them to the Cape, as da Gama had suggested. This course would take them along the Brazilian shore. The south-east trade-wind area extends in an approximate oval from the Cape of Good Hope to Cape Saint Roque in Brazil. The uniformity of this wind, like that of the north-east trade, was well known to da Gama. On his outward voyage he had sailed against it from the equatorial calms to the Cape, and he had found that this head wind had made the sailing slow and caused discomfort to the crew. In da Gama's suggestion for the route to be followed by Cabral's fleet, therefore, a westward diversion was advised, not only with the belief that the Guinea calms might be rounded but even more so that the south-east trade wind might also be avoided. The rounding of this contrary wind area in the hope of finding more favourable winds to the west may have been the chief reason for Cabral's course. The voyage as far as Brazil was the correct course to the Cape.

Unfortunately, Cabral does not seem to have sailed far enough to the south after leaving the Brazilian coast to obtain the benefit of the westerly winds. This error was evidently recognized, for subsequent voyages took their course eastward in the parallel of the Tristão da Cunha Islands. They thus avoided the high pressure area to the north that was so disastrous to Cabral's fleet.

It must not be forgotten that the fleet was destined for India. It was large for the time and carried a valuable cargo. The course to be followed, therefore, was the one that it was believed would ensure the most favourable winds and the greatest safety irrespective of any hopes of rounding the calms or discovery. The discovery of Brazil according to this theory was accidental.

From the foregoing it seems probable that Cabral's fleet was the first to reach the shores of Brazil under the Portuguese flag. The westward diversion of the fleet, during which Brazil was visited, seems to have been made not for one but for several reasons. The chief motive was to follow the most practicable and safest route to the Cape of Good Hope.

CHAPTER 10

CLAIMS OF PRIOR DISCOVERIES OF BRAZIL

The theories that Brazil had been visited by Europeans prior to the voyage of Cabral may be divided into two classes : those claiming that the voyage had been made by navigators in early times who did not return, and those made in the fifteenth century by others who brought back word of discoveries. To the former class belong those theories that are based on Biblical references, on allusions by classical writers, or on evidences to be found on the South American continent. A discussion of these belongs to a field that is not within the scope of this volume. In the second class are the theories based on indications in the charts of Andrea Bianco and Pero Vaz Bisagudo, on the belief that voyages had been made during the reign of João II and that Duarte Pacheco Pereira had visited Brazil in 1498. These have already been discussed as reasons for the diversion of Cabral's fleet to the westward. There remain to be mentioned other claims, probably unknown to Cabral, that have been seriously advocated for the prior discovery of Brazil. These include the Spanish voyages, the voyage of Jean Cousin, and the statements of three persons which, it is believed, indicate that Brazil was previously known.

Columbus visited Trinidad and probably the coast of Pária in 1498, and may be considered the first European to visit the South American continent. The discovery of the mainland during his third voyage was disputed by the Spanish Crown in a celebrated trial during which testimony was taken in 1513 and 1515 by the Spanish Fiscal and Diego Columbus, the son of the great admiral. The question was not settled at that time; but, in view of the evidence there produced and the research of subsequent historians, it is almost certain that he did so. After this discovery Columbus returned to Hispañola, where he remained until his return to Spain in chains. Word was sent back to Spain, however, that pearls had been found along the South American coast. This news caused other fleets to be sent to Pária to seek these new riches and to make further discoveries. The advantage of following a more southerly route from the Cape Verde Islands and thus to take advantage of the north-east trade winds had been apparent during the voyage of

Columbus, so this course seems to have been chosen. It has been claimed that during these voyages the coast of Brazil was followed until Venezuela was reached, and that it was thus discovered prior to the voyage of Cabral. Five Spanish fleets may have sailed during the year 1499, under the commands of Alonzo de Ojeda (who it is said was accompanied by Amerigo Vespucci as a merchant and by Juan de la Cosa as pilot), Cristobal Guerra, Vicente Yañez Pinzon (who had gone with Columbus on his first voyage), and Diego de Lepe. Some believe that there should be added the name of Alonso Vellez de Mendoza. The information that remains concerning these voyages is confused and conflicting. Ojeda claims that on his voyage he first sighted land 200 leagues (Vespucci says 300) before reaching Pária and would thus have visited the coast of Brazil in 1499. The accounts of this voyage by Ojeda and Vespucci have caused much controversy that is too involved to be adequately given here, but it is reasonably certain that Brazil was not visited by them at this time. The references to other Spanish voyages are chiefly given in the probanzas and cannot be considered confirmed, because of lack of sufficient corroborating evidence. The voyage of Vicente Yañez Pinzon, however, has documentary support in its favour. In his testimony given in 1513 Pinzon states that he discovered 'from the Cape of Consolation which is in the part of Portugal and is now called Cape S. Agustines' and that he discovered the whole coast to the west and north-west as far as the mouth of the Drago. In an agreement signed by Ferdinand and Isabella at Granada the 5th of September 1501, his discoveries on the South American mainland were recognized as from the places that he had designated as Santa Maria de la Consolacion and Rostro Hermosa, along the coast to the north-west, past the large river that he called Santa Maria de la Mar-dulce, and all the land as far as the Cape of San Vicente. In this document he is named as royal captain and governor of these lands from the first named place to the river of Santa Maria de la Mar-dulce and the islands in the mouth of that river.

In the same year Angelo Trevisan, the secretary of the Venetian ambassador to Spain, had access to the papers of Peter Martyr relating to the voyages to America. After the departure of Martyr for Egypt on the 14th of September, Trevisan sent copies of these in Italian translation to his former employer, Domenico Malipiero, at Venice.

These accounts of the Spanish voyages were printed in 1504 in a collection known as the Libretto de tutta la navigation de Re de Spagna and subsequently reprinted in the Paesi of 1507. Among them was an account of the voyage of Pinzon that was sent to Venice in December 1501. All of this was unknown to Peter Martyr, who included this account of Pinzon's voyage in the first edition of his First Decade in 1511 and also in the complete Decades in 1516, both of which were in Latin. In the Libretto the statement is made that Pinzon's fleet of four caravels departed from Palos on the 18th of November 1499, and after taking their course south-west from the Cape Verde Islands came in sight of land on the 10th of January 1500. It then continued along the coast for 600 leagues, passing a gulf of fresh water. The coast of Pária was reached, and on the 3rd of June the fleet departed for Hispañola.

The account of the voyage, as given by Peter Martyr in the Seville edition of 1511 and in that of Alcalá of 1516, agrees substantially with that in the Libretto, but it states that the first landing was on the 26th of January. Further evidence that the Pinzon brothers visited the shore of Brazil is indicated on the map of Juan de la Cosa. This map, which is dated 1500 (though there is evidence that the only copy now known was drawn not earlier than 1508), might provide proof that Cape São Agostinho was reached by Pinzon and the coast followed to the north-west as far as the coast of Venezuela. It was in fact originally drawn expressly for this voyage, for on it are prominently shown three Spanish flags along the shore, two caravels, apparently those of the Pinzon brothers, and an inscription opposite Cape São Agostinho stating that it had been discovered by Vicente Yañez in 1499. The coast shows some resemblance to that of Brazil, and there is an indication of the mouth of the Amazon. The map does not show Vespucci's voyage of 1501 or Cabral's voyage to India, although an island appears to the east of Brazil with the inscription "island discovered for Portugal". This map, therefore, contains information collected after the return of Gaspar de Lemos and Pinzon in the autumn of 1500 but before Vespucci reached Portugal in 1501. The voyage of the Pinzons in 1499 along the Brazilian shore was accepted by the early Spanish historians. These Spanish voyages were discussed during the nineteenth century by Navarrete, Humboldt, Varnhagen, Harrisse, Vignaud, and others, and while no agreement was reached, the general opinion has been that the voyages of Pinzon and Lepe, at least, followed this shore. In 1921 Professor Duarte Leite made a critical and unprejudiced examination of these Spanish voyages that was published in chapter iii of the História da Colonização Portuguesa do Brasil with the title "The False Precursors of Álvares Cabral". In 1931 he further discussed the questions involved in his Descobridores do Brasil. As a result of his studies Professor Leite concludes that "In 1499 Hojeda did not cross the equator nor bring to view the Orinoco; Pinzon was not in the Amazon in 1500, and was farther north, not passing beyond Cape Orange; Diego de Lepe and Vellez de Mendoza visited only the greatest of rivers when the splendours of history had already displayed it in the sixteenth century". The claims of these Spaniards to the discovery of the Brazilian coast are according to this author false, and were made either for personal ends or to exclude the Portuguese from possessions on the South American continent. Professor Leite takes up each voyage in succession, and with a full knowledge of the sources and of subsequent criticisms challenges the claims that Brazil had been visited by the Spaniards before the voyage of Cabral. He asserts that these voyages may have been made to the vicinity of Trinidad, but it was the Orinoco and not the Amazon whose fresh waters extended far into the sea. The descriptions of the natives and of the positions of the north star are not correct in these narratives. The distances are greatly exaggerated, and the landmarks given by Pinzon and other navigators in the authentic contemporary documents may with greater reason be located on the coast of Venezuela. The map of Juan de la Cosa according to this criticism cannot be considered to be based upon authentic information regarding Brazil, and either the original map has been altered or a copy made on which the claims of Pinzon were inserted and the line of demarcation shown to the east of Cape São Agostinho. If these claims of Pinzon were fictitious the map was altered or redrawn after 1500; indeed not earlier, as we know from other evidence, than 1508. In view of the present knowledge of the early Spanish voyages there is thus a probability that Pedro Álvares Cabral was not only the first Portuguese but also the first European to visit the shores of Brazil.

Many French historians believe that Brazil was discovered by a navigator from Dieppe prior to the voyage of Cabral. The claim for this discovery is based on a tradition prevalent in Dieppe that a certain Jean Cousin was selected by some prominent merchants of that city to go on a voyage of exploration. He accepted this offer, and set sail in the year 1488. In order to avoid the storms and the sand-banks along the African coast he decided to take a course well out to sea. Arriving at the latitude of the Azores he was carried to the west by an ocean current. This took him to an unknown land at the mouth of an immense river. He claimed possession of this land and, instead of returning directly to Dieppe, went to the south-east, that is, towards South Africa. He discovered Cape Agulhas, and, after noting the coast, returned, arriving home in 1499. There is no proof of this voyage, and the author who suggests it, Desmarquets, is not considered reliable. Unfortunately, the public records at Dieppe were destroyed by the English in 1694, so that the question can never be settled. While this voyage may have been made, it seems more probably that the tradition regarding it was derived from the account of some voyage subsequent to that of Cabral, possibly that of de Gonneville. If it took place it would not have been sufficiently well known in Portugal to have influenced Cabral on his voyage.

It has been asserted that in a will signed before a notary on the 3rd of May 1580, in the presence of a judge and witnesses, one João Ramalho stated that he had been in Brazil since 1490, ninety years before. This statement has caused some to believe that Ramalho had arrived in Brazil on a clandestine voyage prior to that of Cabral and had later taken up his residence in São Paulo. There seems to have been a man by that name in Brazil as early as 1532, when Martim Afonso de Sousa states that he lent him signal services. This João Ramalho was associated with Antonio Rodrigues. Both of them married Indian wives and had considerable influence with the natives. Father Simão de Vasconcellos in his Chronica da Companhia de Jesus states that he was a man "infamous for grave crimes and at that time excommunicated". He is similarly mentioned by Ulric Schmidel and others. The date of the arrival of João Ramalho has given rise to much discussion, particularly in São Paulo. It has also been suggested that he might have been one of the convicts left by Cabral. It is more probable that he arrived in Brazil with one of the later fleets.

Another claim to a knowledge of Brazil prior to Cabral's voyage has been based on a document found by Jordão de Freitas in the Torre do Tombo, dated the 12th of July 1537. In evidence produced at a trial the following statement was made :

"They hope to prove that in the year 1531 (or 1532), in the said month, the ship and people who it is said belonged to the author went to Fernambuquo, a port of Brazil, where was a castle and fortress made by El Rey, our lord, and his Portuguese vassals thirty years ago and more. In the said port the said castle was made, and the port was inhabited by the Portuguese who had their dwelling houses there forty and more years ago. And at the time when it is said that the ship of the author arrived there, there was in the said castle a factory of the said lord and of many Portuguese merchants who had much merchandise there, as well from Portugal for trading as that which they obtained from the land, namely, brazil-wood, cottons, animal skins of different colours, parrots and monkeys and oils and slaves and much other Portuguese merchandise of great value. And they also had much artillery of copper and iron and powder and lances and bestas espinguardes and other offensive and defensive arms for their protection and against their enemies."

Another claim is that indicated in a letter written to Dom Manuel by Estevão Frois, a Portuguese, in 1514. In this he says that he was held in a Spanish prison at Hispañola after a voyage to Northern Brazil, and asks for intervention by the king. In the course of the letter he states that the Spaniards were unwilling to accept his proof that the Portuguese had possessed Brazil for twenty years and more. These claims are probably based on the reports of the early French and Portuguese voyages made to Brazil as private enterprises during the thirty years which followed that of Cabral.

CHAPTER 11

THE VOYAGE AROUND AFRICA TO INDIA

Barros asserts that Cabral set sail to resume his intended voyage on the 3rd May 1500. If so, one might find therein the explanation of his bestowal of the name Terra da Santa Cruz upon the newly discovered country for the Festival of the Invention of the Holy Cross falls upon that day.

When Cabral's fleet left the coast of Brazil it took its course to the Cape of Good Hope, with the evident intention of making a stop at São Bras. This sea had never been sailed previously, and this voyage from Brazil to the African coast may have been longer than any that had hitherto been made without sighting land.

The fleet continued with light winds, and a comet was seen on the 12th of May that was in view for ten days. This was to the crew an ill omen.

On the 23rd of May, according to Barros and Castanheda, on the ninth of that month according to Osorio, as the fleet was proceeding on its way in a high sea and with the wind astern, the wind suddenly veered to the contrary direction and, before the sails could be lowered, four ships were overset by the violence of the wind and their crews thrown into the sea and drowned. The captains of these vessels were Bartolomeu Dias, Symão de Pina, Gaspar de Lemos and Ayres Gomez de Silva. It was subsequently assumed that this disaster had occurred in the vicinity of certain islands but the assumption rested on a slender foundation.

When Vasco da Gama encountered a storm during his voyage to India in 1502, he was, Correa tells us, near the islands of which the Moorish pilot had spoken to Cabral. And the same author relates that after the catastrophe one of the pilots from Malindi told Cabral that the wind had struck upon islands and had rebounded and he thus accounted for its sudden change of direction. It seems extremely improbable that a pilot from Malindi could have any knowledge of islands in the South Atlantic unless he had himself seen them or been informed by others in the fleet of Cabral that they had seen them. It is not impossible that the disaster occurred within sight of the South American coast. Cretico asserts that the fleet followed the coast of the "Terra d li Papagá" for two thousand miles, and John Pory informs us that the first island discovered in the Ethiopian Sea about the Cape of Bona Speranza was that of Don Aluarez, in thirty-and-a-half degrees, where no island is. According to Osorio the disaster occurred ten days, according to Barros, twenty days after leaving the Terra da Santa Cruz.

A furious storm followed the hurricane and the ships with torn sails, and at the mercy of the elements for many days, parted company. Those of Cabral, Simão de Miranda, Nicolao Coelho and Pedro de Ataíde went in one direction, those of Nuno Leitão and Sancho de Tovar in another. Cabral's ship with two others, passing the Cape of Good Hope, and ascertaining their position through indication of land, turned to the north. The ship of Diogo Dias had became separated from the rest of the fleet.

On the 16th of July, Cabral with six ships was off Sofala. These vessels were the flagship and the ships commanded by Sancho de Tovar, Bras Matoso, Nuno Leitão, Nicolao Coelho and Luiz Pirez. A landing was made near the Ilhas Primeiras, north of Sofala on the East African coast. Here two Moorish ships, belonging to a cousin of the King of Malindi, who had so cordially welcomed da Gama, were encountered. One of these was beached by its captain but the other was captured together with the owner of both, a sheikh, Foteima by name, who was returning from Sofala to Malindi. He was an uncle of the Sultan of Malindi and was therefore immediately set at liberty. The captured vessel was restored to him. Cabral then continued his voyage to Mozambique where he appears to have been rejoined by Pedro de Ataíde. The other three ships joined Cabral at Mozambique on the 20th of July.

One is thus constrained to inquire what had become of Simão de Miranda. None of the chroniclers relate that he perished. However, in a letter ascribed to Amerigo Vespucci it is stated that five ships foundered in one storm. The letter was published in "Il Milione di Marco Polo," by Baldelli Boni, at pp. liv-lv. and was entitled "Copia d'una lettera scritta da Amerigo Vespucci dall' Isola del Capo Verde e nel mare Oceano a Lorenzo di Piero Francesco de Medici sotto di 4 di Giugno 1501 relativa a queste prime scoperte orientali." The author of the letter states that, being at Cape Verde on a voyage to the South, he met there two Portuguese vessels belonging to the fleet that had sailed for Calicut fourteen months previously. The writer gives a brief account of their voyage.

There is one assertion in this letter that requires some elucidation. If five ships were lost at sea between Brazil and the Cape of Good Hope and eight still remained, thirteen are accounted for without reckoning that which disappeared before the Cape Verde Islands were reached or that of Vasco de Taide or that which was sent home from Brazil. The name of Simão de Miranda was not amongst the names of the Captains who were at the place of rendezvous at Mozambique and hence it appears probable that the vessel commanded by Miranda also perished in the great storm but at a later date than the other four. Damião de Goes calls Sancho de Tovar the vice-commander of the fleet. If Simão de Miranda perished, Sancho de Tovar may have been appointed in his place.

Mozambique was ruled by a governor who was subject to the Sultan of Kilwa. The former port was entered on the 24th of July. The ships were repaired and refitted. They found the king of that place well disposed, because he feared the Portuguese guns, which da Gama had caused him to respect. Water and other supplies were secured here, and a pilot was obtained to guide them past the islands and shoals along the coast.

Having tarried here for several days, Cabral departed for Kilwa where a certain Ibrahim was Sultan. They reached Kilwa on the 26th. Kilwa had at that period about twelve thousand inhabitants. Here Afonso Furtado went on shore to negotiate a treaty with the king. Furtado had been appointed as factor to go with Bartolomeu Dias and Diogo Dias to Sofala, but he evidently sailed on the flagship and was thus saved from the misfortunes that overcame their ships. Arrangements were made for Cabral and the king to meet in boats at sea. Here a letter from Dom Manuel was presented. The king, however, was suspicious of the intention of the Portuguese and resented the enmity shown towards his religion. This was the principal city of East Africa and one of considerable wealth. Kilwa occupied an independent position on the East African coast, and derived a large revenue from the traders who came to Sofala and to other ports under its control. There was no reason, therefore, for welcoming the Portuguese, who could but be rivals in the trade that these Arabs enjoyed, and the attitude of superiority assumed by the Europeans caused additional hostility. Kilwa, like Mombasa, had nothing to gain from the advent of the Europeans and much to lose. While Cabral was received in an ostentatious and apparently friendly manner, ill feeling towards the Portuguese became increasingly apparent. The Chief Captain did not tarry long at this place for he was informed by a brother of the Sultan of Malindi that Ibrahim cherished evil designs. Without being able to make a treaty Cabral decided to continue his voyage.

No stop was made at Mombasa, because of the treachery that had been displayed there towards da Gama and because of the warfare existing between that city and Malindi. Malindi was reached on the 2nd of August. They were received here in a most friendly manner. Pedro Cabral was received with a like hospitality to that with which Vasco da Gama had been received about two years previously. A meeting was arranged between the king and Cabral in boats before the city, as had been done at Kilwa. Gifts were exchanged, and a letter from Dom Manuel was presented to the king. The King of Malindi was the only Arab ruler with whom the Portuguese were on friendly terms during this voyage. It is apparent that the friendship on the part of the Arabs was not disinterested. One cannot but note the difference in the attitude shown by the Portuguese towards the Arab merchants of Malindi and their king, where they had a common interest, and that shown towards the Arab infidels whom they encountered on the sea. Four days were spent in all kinds of festivities and on the seventh day of the month the fleet departed for India in charge of Gujarati pilots that they had secured. The coast of India, a little to the north of the Anjediva Islands, was sighted on the 22nd of August 1500.

CHAPTER 12

THE DISCOVERY OF MADAGASCAR

During the voyage of Cabral's fleet to India the ship of Diogo Dias had become separated due to the storm. It lost its way sailing too far beyond the Cape and then turned north. Diogo Dias then sailed far to the eastward and came in sight of the east coast of Madagascar, which had probably not been previously visited by Europeans. He only discovered his true position when he arrived at the northern extremity of the island.

The Anonymous Narrative, the letter of King Manuel, and most of the subsequent historians state that this ship reached the African mainland somewhat to the north of Malindi, and after an almost miraculous voyage returned to Lisbon. Corrêa, alone, tells of the discovery of Madagascar. While Corrêa cannot be relied on for the early voyages to India, in this case the information that he gives seems to be correct. After describing the storm in the South Atlantic and the voyage of the other ships around the Cape to Mozambique, Corrêa continues :

"Except Diogo Dias, who, not knowing where he was going, did not arrive at land as soon as he should, and went on the other side of the island of Sam Laurenço. And because they saw it on his day [the 10th of August], they gave his name to it. And when they arrived at it, thinking that it was the coast of Mozambique, they ran along it, keeping a sharp lookout, seeking Mozambique, until they came to the end of the island, which was turning back so that the wind was on the other side, which was against them. On this account they then knew that it was an island and that they erred. Then they went to the island and cast anchor in a good port that made a harbour, protected from the winds of the sea. And lowering a boat they went on shore, where they found a spring of very good water. There were no people, and there were very good fish. He then sent there a convict whom he carried, because the king sent convicts in all the ships to thus adventure in doubtful lands; and the king ordered that they should be pardoned in the event of death or life. This one went inland and found some villages of straw houses, and the people were black and nude. He spoke with them by signs, without any of them doing him any harm. And he returned to the ship. And with him came some of those people, who sold chickens and yams and fruit from bushes, good to eat. And these they exchanged for knives and axes and things of iron, little painted beads and caps and small looking-glasses. Our people did very well there for several days, but because the crew began to fall ill of fever and died, on this account they departed and went with a side wind as much as they could, to take the coast of Mozambique, and they reached the coast beyond Malindi. And they ran along the coast seeking Mozambique by the signs that the pilot carried in the instructions. And they went so far that they passed Cacotorá and went as far as the Cape of Guardafú, since they did not know where they were. And they continued along the shore within the strait until they arrived at the city of Barbora."

So even though Diogo Dias was unaware that he had passed the rendezvous in Mozambique, he still continued to look out for it. No historian who mentions the voyage of Diogo Dias states that he stopped at any of the ports of East Africa south of Mogadishu. His destination was Sofala, but because he became separated from the fleet he sought Mozambique, which seems to have been the appointed meeting place. It must be remembered that Dias did not have an Arab pilot. He undoubtedly knew of the difficult sailing along the coast, and with the feeling that the main fleet had preceded him he may have hoped to join it before it crossed to India with the favourable monsoon. Diogo Dias and Bartolomeu Dias had instructions independent of those carried by Cabral, and the cargo that they carried was for trade with the people of the coast of Africa. The contents of these instructions are not known, but they may have directed that these two ships should proceed north along the coast before they returned, for discovery. In this case, Diogo Dias was but following his instructions.

In Barbora (as Correa and Duarte Barbosa write it) there were many ships and sambuks. The troubles of Diogo Dias and his men were by no means at an end with their advent in this port, for Moorish merchants, who had been in Calicut when Vasco da Gama was in that city, had the ear of the Sheikh and gave him their own version of that which had taken place in India. Thereupon the Sheikh planned the seizure of the Portuguese ship and its cargo and, in order to conceal his intentions, made specious offers of assistance and promised an exchange of merchandise. Diogo Dias sent a boatload of merchandise on shore with his clerk and about fifty of his sick that they might be benefitted by a brief sojourn ashore. The boat was seized by the men of Barbora, the sick were bound, and the ship simultaneously attacked by men armed with bows and arrows and with "zaguchos" or javelins. The condestabre was sick but rose from his couch and ignited the charges in the falconets and berços and by great good fortune three boats of the Arabs were hit and sank.

Meanwhile, the Captain and gunners and some of the sailors had hoisted sail and the ship was soon under way. The enemy did not pursue. But there were not enough sound men on board to work the ship or to hoist the sails if they were lowered. They were therefore left upon the masts and the sheets were untied when the wind freshened.

After three months, during which more deaths occurred and all suffered great hardships, they arrived at Cape Verde reduced in number to thirteen men. Here they met some of their fellow-countrymen who worked the ship for the remainder of the voyage.

They reached Lisbon probably early in 1501 and brought the first intelligence of the loss of four vessels in a great storm, whereat Dom Manuel was deeply distressed. The town in which Diogo Dias and his men had been treacherously beset was destroyed by Antonio da Saldanha in 1518.

The discovery of Madagascar seems not only probable but was a necessary result of the course taken, for had not Madagascar intervened either Mozambique or Malindi would have been reached. In subsequent voyages to India the route to the east of Madagascar was sometimes used and a landing made at the northern point for messages and supplies as at São Bras and Mozambique. At this period the Portuguese were not interested in colonizing; they wished only to purchase commodities raised by others. Madagascar had little to offer in this respect, so its discovery was not considered a matter of great importance. No other claim is made by Portuguese navigators for the discovery of the island prior to 1506, and no other author accounts for its name.

Madagascar was visited by the Arab and Hindu navigators in early times and was known to the Greeks, who may also have been there. During the first centuries of our era there was an Indonesian or Khmer migration, the results of which are still evident in the natives of the eastern shore. It was mentioned by Marco Polo, who probably confused it with Zanzibar, but it was not definitely located and described until the coming of the Portuguese in the sixteenth century. It is shown on the Cantino and Canerio maps, which are supposed to have utilized a map brought back with Cabral's fleet. On these maps it has the shape of a rectangle.

CHAPTER 13

INSTRUCTIONS FOR INDIA AND THE RETURN

Cabral's fleet was the largest that the Portuguese had sent. It went on diplomatic missions and carried cargo for trade. Because of the danger that the ships might become separated, regulations were necessary for signals and ports named to which those that lost the convoy could proceed. In dealing with the Mohammedan and Hindu rulers instructions were desirable for the safety of the members of the fleet, for obtaining treaties, and for commercial relations. When Arab ships were met at sea they were subject to seizure, and regulations were required for the distribution of booty. Directions were also necessary regarding discipline, the operation of the fleet, the succession of commanders, and other matters of a similar nature. Before Cabral's departure, therefore, comprehensive instructions were prepared with great care. All of these no longer exist, but fortunately the most important portion, that which was intended as a guide for Cabral on his arrival in India, has been preserved, and also a letter in which the king gave Cabral additional directions for the return voyage. On subsequent voyages similar instructions were provided, and from these it is possible to supply some portions of Cabral's instructions that are lost.

****

Instructions for Cabral's guidance in India

Cabral went to India as the representative of the King of Portugal on missions of the greatest importance to his country. Though he was a man of only thirty-three years of age who had had little previous experience, there went in the fleet some of the best pilots and navigators in Portugal, so that their duties were in capable hands. The commercial activities were in the charge of Ayres Correia, who was also able to negotiate commercial treaties. It was further arranged that important matters should be discussed at councils composed of the principal men of the fleet, at which Cabral presided. He was also provided with instructions for his guidance, that were intended to provide for every contingency that might arise. Among them were those for his conduct towards the native rulers, that provide a clue to his actions. These instructions reflect the knowledge that the Portuguese had of India and its rulers before Cabral sailed. Unfortunately for him, this was in many respects inaccurate. Cabral followed his orders as exactly as he could, and because he did so he has in some instances been blamed. From those, however, who were with him and who understood his limitations he received no censure. This portion of the instructions explains several doubtful points, because there is no question as to their authenticity. The statement by Gaspar Corrêa that Cabral did not have the command of his ship but that Simão de Miranda held this position and went as Cabral's successor is shown to be erroneous. It indicates that there existed a preceding portion in which a method for signalling was given, and shows also that Ayres Correia carried independent instructions and that Cochin was known to the Portuguese, although it had not previously been visited by them. The instructions were written in a spirit of friendship and conciliation towards the Zamorin, with no indication of hostility except as a last resort. The heading raises the question as to whether this portion was not designed for the particular guidance of Cabral.

The source of this document was Torre do Tombo - Instructions for Pedro Alvares Cabral when he went as Chief Captain of a fleet to India. (Fragments) Maço 1° de Leis, sem data, no. 21. (Alguns documentos, pp. 97-107.) :

"Integral. Jesus. Furthermore as soon as, God willing, you shall have departed from Anchediva you shall go your way to anchor before Calicut with your ships close together and in good order and also dressed with your banners and standards and as much ornament as possible and you will place them where you know that there is the best anchoring ground and the safest for the ships and you shall do no injury to any of the ships that you may find there even if you should know that they are of Mecca or from Anchediva to Calicut before saluting them and showing them a good front and the signal of peace and goodwill and giving food and drink and all other good entertainment to all who shall visit our ships; taking heed however that so many of them shall not come aboard together as to consume many provisions or to be able to take possession of the ships. And after that you have cast anchor and moored the ships and put all things in order you shall send ashore in a boat Balltasar and those other Indians whom you take with you and with them a pair of men from amongst those who appear to you to be fit and apt for the purpose and shall order them to go with the aforesaid Indians to the Zamorin, king of Calicut, and to tell him how always in past times, desiring much to have knowledge of the concerns of that land of India and the lands adjacent, chiefly that our Lord might be served thereby and to ascertain if he and his subjects and the sojourners in his kingdom were Christians and of our faith and persons with whom we should be glad to have friendly and advantageous treaties, we resolved to send our ships to discover the way to India in order to know if the Indians also were Christians and men of such good faith, truthfulness and fair dealing that they should be sought out in order that they might have more perfect instruction in our faith and might be indoctrinated and taught in such matters as pertain to it for that is conducive to the service of God and the salvation of souls and afterwards in order that we might be of service to one another and might traffic with them and they with us and might send to them the merchandise of our kingdoms necessary to them and bring back theirs. And it pleased God, our good intentions being known, that, a short time ago Vasco da Gama, our captain, went in three small ships and, having entered the Indian Ocean, reached his country, the city of Calicut, whence he brought the aforesaid Indians in order that we might have speech with them and obtain information and we send them back to him [the Zamorin] and of them he may learn what is in our country and in like manner as we send them back so he should order the merchandise of which Vasco da Gama was deprived on shore and which was taken from him to be paid for and should give us information chiefly concerning himself and his Christianity and good purpose in the service of God and, in the next place, concerning his good faith and the fair dealing of his people from all of which we would receive much pleasure. And we have resolved to send you with these few ships freighted with such merchandise as (according to the information that we receive) may be necessary and profitable in his country in order that, in our name, you may conclude peace and establish friendship with him if he is pleased so to act towards us as we trust is the case according to that which Vasco da Gama has told us and it seems to us that he ought to be glad to do so since he is a Christian and faithful king for great advantage will accrue to him in his country from peace and agreement with us chiefly because he will be instructed and illumined in the faith, which is a matter that ought to be more highly esteemed than aught else and secondly, because of the great profit that he will receive from the merchandise that we will send from our kingdoms and domains to his country and which our countrymen will bring him; for that which is sent at present is only a sample for we know not if these or other things are more sought after there. And if you should desire to visit him in order to tell him at greater length on our behalf those matters that we command you to tell him and to give him our letters and some things, that for the present we send him as a beginning and token of friendship and if it appears to you that it is very desirable to trust him and his word, yet must you not go ashore without obtaining hostages because of what was done to Vasco da Gama who was detained at Pandarani and also because of certain merchandise of ours that he took as a sample and ordered to be placed on land and that was taken from him and we believe that this was not done by him [the Zamorin] or through his fault but on the demand and by means of some people without faith who neither desire to serve him nor to preserve his honour. And therefore you shall ask him to be pleased to give you the aforesaid hostages who shall remain in your ships until you return to them and if you are satisfied from information received from them that they are so and so, you shall keep them in such manner as seems good to you so that they may be seen and known by one of our people whom afterwards you shall send back with the aforesaid Indians so that if the king of Calicut sends them he may know them so that they may not be able to substitute for them others not of equal importance and standing and to this matter you shall pay great attention. And, if he gives hostages, you shall go ashore and give him what I have already mentioned and shall tell him things that he will be very pleased to hear and that will bring him much profit and honour and you shall beg of him not to think it strange that you should require hostages for it is the custom in these kingdoms that no Chief Captain shall land from his ship in a place where peace has not been concluded without hostages and a safe conduct and that you have always acted in that manner in this voyage, wherefore, although in some places that you have visited and where you have been well received and invited to land you have not landed and would not land even if hostages were given, you have landed here because he is a Christian and a virtuous [prince] and because we have sent you to him and you will tell him that before sending you these hostages he may safely send his factors and the 'carranes' of the country to the ships to whom all the ships shall be shown and the coffers and bales shall be opened and they will see that they are full of merchandise and that we are sending merchants to him for his profit and that they are not robbers as we are told they gave people to understand when Vasco da Gama went there.

And, if you wish, leaving the aforesaid hostages in your ships and in your power and treating them honourably and well but taking care that they shall not be able to escape, you may land with ten or fifteen men such as shall appear to you the best to take with you; the other captains are to remain in their ships and also a captain is to be in your own ship, all for the sake of security, so that the ships shall receive no damage whether you are at sea or on land and you shall give orders that until you return to the ships no one is to go ashore or launch any boat from the ships unless you give orders by one of the men who go with you that this is to be done. Then you shall go to speak to the king and shall give him our messages and shall give him that which we send by you and shall say to him on our behalf that we desire his friendship and a friendly understanding, his advantage and trade with his country and that with this object we send you there with those merchant vessels and that we pray him to give orders that our merchandise shall be sold in safety and that cargo shall be given for our ships, namely spices and other merchandise of the country that may be profitable, and to give orders that you shall obtain these at the price at which they are usually sold in the country in such manner that if any of the merchants who are there disapprove of our trading there they shall not obtain samples of the merchandise of the country in order to take away more of it than they already have. And if on your arrival the [purchase of the] said merchandise should be opposed by those who are there you shall ask him to order such as is necessary for the lading of the ships to be sold to you at its value or, if his own factor prefers to bind himself to give you all the cargo that you require for the ships in merchandise of the quantities and kinds that you shall determine and will fix the price of his goods and for how much he will take ours, you shall act accordingly for the sake of quicker dispatch and to transact business more expeditiously.....to whichever of these methods you agree he shall give his promise and, that being done, you shall commence to have the goods sold that you are taking and to buy what you wish to bring away and so, from the commencement of your sales and trading, he will know what you are and the profits that are to be obtained now and henceforward from our ships.

Item, before going to the king, take means, if it shall be possible, to learn if the duties to be paid there on merchandise entering or going away are the same as Gaspar told us of which you have a memorandum and if you find that it is so you shall tell the king that you are aware that there are high duties in his country and that it appears to you that he ought not to levy such high duties upon us because we have recently begun to send merchandise to his country and in all places it is the custom at the commencement of a trade to make reductions and grant favourable terms to those who come with merchandise and that such is the custom in our kingdoms and that it appears to you that he ought to act thus towards us and our merchandise and propose something reasonable to him in order that there may be purchases and sales and tell him that although we should pay lower duties than the others the number of our ships and the amount of merchandise is, if God will, so great that the duties will yield him much more than they do at present. And if it shall appear to you that the king of Calicut is averse to this proposal in any way and that he is not well disposed to it so that you do not expect to derive any advantage from the proposal in such a case you will be careful not to insist nor to say more regarding it for what you shall have already said will suffice in order that it may not appear to him that you are bringing forward a matter that has been arranged by us and that he will lose some of the duties that have been paid by the Moors. And if, perchance, he should refuse to give the hostages who have been already named or others concerning whom you shall be credibly informed that they are safe and suitable to have in order that upon delivery of them you in person may land, in such case you shall not land; and thereupon you will send to inform him that, since he does not wish to send hostages, it appears to you that he does not desire to talk with you and to see and hear things as we supposed he would and that therefore it appears to you that you ought not to land but that in order to conclude the commercial agreement and to discuss the conditions of it and to deliver that which we send him by you, you request him to send to the ships three or four merchants for this purpose, which being done, you will send an equal number to deliver to him the articles aforesaid and to talk with him on your behalf. Thereupon you shall send Ayres Correa and with him two of his clerks, one a receiving, the other a paying clerk, and you shall deliver to him that which we send and shall bid him speak of the commercial agreement and settlement and delivery of cargo in the manner in which we have already set forth that you yourself should do if you had gone to him and say to him that it appears to you a great mistake and little to his advantage not to give the hostages that you asked in order that you might land, because, if you had visited him, you would have told him many things to his advantage and you would have selected a house for us in which the priests and friars whom we send might lodge in order to instruct him in the faith and how to receive it and to save his soul. And [he shall say that] the merchandise is there and.....from which he will derive great advantage.....honour.....to go to his country.....and supply his subjects with things necessary that may improve his country. And if, notwithstanding, he still refuses to give hostages in order that you may land safely, then you shall request that those [merchants] whom he sends to the ships may remain with you in the ships until they load them.

When this has been agreed upon between you and the king (of which we think there can be no doubt) the aforesaid Ayres Correa shall begin to unload the merchandise and to sell and to buy what may appear to him for the advantage of our service but he shall not discharge all the merchandise at once but only what may appear to him necessary to effect sales and shall at once spend the money received so that he may return speedily to the ships; in this way you will incur the least possible risk on shore.

If the said king should say that he has no hostages to give because it is not the custom to find hostages seeing that his country is safe and secure for all who wish to go to trade there and that it will be so for you if you wish to land in it to trade and to buy and sell and other words to this effect, so that he may still excuse himself from giving hostages in order that you may land as aforesaid as well as other hostages in order that Ayres Correa may dispose of the cargo, you shall send to tell him that what he says is doubtless perfectly true and that you believe that this is not the custom there and that he does not permit it, but that, even although such is his custom and that of his country and although this request to grant hostages appears to him something new, yet he ought to do for you that which you desire not only because you are not a merchant like the others who go to his country, as you yourself know, but because you are our Captain and that you are chiefly sent by us out of love and a desire of peace and friendship because he is a Christian king and one with whom we much desire these things and that for many years and often we have followed this aim with the object chiefly of serving our Lord in order that therefrom the salvation both of the king and his subjects might result. And say that for, this purpose you bring with you every kind of thing that is necessary as well priests as friars and all else that is required and, in the next place, that you are sent in order that such an understanding and agreement may result regarding matters of trade that it may be safe and sure in time to come and may be engaged in all tranquility by those whom we may send hereafter and so it may come to pass that our people may land in his country without fear and his people come to ours if this treaty shall be concluded.

And if the said king of Calicut will not on any account whatever give hostages either to enable you to land in person or to enable Ayres Correa to conduct business in the manner aforesaid, you will then send word to him that his conduct is very displeasing to you because you did not expect that he would show any reluctance and that you are all the more displeased on account of the displeasure that we ourselves will manifest because of his not consenting to nor entering into negotiations for peace, cordiality and agreement as we expected would be done, for you did not come nor were sent by us for this purpose only but also that, after discharging your cargo, you might leave our factor in his city and a storehouse for our merchandise and other persons to be with him whom you bring for that purpose from all which so great profit would accrue to him that he would be well satisfied because his country would become richer and better provided with necessaries and that, since he shows so much reluctance in so small a matter and because he fortifies himself against our love, service and friendship, although greatly against your will for the aforesaid reasons, you will proceed at once to

Callemur [sic] and there conclude your treaty of peace and establish your factor and factory that you brought for his city and with him you will treat regarding all matters in order that we may be well served and you will say that you know that this can be done there as in his city and perhaps more perfectly and securely and that he knows that this is true. And after that you have in the most careful manner done all that you can do in the matter and perceive that he [the King of Calicut] does not alter in favour of the object that we seek, when one day or several days, as best appears to you, shall have elapsed although some delay must result therefrom because of the embarrassment that as you know will arise, you shall then send another message, saying that although you are assured that our affairs would be better conducted and we be better served in Calemur [sic] and that our factor and factory would be very safe there, yet because of the dissatisfaction that you know we would experience thereby because of our sending you chiefly to him and of our desiring peace, friendship and a cordial understanding with him rather than with any other king of India, you have resolved, to disregard all blame that may attach to you in the matter and to transact your business with him and to take in your cargo at his city; and having taken this final decision, you shall send ashore Ayres Correa and his clerks who, acting in all respects as we have already directed, shall endeavour to obtain and to buy a cargo of merchandise as expeditiously as possible and shall do it with every precaution that may appear good to you and take care that what is bought shall be such as is to the greatest advantage.

And whilst you are conducting these negotiations and parleys with the aforesaid king of Calicut, you shall endeavour in whatever manner may appear best to you to ascertain if it is possible to obtain a cargo at Callnur [sic] for your ships and also if, in case you should desire to go thither and there establish your storehouse, this could be done to the advantage of our service and if you would be well, received and also if all the goods would be safe there if you should thenceforward establish yourself there and this as regards merchandise at any future time and you shall inquire concerning the residence of our factor and obtain all possible information of that kind so that you shall not only be well informed regarding that which is necessary to be done but that you may be able to bring full and certain information to us when you return.

Item, although inconvenience must arise from this method of conducting business, seeing that the people are not to land for the purpose, this is the method that must be followed, that is to say, the aforesaid Ayres Correa shall buy all the spicery that those people wish him to buy who offer him their merchandise and will give it at prices at which it can be bought without chaffering as will be set forth at greater length in his instructions and if perchance it should appear that this is a matter of great difficulty for Ayres Correa and something that he cannot accomplish because it is to be done in our [manner], you shall then send with him and his clerks a factor, one who shall appear to you suitable and a clerk shall be assigned to him who, on the purchase of spicery from the aforesaid persons, shall arrange that everything shall be done in good faith and that the vendors shall not be cheated; at the same time the said factor shall always agree with Ayres Correa upon the price to be paid for the goods and upon the price at which our goods are to be sold. With regard to small articles such as precious stones and other things, other factors shall be appointed to deal with these, one factor in each ship who shall go on shore; every day one factor shall go ashore from each ship and shall purchase articles of that kind and shall return every day to sleep on board and in this way all shall be provided for that is conducive to the safety of our servants. And if perchance the king of Calicut should give you the hostages mentioned above on acceptance of whom you are to land in order to speak to him and to give him our present and to do the other things that you are ordered to do, then if you perceive that matters are being so arranged that you can proceed with all security and that he is reliable and that no inconvenience could follow and if you are of opinion that all is well ordered that concerns the ways and means of trading and that all is well ordered in all other respects, you are then to tell him that we send you to him on this first voyage not only to conclude peace and establish a friendly understanding with him and to freight the ships that you have brought with spicery and the products of India and of his country but also in order that you may leave there our factor and establish a factory and may leave there other persons who are to remain there and priests and friars and property of the Church in order that our faith may, be thus perfectly made known and taught him so that he may be indoctrinated in it as a faithful Christian, from all which he will perceive how great is the love we bear him and that we all desire his friendship and personal advantage. And you shall request him to ordain and order that houses shall be assigned you in which the merchandise and those who are to remain with him may be in all security so that all those who remain with him and also the merchandise that you leave behind may be and remain safe at all times, in evidence whereof he should order his written mandate to be given you and whatever other formal assurance you may know to be generally given in that country. And if the king of Calicut gives these letters of safe conduct and such other warrants of safety as you may think that you ought to demand for the greater security of the factor who is to remain there, these warrants being to the best of your knowledge such as are usually granted in that country, then shall the factor remain in that city with the merchandise.....[which still] remains of the cargo and also with all the rest of the spicery.....[as] ordered [by his instructions] and you are to tell him that, seeing that you are leaving behind you the aforesaid factor and other persons and also our merchandise to do which we were chiefly moved in order that he might know how great is our desire for his friendship and advantage and how great is the pleasure that we have therein, you therefore request that he will be pleased to send some honourable persons with you who shall come to visit us not only in order to see us and our kingdoms but also that, after they have received honours and thanks from us, they may know better the goodwill that we have towards him and his interests and you are to endeavour to bring them and, if you bring them, they are to receive all the honour and good treatment from you that is possible.

And if it should so happen that no hostages should be given you in any of the ways already mentioned and if you have great trouble in obtaining cargoes for the ships in the manner already described, (from which circumstances you will know and see clearly that our factor and merchandise, as well as the other persons who are ordered to go and to remain with him, cannot remain in safety in the aforesaid city of Calicut) then, as soon as the ships are ready, you shall send to tell him [the Zamorin] that you had the intention as well as our command to leave our factor and establish our factory there, as is set forth in a previous paragraph together with the rest that you shall see there and when that which concerns the residence of the factor and the intercourse with the king of Calicut has been finally settled in this way at his pleasure and in our interest, then you, having reloaded your ships, shall in conclusion tell him that he ought to have known what great security would have resulted from peace and friendship with us, a peace that would have been perfectly preserved by us and ours at all times to his advantage and the good of his kingdom and people but that, inasmuch as we have learnt that Moors (mouros), enemies of our holy faith, trade in his city and that their ships and merchandise go there and inasmuch as we continually wage war upon them both on account of the obligation imposed upon every Catholic king and because it devolves upon us as if by direct succession, in order that you may acquaint him in detail with the events of the war beyond [the sea] and in order that all matters both great and small shall be clearly understood as is right and proper between him and us, you shall give him to understand that when you encounter ships belonging to the aforesaid Moors at sea you are required to endeavour with all your might to take possession of them and of their merchandise and property and to make use of the Moors who are in the ships to your best advantage and to make war upon them and do them as much damage as possible as a people with whom we are and have for so long been at enmity and also because we comply with our obligations to the Lord our God but that he may be assured that although you may encounter them and although other captains whom we may send in future may encounter them in his harbour and before his city yet, in order to do our utmost to preserve his good pleasure and satisfaction, you shall do them no mischief or damage but shall only so act when you meet those ships at sea as has been already said, where they have done what they could against you and against our people whom they have already encountered. And [you shall tell him] that he may be certain, in order that he may know how that which is due to a king with whom we delight always to maintain great affection, peace and friendship is to be observed that when you or any other of our captains capture the aforesaid ships none of the Indians found in them nor any of their merchandise or property will be injured in any way, but, on the contrary, they will receive every honour and all good treatment and will be safe from injury until they and all that belongs to them can be liberated for war will only be waged against the Moors as our enemies. And [you shall tell him that] it would be well pleasing to us if he could exclude these Moors from his country and from trading in it for that he would, please God, receive from us and ours all the profit that until now he has derived from them and much more and that it would be well and for God's service (and in doing so he would comply with the duty of a Christian king) if he would expel them from his country and not allow them to come there nor to trade in it, seeing that no advantages result from them and their residence, arrival and continuance in it except the profits that he draws from them and these he would draw from our people with God's help and with so great an increase that he would be well satisfied. And [you shall say] that in case Moors and ships of Mecca should be captured by our captains he is to give us assurance by letter that even if for that reason the aforesaid Moors of Mecca who may at such time be in his city or country or any others request him to make reprisals on our factor and factory and merchandise and people with it in order that they shall thus be indemnified for the injury done to them by our people, he shall not [accede to their request] and that no blame will be attached to our people and no injury done to our merchandise but that he will always protect them as being thereto obliged by the [treaty of] peace and amity with us.

Item, you shall tell him that inasmuch as we have learned that it is the custom in his city and country when any merchant dies that his estate, merchandise and property shall become the property of the king and be escheated and that it would not be reasonable that this should apply to our factor because this rule should be observed only in the case of persons who trade in their own merchandise and transact business on their own account which our factor does not do, for everything is ours, [you shall tell him] that he is to give an undertaking that if our Lord God should take away our aforesaid factor and he should die all our merchandise and property and also our storehouse shall not be subject to this custom and that the factor who shall succeed to the other at his death shall be at liberty to do without impediment all that the deceased factor would have done without anything being seized for the aforesaid king and without implicating our people in a dispute, for, as we have said, it would not be reasonable to apply the regulation to or to act towards our people in the same way as he acts towards the other merchants and people.

Item, if in this parley you should find from the progress of the negotiations and if you should foresee such great trouble from the fact of his not giving hostages that you shall be obliged to depart and go to Callemur [sic] you shall then depart with your ships and shall go direct to Callemur [sic] and shall give [to the king] our letters that you take with you and shall tell him that we are sending you to those parts of India in order to conclude peace and establish amity with their kings as we have many times desired to do and as ought to be done between Christian kings and that, inasmuch as you were told that on this your first voyage you would not be able to obtain a cargo in his country for your ships, you therefore went first to Calicut, where you took in cargo, and that, inasmuch as we knew that he was a faithful king and known to be such above all others and that he is very firm in matters that relate to our faith and averse to intercourse with the Moors and to anything for their advantage who are the enemies of the faith and, inasmuch as we greatly desire it for all these reasons and for others that we have known relating to his virtues, we therefore command you to go to him to conclude peace and establish amity with him in our name in order that for the future as.....friends we and ours may avail ourselves of his country and he of ours, as is reasonable and well-pleasing and not only for this purpose....., but also that if he agrees to peace and amity, as we trust he will do, that you may soon leave in his city our factor and people and factory so that in time to come our large and small ships may take in cargo at his city and our merchandise may be sold there and such merchandise as we have samples of may be bought from all which proceedings great honour and profit would accrue to him and to all his country. And inasmuch as perhaps his city is the principal gate of entrance to all the kings of India you are therefore to request that, if he can arrange with you to do so, he shall be pleased and hold it desirable that the aforesaid factor shall remain and that he shall give you warrant for his safety according to the custom of the country, namely his letters and any other warrant of that kind and if he desires to send one person or several persons to come with you to our kingdoms to see what is here, you can assure him that you believe that it will be well-pleasing to us and we will send them back in our ships and they will receive honours and thanks from us and during the voyage they will be treated as you yourself are treated. And if he gives his written assurance, our aforesaid factor shall remain together with all those who are ordered to remain with him and the merchandise and plant that you carry for him and when all has been arranged you shall go to him at the proper time. And at this first parley with the aforesaid king you will endeavour to ascertain if cargoes of spicery can be obtained in his city and if other Indian merchandise is brought there and if he troubles himself about this matter and also if the people there desire to have the kind of merchandise that you bring or other kinds and if other kinds what other kinds, so that we may understand everything aright and moreover it will be the chief care of the factor.....to know and comprehend how the aforesaid king sends.....by them and gives authority to conduct sales there in order that he may be able to buy and have [cargoes] ready against the arrival of our ships, so that, if God please, they may be certain to find cargoes and he shall carefully perform all other necessary duties as is laid down in his instructions. And as soon as you have in good time arranged matters in Canelur [sic] [with the king] and agreed upon the acceptance of the aforesaid factor and as soon as he has landed with everything intended to remain with him in the manner ordained in a preceding paragraph, you shall depart in good time for these kingdoms and if on the voyage you encounter any ships of Mecca and it appears to you that you are able to capture them you are to try to do so but you are not to come to close quarters with them if you can avoid it but with the aid of your artillery you are to compel them to strike sail and to launch their boats and to send in them their pilots, quartermasters and supercargoes so that this war may be waged with safety and so that less loss may result to the crews of your ships. And if their ships should, with God's help, be captured, you shall take possession of the most valuable merchandise that you find in them and convey it to our ships and you shall bring to us all the pilots and quartermasters and principal supercargoes who may come to our ships and you shall liberate for a ransom the others and the crews of the aforesaid ships that you have captured (provided that you have sea-room and that the weather is favourable) and if you are unable to accomplish all this, you shall put them all in one ship, that which has been dismantled the most and shall let them go in it and you shall sink all the others or burn them and shall take due care if, by God's favour, you capture ships to seize all the merchandise, great and small, that they carry.....with all our servants.

And as soon as, please God, you shall have crossed [the Indian Ocean] and arrived at Malindi, seeing that you will then have learned which of the vessels of the fleet are the better sailers and which the worse and slow, you shall act thus at Malindi; you shall separate all the ships that have been fast sailors from the others and shall give orders that they shall continue their voyage to these kingdoms without waiting for the others but you shall give orders that those ships that have been found to be the fastest sailors shall wait for one another and shall observe all the other regulations that you take with you relating to waiting for and signalling to one another so as not to part company and you shall also separate those that are less fast and are laggers and these are to continue their voyage independently of the others in the manner that we have prescribed and explained that the fast ships are to continue it and if it should so happen that your own ship is one of the fast sailors you shall come in company with these and shall appoint a commander of the slow sailors and those that are inferior in sails, - such as one you will select for this purpose who appears to you to be the most suitable and apt and to him you will commit all the authority that you yourself possess and we hereby order that all the other captains and crews shall obey him and comply with his orders in like manner as they would obey you and if [your ship] should be.....one of the laggers you will remain with them and will appoint a commander for the others in the aforesaid manner.....and if Sancho de Tovar should have one of the quick sailors he shall be their commander and if one of the slow sailors he shall be their commander provided always that he is not in the same division of the fleet that you yourself are.

And although we ordain in these instructions in such great detail all that you are to do and to observe yet, seeing that as yet so little is known regarding the time and manner of conducting this business and on account of the difference which perchance you will find in the customs of that country [from those that are observed in ours], if it should appear to you that you ought to alter and arrange matters otherwise in order to conduct and conclude them in a proper manner and as we would desire for our service, we, in the great confidence which we have in you, hold it well and hereby command you to do and follow that which appears to you best, taking in everything counsel with the captains and factor and any other persons whom you think you ought to associate with you in the matter and, finally, that which you prefer to do and agree upon you will follow out and perform.

Item, the Second Captain....."

Additional instructions Given to Cabral

These are in the form of a letter and were evidently an afterthought on the part of the king. They give some additional information regarding the voyage, and show that Bartolomeu Dias carried independent instructions. Unfortunately, these have not been preserved; they would indicate what previous knowledge the Portuguese had of the East African coast and the duties of the Dias brothers.

The source of this document was Torre do Tombo (Armario 26 do interior da casa da Coroa, mago 4, No. 91) :

"Pedro Alvarez, chief of the other captains; concerning your instructions, we hold it for good and our service that you should comply and keep those that are continued below.

Be furthermore advised that on your return in good time, after passing the Cape of Good Hope, you shall not make other port nor a stop in any part, but shall only come directly to this city, save that it is for some necessity, or because it may be appropriate for our service that you should do so, because you cannot avoid or be able to do otherwise, in which case you shall do that which seems necessary for greater safety of the matters of our service; but in whichever of the places in which you may do so, be well advised that in all the fleet great care shall also be taken that there shall not be taken out any merchandise or that anything should be done contrary to our service. And at the island of São Tomé or Cape Verde or of the Azores, in which we have officials, you shall always obey in these the regulations of our customs officer and the officials who look after the matters of our service, as well as those guarded and made in our instructions for the caravels of Mina, by which I hold it for good that you shall not send out your boats if you can avoid it, and having in this all advice and good order; and thus we recommend and order that you do, and as soon as you arrive in good time at this city, you will be advised. And thus we order you that neither you nor any one of the ships and caravels of the fleet, whether they are ours or others who go apart, shall launch any boat or consent that any arrive to you, or go in a boat of any sort until there come to you and to the ships of all the said fleet our factors and officials, and they make and provide that which we order them for our service and as it appears to them that they should do; and thus you are to understand and do, for this we hold for good. And in this manner we order to each one of the captains of the fleet that they comply and as their chief you shall give your instructions that they shall so do.

Furthermore, because it might happen that, with the aid of Our Lord, you should arrive in Callecut or in Calemir, in which two places your cargo should be of such abundance that by chance other ships might carry it if they could load; in this case, if it appears to you that it is for our service that you should do so, we hold it for good that you should buy some ship or ships of those of the land, so that you may load them and bring them with you unto some place where you can come to anchor, to place in our ships what is therein loaded, so that they shall take the place of the supplies that are daily consumed; it appears to us that this would be a good thing to do. And if they can satisfactorily and with security come with the fleet, it would thus be well. If it cannot be accomplished in the manner that is said and which thus appears to us would be to our service, you can do as follows and can still do that which will please us greatly, to place thus in them by purchase such an abundant cargo as we have told you before; and we order that Ayres Correa, our factor, accomplish that which is required for our service and you should authorize and direct him thus as to the purchase of the said ships as well as their cargo.

And if some of those from these parts who go in the fleet should wish to buy such ships of those of the land so that they might load them with some sort of merchandise in addition to the quintals that are authorized by us that they might bring to these kingdoms, we hold it for good that they may do so, and they will be obliged to pay us all our dues of merchandise which thus in similar ships are loaded and carried.

And we command you that on them you shall not place in this matter any embargo whatever. And these chapters you shall join with all the others of your written instructions.

Which I entered in the instructions of the chief captain and of Bertolomeu Dias, to the alvara of the licence in the chapter for Bertolomeu Dias."

Page 112

CHAPTER 14

WHILST IN INDIA

Land was reached at Anjediva, an island frequented by ships, in order to obtain supplies when on their way to Calicut. Here the ships were careened and painted, and preparations were made for meeting the Zamorin of Calicut. Cabral's instructions provided that Arab ships should be captured if found at sea or at places other than friendly ports. He therefore hoped that some might be encountered at Anjediva, but in this he was disappointed.

Leaving Anjediva, the fleet of six ships anchored before Calicut on the 13th of September. All were gaily decked with banners, and a salute was fired. Merchants came to visit them, but Cabral, in accordance with his instructions, could not open negotiations until after certain prescribed preliminaries had been fulfilled. The negotiations related principally to lading with spices, which the rajah agreed to, and promised that the Portuguese should have every facility in procuring them. One of the officers was sent to the Rajah to request that hostages should be sent on board the Portuguese ships. This request was agreed to. Five Brahmins were delivered as hostages who were to remain on board until Cabral should return from a visit to the Rajah. A house near the beach was granted as a residence for the factor and a storehouse.

Several days elapsed before Cabral could land. The lengthy details of the negotiations regarding the obtaining of these hostages, that are given by the historians, are perhaps intended to absolve Cabral from any accusation of timidity, and to show that he was only obeying the instructions formulated for his guidance. It was arranged for Pedro Cabral to meet the Zamorin of Calicut.

A letter, with a strongly religious tone, was sent by Dom Manuel to the Zamorin of Calicut, who was already known to the Portuguese :

"Great and most powerful Prince Zamorin, by the Grace of God King of Calecut. We, Dom Manuel, by His Divine Grace King of Portugal and the Algarves on this side of and beyond the sea in Africa, Lord of

Guinea, etc., send you many salutations as to one we greatly love and prize. God Almighty, the beginning, middle, and end of all things, and under whose ordinance the days and human acts and times run their course, as by His infinite goodness He created the world and the Kingdom of Christ, His Son, Our Saviour, so in His great and infinite power and knowledge He ordained for future time many things for the good and profit of the human race, inspiring through the Holy Spirit the hearts of men that they might be made manifest and accomplished in times more fitting for them and marked out by Him, and neither before nor after. And since this is a truth well known by experience, if with sound and true judgement you will reflect on the great novelty and mystery of the voyage of our men and vessels to you and to those your lands, you must do in those Eastern parts what all of us and we do in the West, where we give many praises to the Lord God because in our day and yours He has bestowed such favours on the world that we are able not only to know through hearing, but to see and know by sight and by intercourse to unite and also be neighbours [one to another]. And while from the beginning of the world until now the inhabitants of those lands were so far removed from these and ever beyond all hope or thought of this, the Lord God now willed to inspire sixty years ago our uncle and vassal called the Infant Dom Henry, a prince of very virtuous life and holy habits, who for God's service and by His inspiration resolved to open out this navigation; and it was continued by the kings our predecessors until now, and, it pleasing Our Lord, He willed to give it the end we desired and that those men who now arrived there in one voyage only should make so long a journey until they reached you, as in all past voyages was made in sixty years; and these were the first men we sent out as soon as, by the Grace of God, we assumed the rule of our realms and lordships. And although this thing is seen to have been done by men, it ought not to be judged as the work of men, for it is not possible for them but of God alone, by whose power what is impossible to men is possible to Him, for since the creation of the world there existed, in those parts and these, great powers and lordships of princes and kings and the Romans and other people who possess the greater part of the earth, of whom we read that they had great will and desire to make this navigation and that they worked at it, but it did not please God to grant them such a possibility in those times, just as we ourselves could [not] have accomplished it if we had not had it from

His hand and will. And since as long as God did not wish it to take place all the men of past times were unable to accomplish it, no one should think that now that He desired it, men are strong enough to oppose and undo it, and it is now a much greater wrong and injury to God to wish to resist His manifest and known will than it was to be obdurate against it before it was known. And among the principal reasons why we render many thanks to the Lord God in this achievement is because we have been told that there are Christian people in those parts, and it will be our chief desire to hold converse with you and to profit and give in great conformity of love and brotherhood, as Christian kings ought to do between each other, for it may well be believed that God our Lord did not ordain such a marvellous deed as this of our navigation only to be served in traffic and temporal profits between you and us, but also in the spiritual of souls and their salvation to which we are more bound. And He holds it for His greater service, therefore, that His Holy Christian Faith should be communicated and united between you and us as it was by all in all the small universe for quite six hundred years after the coming of Jesus Christ, until by the sins of men there arose some sects and contrary beliefs, foretold by Christ that they would come after Him for the trial and manifestation of the righteous and for the deceit of wickedness of those who deserved condemnation and destruction because they would not receive the truth to be saved; and therefore God perverted their knowledge and understanding to do evil and believe lies and be condemned, since they would not believe the truth and consented to falsehood. These sects occupied a great part of the earth between your lands and ours, and therefore our communication with you by land was impeded, but is now again opened through our navigation and made free by God, to whom nothing is impossible. Therefore, knowing all this and wishing to follow up and fulfill, as we ought, that which the Most High God clearly shows us to be his will and service, we now send there our captain and ships and merchandise and our factor who, by your pleasure, will remain there and perform his duties. And we also send religious persons instructed in the Christian faith and religion, and also church ornaments for the celebration of the Divine offices and sacraments, so that you may be able to see the doctrine of the Christian faith that we hold, given and instituted by Christ Jesus our Lord and Saviour to the twelve apostles, His disciples, that after His Holy

Resurrection was by them generally preached and received by all the world. And some of them, to wit, Saint Thomas and Saint Bartholomew, preached in your parts of India, performing many and great miracles, drawing those people from the paganism and idolatry in which all the world formerly lived, and some of the said apostles converted them to the truth of the holy belief and Christian faith. Our Lord ordained Saint Peter as his principal vicar among all his apostles and disciples, who preached in the great city of Rome, which was then the head of the people and idolatry, and suffered martyrdom for Him, and there lies buried. And from that time until now the holy fathers, his successors, set up there by the same ordinance of Christ the chief head and seat of the Christian faith and religion, the Lord God wishing, as is shown, that Rome, which was formerly the mother of error and falsehood, should be and remain the mother of truth, of whose obedience and true doctrine we and all Christian kings, princes, and seignories are. Wherefore, pondering these things, and reasons of the will and service of my High God for Himself, who was and is the cause of our navigation and journey to you, very affectionately and as a brother we ask you to conform to His will and wish and to make your profit and that of your land, both temporal and spiritual, and that you may be pleased to receive and join in our friendship, trade, and intercourse which we thus peacefully offer you for His holy service, and to receive and treat our captain and men with that sound and true love with which we send them to you; for in addition to the very dear reasons and mystery of the will of God as He has shown us, who could see and recognize as His work, there is every reason why you should rejoice that people should come from so far, and with so great a heart, to seek friendship and intercourse with you and bring you such profit as you may get from our lands more than from any others. And if it should happen that owing to ill will and minds obstructive of good, which are never lacking, we find in you the contrary of this, which for every reason we could hardly credit or expect from your virtue, our fixed purpose is to follow the will of God rather than that of men, and not fail through any contrarieties to prosecute this affair and continue our navigation, trade, and intercourse in these lands that the Lord God wishes to be newly served by our hands, not wishing that our labour to serve Him should be in vain, as we no less hope from His piety that it may in purpose, because we firmly believe and hope that, as He created these lands and gave them to you and to His peoples to possess, He will ordain that in His own, His Will will be done, and that there will not fail to be some one in them who will welcome and receive our friendship and our people who go there so much by His will and wish, to whom He so wonderfully opened the way and gave the power to go to them, which thing He himself knows how greatly we desire should rather be through good peace and friendship to Him; and may He be pleased to give us His Grace to know what is His Will and holy service. And as regards this, may it please you to give full faith to Pero Alvares Cabral, noble of our household and our chief captain, in all that he says and requests you on our part and treats of with you. From Lisbon, the 1st of March 1500."

Some of the details of what followed at Calicut are given in the narratives. They tell of the meeting of Cabral and his officers with the Zamorin, of the antagonism shown by the Arab merchants, and of the conclusion of an agreement after a long delay. To please the Zamorin an Indian ship was captured, without provocation, so as to obtain for him a coveted elephant. Because of the opposition of their Arab competitors it was impossible for the Portuguese to secure adequate cargo, and only two of the ships, probably the largest ones, were loaded - the flagship and that of Simão de Miranda or of Sancho de Tovar. This would be done because it would be desirable for the largest vessels to return to Portugal before the change of the monsoon. The caravels and small ships could find protection in the backwaters, if necessary, and return the following season. From the commercial standpoint, therefore, the departure from Calicut was opportune, since it permitted all the ships to be loaded and to return together.

There is much diversity in the accounts of the massacre that followed. But the Portuguese historians agree in affirming that Arab traders were the instigators of it and chief participators in it. The intrigues of the Arabs finally caused an uprising, and the small factory that the Portuguese had established on shore was stormed.

Ayres Correa, the factor, had been warned that the warehouse was likely to be plundered and on a certain night, when the factory was surrounded by several thousand Arabs, one of Correa's servants raised an alarm by shouting "Ladrões, ladrões." Moplah Arabs and some Malabaris immediately scaled the outer walls in many places but were unable to force their way into the factory through the doorways. They succeeded however in climbing to the roof that they broke through and attacked the inmates with darts and arrows. The Portuguese crossbowmen had by this time discharged all their bolts so that resistance was impossible.

Thereupon Correa gave orders to fly to the beach and the Portuguese, reduced in number from eighty to fifty, sallied forth but only thirty-six reached the beach, almost all of whom were dangerously wounded. All but twenty of those who were there were killed or captured. Among these were the chief factor, Ayres Correia, Pero Vaz de Caminha, and three of the Franciscan fathers. Nuno Leitão took little Antonio Correa under his protection and succeeded with great difficulty in conveying him to the beach, where he entrusted him to a sailor who carried him to one of the boats of a rescue party under the command of Sancho de Tovar. These events occurred on the 17th of December, 1500.

Pedro Cabral believed that the Zamorin was not free from blame. Cabral waited a day in the hope that an apology or explanation of the affair might be received from the Zamorin; but none came. Angered by the death of their countrymen and the loss of their property, the Portuguese took vengeance on the Arabs by seizing ten of their ships that were in the harbour. After killing most of the crews they removed the cargoes and burned the ships, together with those of the Arabs who had hidden themselves in the holds. Because it was felt that the Zamorin had had a part in the uprising and had favoured the Moors, the city of Calicut was bombarded for a whole day and great damage done. An enmity was thus caused that went down in the history of that city, and the bombardment was never forgiven by its inhabitants.

From the Portuguese point of view these acts seemed justifiable. They had come to secure the commerce of India with the permission of the Pope and they felt that it was theirs by the will of God. In its acquisition they had been opposed by infidels and heathen whom they considered inferiors. The Portuguese had the crusading spirit from centuries of war with the Moslems. The intrigues of the Arabs and the vacillation of the Zamorin were treachery and an affront to the honour and prestige of their king. The riot instigated by the Arabs, and, as they believed, sanctioned by the ruler, demanded the most severe punishment that they were able to inflict. They realized also that they were few in number and that those who would come to India in the future fleets would always be at a numerical disadvantage; so that this treachery must be punished in a manner so decisive that the Portuguese would be feared and respected in the future. It was their superior artillery that would enable them to accomplish this end. A decisive blow at the chief ruler of the Malabar coast would demonstrate their superiority and win for them the friendship of the subject states whose allegiance they sought. This bombardment of Calicut was the beginning of a policy of armed aggression to secure for the Portuguese the domination of the Indian seas. It was the first step in an active warfare against the Arab merchants in India.

The attitude of the Arab traders can easily be understood. They and their ancestors had won a large part of the commerce of the Indian Ocean from Sofala to China. This had been obtained by peaceful means through the spread of their faith and in fair competition with the native merchants. When recourse was had to war, on land or sea, their methods of combat were the same. Their trade had been threatened by the Chinese, whose junks also had come from a distance, but these had little by little retreated and the meeting-point had been pushed back from Cambay, Calicut, and Sri Lanka to Malacca. Through Egypt and from pilgrims to Mecca they had learned of the people of Europe, and had seen some of them in the renegades who wandered occasionally to their shores. To the Arab merchants the arrival of the Portuguese by the long sea route to take from them their trade could only have been understood as the beginning of a commercial war. They had driven back the Chinese by fair means and they may have felt that the Portuguese could be similarly treated. The Portuguese, however, had no intention of sharing this trade with the Arab and Hindu merchants. They came to monopolize it, and this was shown in every act. Nor would the Arabs share trade with the Portuguese, for the Arabs were also monopolists. With arrogance and presumption the Portuguese demanded that their ships be loaded first, and that they be given every preference. The letter that Dom Manuel sent to the Zamorin, which was interpreted to him by Arabs, requested that he should exclude the Arabs from his trade. The Arabs must have realized that, while they were tolerated in friendly ports, at sea the Portuguese were to treat them and the pilgrims to Mecca as enemies to whom no quarter was to be shown. Not only was their trade at stake but their lives as well. The letters that Cabral carried to the Arab rulers also condemned their religion, although the attitude of the Mohammedans towards Christianity had usually been one of tolerance. It was not surprising then that with war openly declared against them the Arabs fought back. This was not done with arms, because they realized that here they were deficient, but with strategy. The incident at Calicut was to them but a counter-attack in war.

So far as the Hindu merchants were concerned, they traded chiefly with their own people, but for the sale of commodities needed by Europe and the Mohammedan world they relied on the foreign Arabs. These spoke their languages, knew their customs and commodities, and through centuries of friendly intercourse had built up commercial relations that, in general, were satisfactory. The Hindus knew nothing of Europe and had seen few of its people. They saw little difference between the European commodities that the Portuguese brought them and those which came from Mohammedan sources. To the Hindus the arrival of Vasco da Gama and Pedro Cabral was but the coming of new merchants to buy their wares, and so long as they conformed to their customs they were welcome. That they were Christians did not exclude them, because in Malabar there were many Christians as well as Jews who lived there as an inferior caste. The attitude of the Indian rulers towards the Portuguese, therefore, was friendly. They were mystified by the arrival of Vasco da Gama and Pedro Cabral. These strangers had come by a route they could not understand. They did not speak their language, and the Arab merchants did what they could to belittle and malign them. Had there been a Portuguese interpreter on Cabral's fleet who could speak Malayalam fluently, the relations of the chief captain with the Zamorin would have been much closer. As it was, every move was watched with mutual suspicion. Cabral's attitude seemed unnecessarily belligerent, and in his treatment of the Zamorin there was an air of condescension. The Zamorin knew the Arab traders and believed much that they told him. He did not know these new foreigners, and was not sure that they had not come to dispossess him of his kingdom. He was also led to believe that the Portuguese were not as strong as they claimed and that he would gain more through taking the property that they left on shore than he could in future trade.

The true story of the events that led to the massacre at Calicut will never be known. The Zamorin may not have been able to control the mob that attacked the Portuguese factory. After it occurred he probably could not have called Cabral back, to apologize, without making a definite break with the Arab merchants and placing himself in the power of these new foreigners, whom he did not understand or trust. The Zamorin was not greatly concerned with the burning of the Arab ships. The bombardment of his city, however, he must have felt was unwarranted and a vital affront to himself and to his people. The rage that Cabral felt because of the massacre was equalled by that of the Zamorin at the damage done to his city. The bombardment of Calicut was a turning-point in the history of the Portuguese in India. The people of Calicut never trusted the Portuguese again nor could they be trusted by them.

Unable to do further damage at Calicut, Cabral's fleet sailed for Cochin, which was reached on the 24th of December. Dom Manuel had heard through Gaspar da Gama that another port lay farther along the coast, but he was not sure of its value. In his instructions Cabral had orders to proceed there in case he was unable to secure satisfactory treatment at Calicut. When Cabral arrived at Cochin he learned that the king of that city was aware of the treatment he had received at Calicut. This knowledge had spread as well along the coast of India. The Zamorin of Calicut, as overlord of the smaller kingdoms of the coast of Malabar, including Cochin, was much feared and hated, so that when word was received of the damage done to his city it was welcome. The rulers of these minor kingdoms felt that in the Portuguese they might have an ally who could reestablish their independence and also pay well for their products. Messengers came to Cabral from Cananore and from Quilon, in Travancore, inviting him to trade at those ports. Cabral replied that he would do so at some future time. The relations with the King of Cochin were amicable. A cargo of pepper was taken on here. Cinnamon and drugs were also purchased and benzoin, musk, china ware, fine cloth and veiling. Spices were also taken on at Cranganore, a town on the backwaters inland from Cochin, during the two weeks that the Portuguese stayed there. The smaller ships of the fleet took their cargoes at Cranganore; the larger ones, that had already been laden at Calicut, probably remained at Cochin, because Cabral, in spite of the apparent friendly attitude of the king, would hardly have taken the risk of having his whole fleet in the backwaters at the king's mercy.

Meanwhile, the Zamorin of Calicut had hurriedly assembled a fleet of some eighty ships, many of them large, to intercept the return of Cabral. The King of Cochin offered the latter his aid, but it was not accepted because the Portuguese felt that with their artillery they could defeat even this number. On second thought, however, they decided to return at once to Portugal. With them went two Christians from Cranganore, and, on account of their unexpected departure, the Portuguese took two hostages home with them. The Portuguese in the factory that had been established on shore were deserted. On the return voyage a stop was made at Cananore. Cananore was the last port that was visited in India. The king there insisted on furnishing whatever cargo they might need. He offered to sell this on credit until the next voyage, but Cabral still had money for its purchase.

One hundred bahars of cinnamon were taken on board and immediately thereafter, on the 16th of January, 1501, the fleet commenced its homeward voyage.

Cabral had gone to India as the representative of the Portuguese king, with full power to act in any emergency. He fulfilled his obligation under difficult circumstances in a dignified and conscientious manner.

The instructions for his conduct in India were based on the assumption that the Zamorin of Calicut was a Christian and on this account should be friendly. When Cabral found that this was not the case he was obliged to formulate new policies. Cabral had the religious mission of the fleet much at heart. He carried with him an image of Our Lady of Hope (Nossa Senhora de Esperança), which still exists. This image was placed in a chapel near Belmonte after Cabral's return, in care of the Franciscans.

He may be criticized for the temerity that was shown regarding the securing of hostages, but suspicion was the attitude in Europe in his time. He realized that treachery might be expected from the Moorish traders and that they would do everything possible to make his relations with the Zamorin difficult. He was far from home with a small fleet and with little knowledge of the local conditions. His cruelty and intolerance may similarly be condoned. The preparation of the treaty was entrusted to the chief factor, Cabral being precluded from participating in the negotiation because of his lack of knowledge of either Arabic or Malayalam. An older and more experienced man might have been able to counteract the intrigues of the Moors. Cabral's youth and inexperience were his most serious handicaps. The seizure of the Moorish ship at Calicut was against his best judgement, and here he deferred to the experience of Ayres Correia, in whom he had great confidence. The destruction of the Moorish ships and the bombardment of Calicut were decisive steps that may seem unduly severe punishment for what was possibly an unauthorized riot, but Cabral was ill and this decision was urged by his council.

One of the duties assigned to Cabral was to impress the rulers in the East with the importance and wealth of his country. He seems to have had this much in his thoughts, but his method of showing it was not always fitting. The removal of the ships' silverware to his temporary lodgings when he landed in Calicut must have seemed strange to a people unaccustomed to its use.

During the greater part of the voyage Cabral remained on board his ship. The real work and the negotiations with the native rulers were carried out by the factors.

CHAPTER 15

PRIEST JOSEPH'S DESCRIPTION OF INDIA

While the fleet was being loaded with spices at Cochin two Christian priests, Priest Joseph and Priest Mathias from the neighbouring settlement of Cranganore, sent word to Pedro Cabral asking permission to be taken to Portugal so that they might go from there to Rome and Jerusalem. Priest Mathias died either on the voyage or soon after his arrival in Portugal, but his brother, Priest Joseph, reached Lisbon in safety and was well received by the king. During the long voyage to Portugal and during his stay there Priest Joseph gave a detailed description of South-west India at the time of Cabral's time there. Fracanzano wrote the introduction. Where he obtained his information is not known, because he states that he had never seen Priest Joseph.

****

"How Joseph the Indian came to Portugal on board our caravels, and the King caused him to be accompanied to Rome and to Venice

The King of Portugal, having learned at other times, through his ships and other Portuguese, how to go from the northern parts to the parts of India, and taking the counsel of some of his people who had come from those parts in the past, the aforesaid King Hemanuel decided in the year 1500 to send twelve ships and caravels. The captain of these was Pedro Aliares. He, having received the standard of his captaincy on the 8th day of March of the said year, departed from Portugal. And sailing through very great storms and perils until the 13th day of the month of September [the 14th of September in the second edition] of the aforesaid year, he reached Calichut with seven caravels. Four of them had been lost in a storm and one went to Zaffal. They remained in that place of Calichut for three months, but finally, because of certain differences, they came to blows with those of the land. And after some of the men from the caravels and also many of the aforesaid place were killed, they departed on the 24th day of November of the same year and the aforesaid ships and caravels reached Cuchin, a place one hundred and ten miles distant from Calichut. That place of Cuchin is situated on the sea, and its lord is an idolatrous king who belongs to the sect of the King of Calichut. The caravels above mentioned were received by the king of that place and they were made welcome. While they were in the aforesaid place, contracting various merchandise, as appears in the third book, seventy-eighth chapter of the voyage previously written, there came from a city called Caranganor, about twenty miles distant from the aforesaid place of Cuchin, two Christian brothers, who boarded the caravels wishing to come to Western parts in order to be able to go to Rome and to Jerusalem. Since about eighty sails came from the region of Calichut to intercept the aforesaid caravels, these departed and together with them the said two Christians and others of the kingdom of Cuchin who had been given as hostages by agreement. Leaving on land an equal number of their own Portuguese, they took their route towards Portugal. Of those two brothers, one died on the way; the other, named Joseph, lived. Later, at the end of June 1501, they arrived at Lisbon. When they had reached the aforesaid place, the aforesaid Joseph remained until the month of January. And when he departed from the said place there was given to him by the majesty of the Most Serene King, one as a companion who should accompany him to Rome, Venice, and Jerusalem. And thus, having been at Rome, he then came to Venice in the year 1502, in the month of June, and remained there for many days. During that time the aforesaid Joseph gave news of the things written below.

The quality of Joseph, with his country, and the Gentiles

Joseph, mentioned above, is a man forty years of age, slender, dark by nature, and of ordinary stature. According to the judgement of those who have seen him and spoken with him he is an ingenuous man, truthful, and of the highest integrity; and in so far as could be understood by them, he is of exemplary life and may be said to be a man of very great faith. This has been learned from him; in the first place, that he is from Caranganor, which is ninety miles distant from Calichut on a certain bay called Milibar and fifteen miles distant from the sea; and as for its area, the city is said to be without walls and to be very long, a length of thirty miles, but inhabited only here and there in the manner of villas. Through that city run many rivers. Almost all the houses face the water. Two sorts of people live in the said city :

namely, Christians and Gentiles. And in order that this name of Gentiles may be known to every one, those are called Gentiles, who in ancient times worshipped idols and various kinds of animals, as will be narrated later. The king of the above mentioned city is an idolater. A small number of Jews are also found there, but they are much scorned, and a considerable number of Moors, mostly merchants, who voyage here from Cairo, Syria, Persia, and other places, to trade, for this place is the source of diverse sorts of merchandise.

The inhabitants of Caranganor and their churches and sacrifices

The country, in so far as concerns the Gentiles, is divided into three parts : first, the gentlemen, who in their language are called naires; second, the farmers, who are called canes; third, the fishermen, who are called nuirinan. And this class of fishermen is the lowest, and they are molested by every one when they go through the country. And if they should meet any gentleman, it is necessary for them to flee before him; otherwise they would be ill treated. Each has separate temples. The women also have their own temples separate from the men. They offer in their temples the first fruits of the land such as roses, figs, and other things. These Gentiles worship one single god, creator of all things, and they say that he is one and three, and in his likeness they have made a statue with three heads. It stands with the hands joined and they call it Tambran. A curtain is drawn before that statue and it is opened at the time of their sacrifices, as we shall relate here. They have various other statues of animals, but they do not worship them. And when they enter their churches some take earth and put it on their foreheads, and some take water. And they go to church three times a day, in the morning, at noon, and in the evening. They then make certain general sacrifices in this manner. They have certain of their men appointed with trumpets, horns, and tambors, who call them to church at the right hour. And after they have assembled, the priest, dressed in a certain large vestment, stands near the altar and begins to chant various prayers, and another replies to him. Then the people answer in a loud voice and this they do three times. Then out of one door goes a nude priest with a large crown of roses on his head, with large eyes, and with false horns. He carries in his hand two bare swords, and runs towards his god, and drawing the curtain entirely before it, he puts one of the swords into the hand of the priest standing at the altar. Then, with the other bare sword, he inflicts on himself many wounds, and thus, bleeding, he runs to a fire burning there in the temple and he leaps back and forth through it. Finally, with his eyes closed, he claims that he has spoken with his idol, who orders that certain things be done and instructs the people how they are to govern themselves. There are many other kinds of sacrifices that Joseph, because he did not understand the language and because he had not had many dealings with Gentiles, has not been able to explain entirely. Concerning their temples and religion enough has been said.

Customs of the King and the inhabitants, and where there are many Christians

The Gentile or idolatrous king has many wives, as do all the other Gentiles. Nor in their chastity is there modesty among them. When the king himself dies or any of the other Gentiles, their bodies are burned. The wives, in perfect possession of their faculties, voluntarily burn themselves alive eight days after the death of their husbands. And this, the aforesaid Joseph says, he has seen with his own eyes. The true sons of the king, after the death of the father, do not inherit the kingdom, but the nearest relatives other than the sons. The reason is this, that the wives of the king have this custom, they have relations with various persons, and on this account their sons are not considered worthy of the kingdom. And in the burial of their king they use the greatest ceremony. The Gentiles go dressed after this fashion : on their heads they wear a cap, that is, the king a cap of gold, and the other important men of velvet or brocade; the others go without. They are nude; they cover only their privy parts with linen cloths. They wear bracelets on their arms with various precious stones, finely worked. Likewise, they wear bracelets on their legs and rings on their toes, set with very fine precious stones. These, in their opinion, are of great price. They bathe their bodies two and three times a day, and they have many places assigned for bathing. The people, both men and women, are very handsome. They have their heads dressed in a careful manner, and on their heads they wear many jewels. When the Gentiles above mentioned write, they scratch on the leaves of trees with an iron point. Their language is the Indian, or Malanar. And enough concerning this. As we have said above there are many Christians in this place of

Caranganor, of whom some mention has been made in this chapter. Concerning each more will be said. And therefore it should be known to all that the Indus river is the beginning of India. Towards the west is the Island of Ornus, which is at the beginning of the Persian Gulf. No other Christians are to be found except in the aforesaid place of Caranganor, but in India there are very powerful Christian kings of Caranganor like those of Cataio. These Christians of Caranganor are of very great number. They obtain their houses at a certain price from the Gentile king, whom we have mentioned above, and they pay their rent each year, and in this manner they live there.

Their houses and how their Pontiffs govern their church

Their houses are made of board walls in different floors. Like those of the Gentiles, they are covered with boards of other kinds of wood. The temples of the Christians themselves are made like ours, except that their churches have only the cross, and on the top of the temples there is also a cross. They have no bells and when they call to worship they use the Greek rite. These aforesaid Christians in divine matters have as their head a pontiff, twelve cardinals, two patriarchs, bishops, and archbishops. The aforesaid Joseph referred to having departed with his superior, bishop of the aforesaid city of Caranganor, they boarded a ship and went towards the island of Ormus, which is 1500 miles distant from the aforesaid place of Caranganor. And from there they went by land a three months' journey. He came in company with the aforesaid bishop as far as Armenia, to find his pontiff. This bishop was consecrated by him, and Priest Joseph aforesaid was ordained for mass. All the Christians of India and of Cataio do likewise. His pontiff calls himself Catolicha and he has his head shaven in the form of a cross. He nominates his patriarchs, as has been said above; that is, one in India, the other in Cataio; he sends the other bishops and archbishops, as has been said above, to their provinces as seems best to him. Of this, Catholicos mention is made in Marco Polo where he treats of Armenia. In that place he says that there are two kinds of Christians, one of which is called Jacopiti, the other Nestorni. And he says that they have a Pope who is called Jacolita, who is this Catholicos, as the above mentioned Priest Joseph relates. He says in addition that the said Pope creates bishops, archbishops, and patriarchs, and sends them to India.

There may be some who will ask what authority this Pontiff has. Our Pontiff Alexander asked Priest Joseph, when he was in Rome and speaking with His Holiness concerning the parts of India, who had given this authority to his Catholicos. And Priest Joseph replied to him that at the time of Simon Magus, Saint Peter was Pontiff in Antiochia, and the Christians in the region of Rome, being molested by the art of this Simon Magus, because there was no one who could oppose him, sent to supplicate Saint Peter to allow him to be transferred to Rome. Leaving his vicar he came to Rome. And this vicar is the one who now calls himself Catholicos and he rules in the name of Saint Peter. As for the making of the said Pontiff or Catholicos, the twelve cardinals above mentioned gather in the province of Armenia, where they elect their Pontiff. The authority for this, they say, they have from the Roman Pontiff.

How they consecrate and bury the dead. Feasts and their festivals

They have, in addition, priests, deacons, and subdeacons. The priests in truth have no tonsures, but on the tops of their heads they have a few hairs. Children are baptized forty days after birth, if a case of necessity does not occur. They confess themselves, and take communion as we do, but they do not have extreme unction. In place of this they bless the body. They have holy water at the entrance to the churches. They consecrate the Body and the Blood of Our Lord, as we do, with unleaven bread. And he says that, since they have no wine, for in those parts grapes do not grow, they take raisins, of which a very large quantity comes from Cataio, and they put them in water, and they strain it and obtain a certain juice, and with this they consecrate. They bury their dead as we do. And they have this custom, that when any one dies, many Christians assemble together and eat for eight days, and then they pray for the dead. They make wills, and in case they do not make them, their property goes to the nearest relatives. After the death of the husbands the wives are paid their dowers, and then they leave, and after a year they have the right to marry. They have four evangelists and four Gospels of the Passion. They observe Lent and Advent. On Good Friday and Holy Saturday they fast until Easter Day. They preach on the night of Good Friday. And during the year they have the feasts mentioned below : the Resurrection, with two holy days following; the Octave of Easter, on which they have a greater festival than all the others of the year, for they say that on that day Saint Thomas put his hand in the side of Christ and recognized that He was not a spirit; the feasts of Saint Thomas, of the Trinity, of the Assumption of the Blessed Virgin Mary, of the Nativity, and of the Purification, the feast of the Nativity of Our Lord, and Epiphany. They celebrate the feasts of the Apostles, and Sundays, and have two feasts the first day of July in honour of Saint Thomas, for Christians as well as Gentiles hold him in the greatest veneration. They have monks clothed in black who live in the greatest poverty and chastity, likewise nuns. The priests live in chastity, and if they are discovered in any infraction, they lose the right to say mass. The Christians cannot be divorced. All people have communion three times a year. They have most excellent doctors and students of letters. They have prophets as we do. Priest Joseph, mentioned above, says further that there are many books of learned men who have spoken concerning the Bible and the prophets. The Christians dress as Moors do, that is, in linen cloth. They have the year divided into twelve months, and they have even the intercalary day. Their day is really divided into sixty hours; they recognize these hours by day from the sun and by night from the stars.

Caranganor during the Winter, and their ships

The people of Caranganor, mentioned above, are located between the equinoctial circle and the Tropic of Cancer, and according to what Priest Joseph told, they have thirteen and a half hours in the longest day of the year and ten hours in the shortest, speaking in terms of our hours and not theirs. When the sun is in the sign of Taurus, they have a perpendicular shadow and when in Cancer the shade is south; when the sun is in Virgo it makes a perpendicular shade, but when it is in Capricorn, the shade is north. The actual movement of the season is from the middle of May to the middle of August, and in that time they do not navigate those seas on account of the very heavy storms. In that part of India there are innumerable ships that sail to the west, to Persia, to Arabia, and to the Red Sea; to the east, to India, Cataio [China], Taprobana [Sumatra], Faillan [Sri Lanka], and many other islands. These ships are very large. Some have twelve sails and countless sailors, and others less, according to their burden. There are some that have sails of matting; these come from the islands; others have sails of cotton and of good fustian like ours. The ships are made with iron nails. This I say because there are some who say that they are fastened together with wooden pegs. And concerning this, wishing to have exact information from the aforesaid Priest Joseph, he was shown the construction of our ships. He laughed and said that theirs were like ours. The pitch is made of incense and other mixture. Formerly, on launching the ships into the water, they were accustomed to use two elephants, one at each side, and because sometimes the aforesaid elephants caused the death of their men, they no longer use this method, but have a great number of people come, who launch them. They have bombards, one kind of iron and another of wood, but they are not like ours and are less powerful. And more concerning this.

Concerning their money and the things that grow plentifully there

There are three kinds of money : one they call the sarapho of gold, which is of the weight of our ducat; the second, of silver, that they call parante, is worth six soldi; the third is called tare, three of which make one of our soldi. All of these coins have letters of their king engraved on them. In the aforesaid parts no gold or metal of any kind is found, but it is found in certain mountains near there, at a distance of about two hundred and fifty to three hundred miles. The province in which the site of Caranganor is located is entirely level, and has mountains at a distance. It has a hot climate, and every one is dark. Those who are in the mountains are white, and live for a very long time, as Priest Joseph says; there are men a hundred years old who have all their teeth. The land of Caranganor is very fertile, except that it does not produce grain or horses. And the grain, in fact, comes from some islands near there. And the same conditions exist in Calichut and Combait. This is due to their sandy soil. The horses come from Ormus and from their mountains. They work them only in carrying merchandise from place to place. Nor do they use them in fighting; they fight on foot. Their weapons are bows and arrows, swords and bucklers like rodelle; they have lances and they are great sword jugglers. There are some who make armour for themselves from the back of the skins of certain fish, which are very hard, and some make them of iron. They have many kinds of animals : oxen, cows, horses, buffaloes, sheep, and many other kinds, all of which they eat for food except the oxen, which the Gentiles worship. They have elephants in very great numbers; they have small animals such as hens and geese in very large numbers. They have no pigs. And because we wanted particularly to know the value of some things, Priest Joseph was shown hens and a ducat. He replied that a hundred hens could be had for a ducat.

Rice bread, and palms that produce India nuts

This province produces a very large quantity of rice and likewise of sugar. This rice they use ground, grinding it with sugar and oil. And it makes the most perfect bread, and they eat this instead of bread. They also have twenty kinds of herbs, and all are nutritious. These they eat, and especially some roots of herbs. They have no rosemary or boxwood, likewise no peaches or apples, or vines, because all the aforesaid things were shown to the said Joseph, who said that trees of that sort did not exist in his region. But they have countless others and especially fig trees, of which they have a very large number, and these have larger figs than ours, so much so that whatever might be written about them would seem a thing incredible rather than otherwise. They have another tree that they call palm. The tree, in our manner, produces the India nuts and, as we have understood from the aforesaid Priest Joseph, from this are obtained four things : namely, wine, vinegar, sugar, and oil. And because it would seem a strange thing to many how so many things come from one tree, I do not wish to pass over in this chapter the text of Strabo, in book sixteen, where he speaks concerning the palm, and which is similar to what Priest Joseph says. Later it will be related what methods they use in making the aforesaid things. But the chapter begins thus : "Other things are furnished by the palm, for from it bread and honey and wine and vinegar are made and various textiles. Blacksmiths use the pith instead of charcoal; steeped in water, it is given to oxen and sheep for fodder."

How they make wine, vinegar, sugar and oil from the palm

The making of the four things above mentioned is in this manner. The aforesaid person says that in the month of August those inhabitants go and cut the branches of the said palms, as is done among us when we trim the vines, for this season is judged to be spring among them, because the trees are in sap and sprout like the vines with us. When these branches are cut from the trees they produce a certain white liquid. They put vessels under them and collect it. For the first three days after the aforesaid liquid is gathered, it is as wine to him who drinks of it; after the three days are passed, it changes to vinegar. In case they wish to make sugar or honey or boiled wine in our fashion, they take that liquid of the first three days and put it over the fire in some vessels, and by means of the fire, the water is reduced to a small quantity and becomes sweet, as has been said above, by force of fire. And over it they put the water and mix it every day for twenty days; then they put it through a strainer and use it instead of wine. According to their report, it is of the greatest excellence. Of the fruit of the aforesaid tree, called palm, they use the inside of the nut to make oil. And thus the four things are clearly explained. And, furthermore, of the wood they make charcoal, and of the bark, ropes and baskets. In conclusion it is the most perfect tree that is found, to our knowledge. In that region there grows a very large quantity of pepper, which dries because of the great heat of the sun. And its trees are of mediocre quality. And more grows in that place than in all the other parts of India; likewise ginger, myrobalans, cassia, and other spices, which are bought and marketed by Moors who barter in that region. These carry them to Cairo and to Alexandria and to Damascus and to Persia, and even, as the aforesaid Priest Joseph says, a greater quantity thereof goes beyond the mountains and to Cataio than comes to our regions, as we shall presently relate. Since we have told about the city of Caranganor, its customs, religion, and manners, and its fertility, we shall now return to the city of Calichut.

Concerning Calichut and its King, with its usages and merchandise

The city of Calichut is located ninety miles westwards from Caranganor on the shore of the sea, and has there a most perfect harbour. That city is larger than Caranganor, and its lord is an idolater of the same sect as the lord of Caranganor, who does not differ in anything from the customs of the aforesaid king. Because we have said enough above both concerning his religion and everything else, we shall not go into further detail. In this city a countless number of

Moorish merchants trade. They deal in coral, zanbeloti, carpets, and other merchandise. There are also some merchants who are called Guzerati, who also trade in various commodities. In this city almost all of India comes together, and this was even more so formerly when those from Cataio used to trade there. These people from Cataio are Christians, and they are as white as we are, and they are very valiant men. About eighty or ninety years ago they had a factory in Calichut, and because the king of that place committed outrages against them they rebelled, and having gathered a very large armada, they came to the city of Calichut, which they destroyed. From that time up until the present, they have not come to trade in the aforesaid place, but have gone to a city of a King Narsindo, which is called Mailapet [Malacca], about nine hundred miles towards the east by way of the Indus [Ganges] river. These people are called Malasines [Chinese]. They carry varied merchandise; that is, cloth of silk of five sorts, copper, lead, tin, porcelain, and musk; and these are the ones who take the coral, and a good quantity of spices. It is said to be six thousand miles from Calichut to their region. They wear on their heads fezzes of great value, and they are very rich merchants. To return to the city of Calichut : the king of the aforesaid city is named Baufer. He has a large palace in which he keeps seven thousand men for the safety of his person. By night he makes the guards go around among the houses because the city is not walled, and three hundred men are assigned to this guard. In addition, he has a very large palace in which he has four separate audience chambers : one for Gentiles, one for Moors, one for Jews, and one for Christians. And when it happens that any one of these four nations wishes an audience, he goes to the place assigned to him, and there they are heard by the king. But first they are obliged to wash themselves, for otherwise the king would not speak to them. Besides, the said Gentiles have a custom, that when they go upon the sea, they do not eat under any circumstance, for if they do, they would be deprived of ever again seeing their king. We shall not take time to relate again what we have said above, that the women, after the death of their husbands, according to custom, are burned alive. And because one might marvel thereat it is not a strange thing, for the Indians have always had this custom not only among the women but also the men. They seem in this manner to attain certain immortality, as Strabo says in the fifteenth book when he treats of the legates or ambassadors of

India sent from Porro, the king of that country, to Caesar Augustus. The same thing is related by Nicholaus Damascenus of Antioch, etc.. Furthermore, in the city of Calichut, above named, much merchandise is handled, as I have said above, and at certain times of the year certain fairs are held to which all the people of Cataio, India, Persia, and Syria come. And upon our asking Priest Joseph whether any mention of our regions is made in that place, he said that none are mentioned except Rome, and France and Venice. And he reports that the money of Venice is very highly esteemed. The said Priest Joseph, having been ordered to appear before our Most Illustrious Signoria, showed some ducats of the Doge of the House of Sten, that he had brought from those regions.

Concerning the Kingdom of Cambaia, Ormus, and Guzerat

Now that we have spoken concerning Calichut, we shall go towards the west to the kingdom of Combait, which is twelve thousand miles distant from Calichut [this is evidently a misprint in the text for twelve hundred miles]. And from Combait it is three hundred miles straight towards the west to the island of Ormus. It is located at the beginning of the Persian Gulf and twenty miles away from the mainland which is called the cape of Mogolistam which is the beginning of the gulf. This island is one hundred and fifty miles around. Its lord is a Mohammedan. And it has a great city, very populous. And it produces countless things and merchandise. In this place glass like ours is made; pearls are gathered; horses are produced in large numbers. These they then take throughout India to carry the merchandise. Between this cape of Mogolistam, which is opposite the island of Ormus, and the city of Combait, there are found many lands inhabited by Moors : the first is named Sobelch, the second Semanaht, the third Chesimii. Then inland is the city of Guzerat and on the shore of the sea is located Combait, which is, as we have already said, three hundred miles from the Cape of Mogolistam. This city of Combait is deeply engulfed. And the gulf on which the city is situated is called the gulf of Guzerat. And the province is now called Guzerat, but in ancient times it was called Bedrosia. And because in this place we have made mention of Guzerat, we shall explain concerning its conditions. This province has many cities and castles. They are a powerful people and great merchants. They are idolaters; they worship the sun and the moon and cows, and if any should kill a cow he would be killed for this. They do not eat anything that meets death. They do not drink wine. The men are whiter than the natives of Calichut. They are the greatest conjurers in the world. They wear their hair well oiled, and they have beards, and they arrange their hair as the women do. They take only one wife and they are very chaste. Their food is vegetables and herbs that the land produces, in accordance with the ideals of Pythagoras. We have spoken of Guzerat. Now we shall tell of the city of Cambaia.

The site of Cambaia and other places, also of the King and its spices

The city of Cambaia is located in the Gulf of Guzerat. It is very large and very populous, and according to common opinion, it is the noblest city in all India. They call it the Cairo of India. It is walled and has very imposing dwellings within its walls. Formerly its lord was a Gentile and idolater; at present he is a Mohammedan. This is the reason : when the number of Mohammedans increased more than that of the Gentiles, the Mohammedans took over the government of the province, which is almost entirely of Gentiles, as also the land. In this place grows lac, and incense in greater abundance than in any other part of the world. They are very great merchants and have a considerable number of ships with which they sail to Ethiopia, to the Red Sea, the Persian Strait, and India. From this city of Cambaia to the cape of the gulf, which is called Diongul, it is three hundred miles. In this gulf are found many cities which it would require a long time to describe. Near this cape of Diongul is found an island called Maya, and from this cape of Diongul towards the east is found a cape called Ely, the two being two hundred and fifty miles distant from one another. And from there to Calichut it is more than six hundred miles.

Concerning King Narsindo and a church of Saint Thomas

Up to this point we have told about all the country that is found along the sea, beginning at Ormus, as far as Caranganor and the kingdom of Cuchin. We shall now tell about the regions inland. Towards the mountains and about three hundred miles distant from the sea is to be found a very powerful king, who is named King Narsindo, and he has a great city with three circuits of walls. It is called Besenegal [Bisnagar]. This king, as Priest Joseph told, he has seen with his own eyes. When he goes with an army against his enemies, he takes with him eight hundred elephants, four thousand horses, and innumerable foot soldiers, and he says that his camp from south to north is thirty miles long, and from west to east, of equal breadth. Consequently it may be supposed that his kingdom is very extensive, and furthermore, according to what Priest Joseph says, it is three thousand miles around. Its faith is idolatrous. Now we return to the regions next to the sea, and first begin from Cuchin towards the east and India. A hundred miles eastward from Cuchin is found a cape that is called Cumari. From this Cape of Cumari to the Indus [Ganges] river is a distance of five hundred miles. Within this space there is a huge gulf that is called the Gulf of Oriza. And there is a large city named Oriza near which the Indus [Ganges] river flows. On this same gulf is located a city on a promontory extending into the sea; it is called Milapar [Mailapur]. In that city is a church of Saint Thomas as large as that of Saint John and Saint Paul in Venice. In it is placed the body of Saint Thomas. There, many miracles are performed, and Gentiles and Christians hold it in the greatest reverence. There are to be found above in this Indian Sea many islands, among which two are worthy of mention. The first is Saylam [Sri Lanka], two hundred miles distant from the Cape of Cumari [Comorin]. On it horses are raised. After this, towards the east is the Island of Samotra [Sumatra], or Taprobana, which is a three months journey from Calichut. Then farther on is found Cataio and other regions, concerning which we shall not write further, on account of not having been able to learn more from Priest Joseph, mentioned above. Many things might be said concerning the spices and the other merchandise pertaining to India and the parts about which we have written in this our progress, but because they are not pertinent things to the narrative of Priest Joseph but rather an addition, and because we do not wish to proceed further, but to tell the simple truth, we have decided to end the present subject."

CHAPTER 16

THE VOYAGE TO CAPE VERDE

Taking with him an ambassador from the king at Cananore, Pedro Cabral sailed towards the African shore. Cabral carried instructions that required him to capture Moorish ships at sea whenever possible, to secure loot, part of which was to go to the king, and the remainder to be divided among the members of the fleet.

When the ships were on the high seas a strange sail hove in sight. The Chief Captain signalled to it to strike sail, which it immediately did and a boat was launched. It was with evident regret that it was later released when it was ascertained that it was an Indian ship and did not belong to the Arabs. It proved to be a ship of Cambay homeward-bound from Malacca, that was richly laden with a cargo of spices and sandalwood.

Valuable presents were conveyed to the Chief Captain for which the Cambay captain would accept no payment in money but begged for a flag that was given to him, - a Portuguese royal standard bearing the Armillary Sphere and the Five Reals (Quinas Reaes). The captain was dismissed with many compliments and with a letter to the Nawab wherein Cabral wrote that he had taken nothing out of the ship because its captain had obeyed the King's flag and that the officers of the King of Portugal would always act thus towards those who obeyed, - that is to say - who acknowledged the supremacy of the King of Portugal upon the eastern seas.

The coast of Africa was sighted between Malindi and Mozambique and, as the summer was well advanced, the pilots advised Cabral not to turn back to Malindi.

As the fleet approached the opposite shore, the pilots advised caution, but the Spanish captain, Sancho de Tovar, insisted on taking the lead. In consequence of hugging the coast in disregard of the advice of his pilot, he ran his ship aground on a sandbank, and the vessel began to fill. All persons on board and all the light tackle and also the anchors and cables were removed to the other ships but the cargo was abandoned because there was no space on the other ships in which to stow it, and the ship was set on fire.

Unable to call at Malindi, the fleet then proceeded to Mozambique to take in supplies and to put the ships in order for the long voyage around the Cape.

When the fleet reached Mozambique, the Chief Captain and council resolved to detach from it the naveta of which Luis Pirez was captain and to send it to Sofala under the command of Sancho de Tovar, for Luis Pirez was dangerously ill and had been removed to the ship of the commander-in-chief.

Another caravel, belonging to Italian merchants, the Anunciada, since it had been found to be the fastest, was placed under the command of Nicoláu Coelho and sent ahead of the others to advise the king of the results of the voyage.

Gaspar da Gama and several merchants of Mozambique accompanied Sancho de Tovar and one of the Malindi pilots, who was skilled in the navigation of the coast, also went with him. The Mozambique merchants took with them Cambay cloth and red beads to barter with the people of Sofala, and Sancho de Tovar had red silk, mirrors, barrets, Flemish handbells and cut-glass beads as presents to the king who was of African blood and to barter for gold beads. The European merchandise realised from twelve to fifteen times as much at Sofala as it would have done in Lisbon and payment for everything was made in gold. When he had disposed of the merchandise and taken in wood and water, Sancho de Tovar took his departure, bearing a letter from the king to the Chief Captain urgently requesting him to send more ships to Sofala.

Pedro Cabral ordered his ships to be careened and caulked at Mozambique, for when rain fell it penetrated between the planks of the decks. When this work was finished and he was about to sail, the Malindi pilots counselled him to navigate with great care when he was off the coast of Sofala, for sudden and violent squalls might be encountered in that quarter at that season of the year. Before setting sail, Cabral sent a letter to the Sultan of Malindi by the master of a sambuk that had arrived from that port. He thanked the Sultan for the provisions sent by the sambuk, consisting of biscuit, dried fish and flesh and sheep, gave the Sultan an account of the events that had transpired in India, informed him that a small ship had been despatched to Sofala and explained the cause that had hindered him from revisiting Malindi. He then took his departure from Mozambique. The prognostications of the pilots were justified by the event, for a gale arose, so violent and sudden that the ships were driven seaward under bare poles and would have been in greater peril had they not been deeply laden. They were separated.

After leaving Mozambique on the homeward journey, the ship of Pedro de Ataíde, became separated from the fleet. This went to São Bras, apparently with the idea that Cabral might stop there to wait for it. Pedro de Ataíde left a note there in a shoe suspended from a branch of a tree for the benefit of later ships, telling of what had occurred in India. This note was subsequently found by João da Nova, who departed from Portugal in four small ships on the 5th of March 1501, over three months before Cabral's first ship returned.

Cabral's flagship and that of Simão de Miranda, both heavily laden, continued alone on their homeward voyage.

Before the ships became separated it had evidently been arranged that they should stop at Beseguiche, a harbour near Cape Verde, after their long voyage from the Cape. Here they could secure wood, water, and fresh fish, the sick could be cared for, and the ships put in order for their return to Lisbon.

Diogo Dias seems to have arrived first, which was almost miraculous. He was found there by Nicoláu Coelho in the Anunciada. While these two vessels were apparently awaiting the arrival of the flagship for instructions, the three ships of Amerigo Vespucci arrived. These had left Lisbon on the 13th of June on a voyage to Brazil to explore the coast that Cabral had found, and for trade. His fleet evidently continued its voyage before the arrival of the ships of Cabral and Simão de Miranda. Before departing to Brazil, Amerigo Vespucci took advantage of this encounter to send a letter back to Lisbon to be transmitted to Florence. The intention was to tell of what he had learned regarding the voyage of Cabral, as he learned it from the interpreter, Gaspar de India, and others.

CHAPTER 17

THE LETTER OF AMERIGO VESPUCCI

Gaspar de Lemos had returned to Portugal from Brazil some time during the summer of 1500, bringing with him letters to the king from members of Cabral's fleet and particularly one from Pero Vaz de Caminha. The return of Gaspar de Lemos and the report of the discovery of Brazil evidently did not create great excitement in Portugal. There is no mention of his arrival in any existing document. De Lemos may not have brought back any of the parrots that seemed such novelties when Cabral's fleet returned, nor is there any indication in the letter of Caminha that brazil-wood had been found. Both of these appear very prominently on the Cantino map, where they seem to be associated with the voyage of Vespucci.

In Caminha's letter, he states that Cabral and his council advised the king to send another fleet to make further discoveries, because Cabral could not delay his voyage to India to do so. In addition to these letters news had certainly been received from Spain that Vicente Yañez Pinzon had reached Palos in September of that year and reported that he had visited the South American shore and had brought back a cargo of brazil-wood. It was therefore decided by the Portuguese that an expedition should be sent to continue the discovery of Pedro Cabral and to claim this land as within their sphere.

According to Duarte Galvão an expedition under the command of Gonçalvo Coelho departed from Lisbon for Brazil in March 1501, and returned in September of the next year. This, he states, reached land at 5° S and coasted along the shore as far as 32° before it returned. There seems to be no conflict between this voyage and that of Vespucci except as to the date, which Galvão may have mistaken. Amerigo Vespucci was not a navigator, but was a banker who was interested in cosmography. The command of this fleet might therefore have been under Gonçalvo Coelho, and Vespucci might still have gone with it and represented the King of Portugal or the Italian merchants.

The selection of the leader for this voyage was not an easy matter.

Many of the navigators who had knowledge of the Atlantic Ocean and to whom this enterprise might be entrusted had gone with Cabral's fleet. There were others, but they probably wished to share in the profits of the voyage to India. It was undoubtedly at the suggestion of Bartolomeo Marchioni that the name of his fellow countryman, Amerigo Vespucci, was proposed. Vespucci may also have agreed to finance this expedition, at least in part, in the hope of securing brazil-wood.

While Dom Manuel had reason to believe that the land discovered by Cabral was within the Portuguese sphere, he may also have believed, since it was not known to be mainland, that the coast began its westerly direction somewhat to the south and would thus reach the Spanish sphere. On this account Vespucci, who could go representing both Spain and Portugal, would be a desirable leader.

Vespucci was well fitted to accompany this expedition. He knew about the earlier Spanish voyages, as he had previously gone at least twice to America and was interested in cartography. He also had the confidence of the Catholic kings, so that there would be no controversy as to whom the land he discovered might belong to. Word was sent to Vespucci by Giuliano di Bartolomeo del Giocondo, a fellow Florentine, requesting him to come to Portugal. Vespucci accepted the charge, and during the early part of May departed from Lisbon with a fleet of three vessels. Since there was ample time, they spent a few days securing a supply of fish along the African coast and then continued to Beseguiche for water and wood. It is here that they encountered the two ships of Cabral's fleet, and from where Amerigo Vespucci sent his letter back to Lisbon.

The authenticity of this letter has been questioned by some historians for two reasons: because of the belief that it was not in the handwriting of Vespucci, and because it was not, judging by the printed accounts of his voyage which were assumed to be authentic, the kind of letter that he would have written. It is true that the letter is not in Vespucci's hand and is a copy. The copy, however, was made by Piero Vagliente at Florence and forms part of a collection of thirty-two accounts which otherwise appear to be authentic. Vagliente was closely associated with Nicoló Sernigi of Florence and thus with Girolamo Sernigi of Lisbon and would be in a position to obtain copies of letters addressed to Lorenzo de' Medici which, because of their interest, he would naturally include in his collection. Vespucci had gone to Seville at the age of forty to represent the Medici, with whom he had previously been associated.

His letters, therefore, would be in the Florentine dialect, as are those which Vagliente copied, and not in the mixture of Spanish and bad Italian found in the printed accounts of his voyages, particularly in Mundus Novus and the letter to Soderini, which may have been first printed elsewhere for popular distribution.

The letter from Beseguiche is the sort of letter that Vespucci would write. He was interested in cartography. In it, therefore, many place names are found. He seems, in fact, to have been more concerned with the geography of the East than with the voyage itself. On comparing this letter with other accounts of Cabral's voyage there seems to be little doubt that it is genuine.

Vespucci evidently met some of the Florentines on the Anunciada, particularly the representatives of Marchioni, who showed him the jewels that they had obtained. He naturally would not mention them by name, because of the injunction of secrecy regarding the voyage that Dom Manuel had imposed.

The original of this letter is not known to exist. The copy, however, is prior to 1514. This was to be found in the Riccardiana Library (MS. 1910). It was first published by Conde Baldelli Boni in volume i of his Il Milione di Marco Polo in 1827, and subsequently reprinted by F. A. de Varnhagen in Amerigo Vespucci (Lima, 1865), pp. 78-82. The translation that follows is from the published text.

****

"Beseguiche, the 4th of June 1501

My magnificent Patron. The 8th of May was the last time I wrote you, when I was in Lisbon ready to depart on this present voyage which now, with the aid of the Holy Spirit, I have commenced, and I thought that until my return I could not write more to you. And it appears that chance has given me another opportunity that enables me to write not only of distant land but of the high sea.

You have learned, Lorenzo, as well by my letter as through the letters of our Florentines of Lisbon, how I was called while I was in Sevilla by the King of Portugal; and he begged me that I should dispose myself to serve him for this voyage; in which I embarked at Lisbon on the 13th of the past month. And we took our way to the south. And we so navigated that we passed in sight of the Isole Fortunate, which are today called the Canary Islands, and passing them at a distance, taking our navigation along the coast of Africa, we navigated so far that we arrived here at a cape that is called el Cauo Verde, which is the beginning of the Province of Ethiopia, and it is on the meridian of the Fortunate Isles and has a latitude of fourteen degrees from the equinoctial line. Here by chance we found, riding at anchor, two ships of the King of Portugal, that were returning from the parts of East India, which are of the same ones that went to Calichut fourteen months ago which were thirteen ships; with which I have had very great discourse, not so much of their voyage as of the coast of the land that they passed along, and of the riches that they found and of those things that they took, all of which I will give brief mention below to your Magnificence; but concerning cosmography, because there was not in this fleet a cosmographer or even a mathematician, which was a great error, I will tell it in the same disconnected manner as they told it to me, save that I have somewhat corrected it with the Cosmography of Ptolemy.

This fleet of the King of Portugal departed from Lisbon in the year 1499, in the month of April, and they navigated to the south as far as the islands of Cavo Verde, which is distant from the equinoctial line about fourteen degrees, and beyond every meridian towards the west, which would indicate that they were six degrees, a little more or less, farther to the west than the island of Canaria, since it is well known how Ptolemy and the greater part of the schools of cosmography place the end of the inhabited Western world at the Fortunate Islands. Here they took the latitude with the astrolabe and with the quadrant; and I have found it to be thus. The longitude is a more difficult matter because of the little that can be known about it except by much observation, and watching the conjunction of the moon with the planets. Because of this longitude I have lost much sleep and have shortened my life ten years, and I believe all was well spent, because I hope to come to fame at a distant time if I return in safety from this voyage; God will reward me to the greatest extent in that all my work will redound to His holy service.

Now I turn to my subject : as I say, these thirteen ships above mentioned navigated towards the south of the Cape Verde Islands with a wind that they say was between south and south-west. And after having navigated twenty days about seven hundred leagues (each league of which is four and one half miles) they went ashore in a land where they found white and nude people of the same land that I discovered for the King of Castile, except that it is farther to the east, of which by my other [letters] I have written you. There they say they obtained every refreshment. And from there they departed and took their navigation towards the east, and they navigated by the south-east wind, taking a quarter to the east, and when they were a distance from the said land, they had such a storm of the sea with south-west wind, and it was so rough, that it overcame five of their ships, and submerged them in the sea with all the people. May God have mercy on their souls. And the eight other ships, they say, went with bare masts, that is without sail, for forty-eight days and forty-eight nights with a very great storm; and they went so far that they were with their navigation beyond the wind of the Cape of Good Hope which is shown on the coast of Ethiopia, and is located beyond the tropic of Capricorn ten degrees on the southern side. I say that it is in the height of the equinoctial line towards the south, thirty-three degrees. The aforesaid found the location of the parallel. They found the said cape to be sixty-two degrees from the inhabited West, a little more or less, so that I may say that it is situated in the meridian of Alexandria. And from here they then navigated towards the north to the north-east, navigating continuously along the coast, which in my opinion is the beginning of Asia, and the province of Arabia Felix, and of the land of Prester John, because here they have news of the Nile, which is to the west of them, which you know separates the parts of Africa from Asia. And on this coast there is an infinite population and cities, and in some they made port, and the first was Zafale, which they say is a city of such greatness as is Cairo, and it has a mine of gold; and they say that they pay tribute to their king two hundred thousand miccicalli of gold every year, and that each miccicalle is worth a castellana of gold, or thereabouts. And from here they departed, and they came to Mezibinco, where it is said there is much aloes and an infinite amount of lac and much silken cloth. And it has as great a population as Cairo. And from Mezibinco they went to Chiloa, and to Mabazai and from Mabaza to Dimodaza and to Melinde, then to Mogodasco and Camperuia, and to Zendach, then to Amaab, then to Adabul and Albarcon. All these cities are on the coast of the ocean sea. And they went as far as the strait of the Red Sea, which sea you must know is not red, and it is like ours but has only the name of red. And all these cities are very rich in gold, and in jewels and cloths and spicery and drugs and in things of their own production that they trade with the cargoes from the parts of India; this, as you will understand who know, is a thing long to relate.

From Albarcone they crossed the strait of the Red Sea and went to Meca, where went a ship of the said fleet, which at this time has arrived here at this cape. And thus far is written concerning the coast of Arabia Felice. Now I will tell you of the coast of the Red Sea towards India, that is within the strait of this sea.

At the mouth of the strait is a port in the Red Sea that is called Haden, with a large city. Beyond, towards the north, is another port that is called Camarcan, and Ansuva : then there is another port that is named Odeinda and from Odeinda to Lamoia, and from Lamoia to Guda. This port of Guda is near Mount Sinai (which, as you know, is in the Arabian desert) which they say is the port of all the ships that come from India, and from Mecca. It is in this port, they say, that they unload all the spices and drugs and jewels, and everything that they bring here. The caravans of camels come later from Cairo and Alexandria and conduct them there, where they say they go eighty leagues through the desert of Arabia. And they say that in this Red Sea they do not navigate, because of the many rocks and the shoals that are there. And many other things were told me of this sea which, not to be too prolix, are omitted.

Now I will tell of the coast of the Red Sea from the parts of Africa. At the mouth of the strait of this sea is Zoiche, the lord of which is a Moor who is called Agidarcabi, and it is said that this is three days this side of the port of Guda, that it has much gold, many elephants, and infinite supplies. From Zoiche to Arbazui. From these, the two ports of Arboiam and Zala in which Prester John is lord. And opposite is a port that is named Tui and that belongs to the great Sultan of Babylonia. Then from Tui to Ardem, and from Ardem to Zeon. This is as much as I have been able to learn concerning the Red Sea : I refer to one who knows it better.

It remains for me to tell what I learned of the coast of Mecca, which is within the Persian Sea, which is as follows. They left Mecca and went along the coast of the sea to a city that is named Ormuz, which is a port in the mouth of the Persian Sea. And thence from Ormusa to Tus and from Tus to Tunas, then to Capan, then to Lechor, then to Dua, then to Torsis, then to Pares, then to Stacara, then to Ratar. All these ports, which are thickly populated, are on the coast of the Persian Sea. I believe there may be more in my mind to which truly I might refer, concerning which a man worthy of trust who is called Guasparre, who had gone from Cairo as far as a province that is called Molecca, which is situated on the coast of the Indian Sea, told me. I believe that it is the province that Ptolemy called Gedrosica. They say that this Persian Sea is very rich : but all is not to be believed, therefore it is left to a pen better than mine to relate the truth.

Now it remains for me to tell of the coast, which goes from the strait of the Persian Sea along the Indian Sea, according to what many who were in that armada told me; and chiefly the said Guasparre, who knew many languages and the names of many provinces and cities. As I say, he is a very authentic man, because he has twice made the voyage from Portugal to the Indian Sea.

From the mouth of the Persian Sea one navigates to a city that is called Zabule; from Zabule to Goosa, and from Goosa to Zedeuba, and then to Nui, then to Bacanut, then to Salut, then to Mangalut, then to Batecala, then to Calnut, then to Dremepetam, then to Fandorana, then to Catat, then to Caligut. This city is very large; and the armada of the

Portuguese went to remain there. Then from Caligut to Belfur, then to Stailat, then to Remond, then to Paravrangari, then to Tanui, then to Propornat, then to Cuninam, then to Lonam, then to Belingut, then to Palur, then to Glencoloi, then to Cochin, then to Caincolon, then to Cain, then to Coroncaram, then to Stomondel, then to Nagaitan, then to Delmatan, then to Carepatan, then to Conimat. As far as this the fleets of the Portuguese have navigated, although they cannot determine the longitude and latitude of the said navigation, which is an impossible thing to do for those who do not have much practice in maritime matters, through which understanding would be possible. And I have hope in this my navigation to revise and correct a great part of the above and to discover much more, and on my return I shall give of all a good and true relation. May the Holy Spirit go with me. This Guasparre, who told me the above-mentioned things, and many Christians agreed with him because they were in one of these, told me later the following : he said that he had been inland in India to a kingdom that is called the kingdom of Perlicat, which is a very great kingdom, and rich in gold and in pearls and in jewels and in precious stones, and he told me that he had been inland to Mailepur and to Gapatan and to Melata and to Tanaser and to Pego and to Starnai and to Bencola and to Otezen and at Marchin. And this Marchin he said was near a large river called Enparlicat. And this Enparlicat is the city where is the body of Saint Mark, the apostle, and here there are many Christians. And he told me that he had been in many islands and chiefly in one that is called Ziban, which he said he had sailed three hundred leagues and that this much had been at sea, the river, another four hundred leagues. He told me that it is a very rich island in precious stones and pearls and spices of every sort, and of drugs and other riches, such as elephants and many horses; so that I believe that this is the island of Taprobana, according to what he represented it to me. And further, he told me that he had never heard Taprobana mentioned in those parts which, as you know, is wholly in front of the above mentioned river.

Furthermore, he told me that he had been in another island that is called Stamatara, which is of equal greatness with Ziban and Bencomarcano, as well as being as rich as they are; so that, Ziban not being the island, Taprobana may be Scamatarra. From these two islands there come to

Persia and to Arabia an infinite number of ships laden with all sorts of spices and drugs and precious jewels. And they say that they have seen a large fleet of ships from those parts that are very large and of from forty thousand to fifty thousand cantara capacity and which they call giunchi, and they have the masts of very large ships and at each mast three or four cabins. The sails are those of junks. They are not made with iron but are interlaced with cords. It appears that this sea is not tempestuous. They have bombards, but they are not in the sailing ships, nor do they put to sea much, because they continually navigate in sight of land. It happens that this fleet of Portugal, to comply with the request of the King of Calicut, took a ship that was loaded with elephants and rice and more than three hundred men. A caravel of seventy tons took it. And on another occasion they sank twelve ships. Then they came to islands called Arenbuche and Maluche and many other islands in the Indian Sea, that are those which Ptolemy tells of, and which are in the neighbourhood of Taprobana, and all are rich.

The said armada returned to Portugal, and on the return voyage, when there remained eight ships, one of them laden with many riches, which they say were valued at one hundred thousand ducats, was lost, and five were lost in storms. As for the flagship, until today it has not arrived here, as I say above; I believe that another day it will come in safety. May God grant it.

What the said ships carried is as follows. They came loaded with an infinite amount of cinnamon, green and dry ginger, and much pepper, and cloves, nutmegs, mace, musk, algabia, istorac, benzoin, porcelain, cassia, mastic, incense, myrrh, rose and white sandalwood, aloe-wood, camphor, amber, canne, much lac, mumia, anib and tuzia, opium, aloe patico, folio indico, and many other drugs that you know it would be a long thing to relate. Of jewels I know only that I saw many diamonds and rubies and pearls, among which I saw a ruby of one piece, round, of the most beautiful colour, that weighed seven and one-half carats. I do not wish to relate more because the ship.....it does not allow me to write. From Portugal you can learn the news. In conclusion, the King of Portugal has in his hands a very great traffic and great riches. May God grant prosperity. I believe that the spices come from these parts to

Alexandria and to Italy, according to quality and demand. Thus goes the world.

Believe, Lorenzo, that what I have written thus far is the truth. And if the provinces and kingdoms and names of cities and islands do not agree with ancient writers, it is a sign that they are changed, as we find in our Europe when, through a marvel, one is known by an old name. And for the greater clearness of the truth, Gherardo Verdi, brother of Simon Verdi di Cadisi, was present, who comes in my company, and to you he sends his respects.

This voyage that I now make, I recognize is dangerous as to the frailty of this our human life. None the less, I make it with a free mind, for the service of God and for the world. And if God is served through me, He will give me virtue to such an extent that I may be directed to His every wish, if only to give me eternal repose for my soul."

CHAPTER 18

THE RETURN TO LISBON

Cabral had rounded the Cape on the 22nd of May 1501, and probably arrived at Cape Verde about the beginning of July.

When his ships reached Beseguiche, near Cape Verde, Diogo Dias recounted to the Chief Captain that he had sailed to Magadoxo, where he was received with feigned hospitality by the inhabitants but, when he sent a boat ashore to obtain water, it was seized by Arabs and the ship was attacked by other Arabs in sambuks. This was probably done as a measure of reprisal because of the bombardment of the town by Vasco da Gama in 1499. So few men were aboard that Diogo Dias was unable to repel the attack and therefore cut the cable and hoisted sail.

Cabral sent the Anunciada to Lisbon and with it the remaining crew of the caravel of Diogo Dias. The vessels of Pedro Cabral, Simão de Miranda and Diogo Dias remained until the arrival of Sancho de Tovar from Sofala and of Pedro de Ataíde. Shortly after these reached Beseguiche, the ships of Pedro Cabral and Simão de Miranda departed for Lisbon and were soon followed by those of Sancho de Tovar, Pedro de Ataíde, and Diogo Dias.

The return of Cabral's fleet had been awaited for weeks, not only by the people of Portugal but by those in other parts of Europe, and particularly by the merchants of Venice. The Anunciada - captained by Nicolau Coelho - arrived in Portugal on the eve of Saint John's, on the 23rd of June 1501. When the Anunciada sailed up the Tagus and anchored at Belem, the news spread rapidly and people hurried to inquire for relatives or friends and to learn the results of the voyage.

In Bartolomeo Marchioni's letter, written in July 1501, he writes of three of the ships already having arrived. Pedro Cabral reached the Tagus on the 31st of July 1501. The Anonymous Narrative describes Sancho de Tovar as arriving the following day. The dates of the arrivals of the other captains, including Simão de Miranda, Pedro de Ataíde, and Diogo Dias are not precisely known.

"Seven ships", writes the Venetian Envoy, "have made the return voyage in safety; one ship ran aground but the ship's company was saved; it was a vessel of six hundred tons or thereabouts; as yet only one ship, a vessel of three hundred tons, has returned to port; they say that others are close at hand; the one of which I speak arrived on the Eve of Saint John; I happened to be with the king who called me to him and said that I ought to congratulate him on his ships having arrived from India with cargoes of spices and I therefore did so as became me; he ordered a banquet to be given that night at the palace and that joy-bells should be rung all through the country; next day there was a solemn procession; when I again presented myself to the king he reverted to the subject of his ships and said that I ought to write to Your Highness that henceforth you should order your galleys to fetch spices hence and that It would please him if you would do so and that you might consider yourself at home here and he would compel the Sultan to fetch no spices."

On the return of the fleet Cabral was well received. However, because of the losses, less enthusiasm was aroused than that which followed the voyage of Vasco da Gama. There was great sadness because of the loss of five ships at sea with all on board and of the death of many others through sickness or in the massacre at Calicut. The commercial results of the voyage were gratifying because, while Cabral's ships had not all returned laden with spices, a sufficient number would soon arrive to show that future trade with India was possible by the all sea route and that Portugal might look forward to more fortunate voyages. The cargoes brought by five of the vessels that returned from India were of sufficient value to repay all the outlay incurred in equipping and despatching the fleet, to indemnify the Crown for the ships and the cargo that had been lost and to yield in addition a profit equivalent to the amounts so expended and so lost.

Castanheda tells us that Pedro Cabral had sailed with three objectives in mind : to make peace and friendship with the King of Calicut, to establish a factory in that city, and to instruct the Christians of India. Cabral, in fact, so antagonized the Zamorin of Calicut that no factory could be left there, and he found that the people were idolaters and not Christians, as Vasco da Gama had supposed. All of the Franciscan fathers who went to instruct them and who survived the massacre returned with the fleet.

Even though a portion of Brazil within the Portuguese sphere was discovered and Madagascar was probably first visited, these at the time were popularly considered as hardly more than incidents of the voyage. They were believed to be valuable only as places where wood and water could be obtained. The fact that Sofala, celebrated for its gold, was first visited by a Portuguese ship during Cabral's voyage seemed of greater importance. The voyage was of evident value to the cartographers. Vasco da Gama had brought back much of interest for them, but further information was sought and seems to have been obtained by members of Cabral's fleet. In the letter said to have been written by Dom Manuel to King Ferdinand in 1505 there is a statement that the Portuguese king had a map showing Cabral's voyage. The Cantino map shows a Portuguese standard at Sofala as well as at Mozambique, Kilwa, and Malindi. Since Vasco da Gama did not visit Sofala, this flag probably indicates that the map was made, in part, from information obtained during the voyage of Cabral. It is possible that a map was made during this voyage that is now lost, but that formed the basis for much that is given in the Cantino map of 1502.

The loss of ships had been great. Of thirteen that departed from Lisbon but five returned from India with cargo, six were lost at sea, and two returned empty. The large loss of property was partly compensated for by the profits, but the loss of life during the voyage because of shipwreck and disease shed a gloom over the nation. There was thus reason for the king and the people to be disappointed. But the losses and the inability of Cabral to attain his objectives were not his fault; they were his misfortune. His achievements, as viewed at that time, consisted in the establishment of friendly relations with two minor kingdoms on the Malabar coast, Cochin and Cananore, where spices could be obtained in the future, in the establishment of a factory at the former place, the first permanent factory in India, in finding an early Christian settlement at Cranganore, in visiting Sofala, and in ascertaining a practical sea route to the Cape.

It was during the voyage of Cabral that the Portuguese had the first authentic information regarding the Christians in India. That Christians were to be found there had been known previously in Europe through the writings of Marco Polo and of Friar Jordanus, Marignolli, and others, but accurate knowledge regarding them had not hitherto been available. During Cabral's voyage, Cochin and Cranganore were visited for the first time by the Portuguese, and at the latter place Christian and Jewish settlements were found. They were not known either to Pedro da Covilhan or to Vasco da Gama, neither of whom went south of Calicut.

In Europe, the voyage of Cabral added greatly to the prestige and credit of Portugal. What Portugal gained in securing the spice trade of India was chiefly a loss to Venice. In that city the return of Vasco da Gama had been known, but its full import was not realized. It was received by the people, then distraught with many problems, as news of interest, but they wished to believe that this new found route, because of the long and dangerous voyage, the loss of life by disease, and the antagonism of the Arab traders, could not work to their disadvantage. When, however, news subsequently reached Venice through the letter of Il Cretico that Cabral's fleet had succeeded in bringing back a cargo, consternation spread among its merchants, to whom the monopoly of the trade in spices was an important source of income, and among the people because it touched their daily lives. From Venice the spices had been distributed through Europe by her galleys to Flanders or to Aigues Mortes for the markets in France, or by land to the cities and fairs beyond the Alps. The news of the return of Cabral's fleet was, therefore, a matter of general concern to the rest of Europe, since the opening of this trade route might mean : the shifting of the market for spices and drugs from Venice to Lisbon.

The voyage of Pedro Álvares Cabral occupies an even more important place in history than it did at that time. In the discovery of Brazil for Portugal, Cabral added to his native land a country that has exceeded in area, wealth, and opportunity that of Portugal itself, to which, though politically independent, it is still tied by bonds of kinship and affection. It is true that the Portuguese would have discovered America in the course of their voyages to India, probably within a decade, had Columbus not crossed the Atlantic, but this does not lessen the importance of the voyage of Cabral as the first chapter in the history of Brazil.

In the long voyage to the Cape of Good Hope Cabral's fleet covered seas never before navigated and determined the practical course for sailing ships to the Cape, which is still followed. The discovery of Madagascar, though considered of little importance at the time, brought that island to the attention of Europe, which had hitherto been unaware of its existence except in a most mythical way. The attack on the Arab ships at Calicut began a war to expel the Arabian Moors from Indian seas. During Cabral's voyage the advantage was clearly seen of a policy of taking the part of the petty rulers against their overlords in order to obtain favourable trade conditions and a basis for domination. This policy, continued by Vasco da Gama during his second voyage, was definitely formulated by Francisco de Almeida and put into execution by Afonso de Albuquerque. During Cabral's voyage the system of establishing fortified factories where merchandise could be accumulated was begun, and thus the delay of the fleet until purchases could be made was obviated. These policies of controlling the seas, of developing friendly relations with the petty rulers, and of establishing factories rather than undertaking territorial conquests, were continued during the Portuguese period.

The attainment of the commerce with India by sea, commenced during the voyage of Cabral, was the result of a number of conditions that were particularly fortunate. Perhaps in no other period of the world's history could this have been accomplished with equal success. The discoveries along the west coast of Africa, confirmed by bulls of the Church, gave to Portugal a prior claim to the route by way of the Cape. The discovery of America led to a division of the whole non-Christian world between Spain and Portugal, a division that was confirmed by the Pope and in general accepted by the nations of Europe. The close bonds between the crowns of Spain and Portugal favoured the aims of Portugal. In East Africa and in India the petty jealousies and the weakness of the native rulers made the arrival of the Portuguese at this time opportune.

When the Portuguese entered Eastern waters the relations between

Egypt, Persia, Venice, and Portugal were complex. Politically, Venice, Egypt, and Persia had much in common because of the danger threatened to their several interests by the aspirations of Turkey, and Venice for this reason sought Portuguese aid. From that standpoint also, both Venice and Persia were glad to see a European power in Indian seas.

The superiority of Portuguese ships, the practical experience of their navigators, and the greater efficiency of their artillery made the future control of the Indian seas possible. The lower cost of transportation enabled the Portuguese to overbid the Arab merchants for spices. It also enabled them to bring, to the East, European commodities not hitherto available there. The elimination of intermediate expense decreased the flow of precious metals to the East. The development of better trade conditions, the establishment of factories, and the encouragement of the proper cultivation of saleable spices enabled the rapid development of a Portuguese monopoly in India.

Pedro Cabral's voyage is of importance not only because of its position in the history of geography but because of its influence on the history and economics of the period. Few voyages have been of greater importance to posterity and few have been less appreciated in their time. This voyage was the beginning of the commercial relations between Europe and the East by an all-sea route. The diversion of the commerce of India from the Red Sea route to that by way of the Atlantic was one of the chief causes for the eventual decline of the prosperity of Venice and for the fall of the Mamelukes of Egypt. It was also responsible for the development of Portugal from an unimportant state to a nation that for a few years was one of the richest in Europe.

CHAPTER 19

THE ANONYMOUS NARRATIVE

One of the earliest and the most complete contemporary accounts of the voyage of Cabral was written by a member of the fleet. From what is known of the voyage of Cabral from other sources the Anonymous Narrative is substantially accurate. It was written by one who was on the voyage and who lived to return. It thus ranks second only to the letters of Pero Vaz de Caminha and Master John as an authoritative source. The author is unknown, but he was without doubt a Portuguese. From the careful and concise manner in which the account was written it appears to have been either an official record of the voyage or a narrative intended for publication.

Some clue as to the identity of the Portuguese author may be obtained from the narrative itself. He was on Cabral's ship or that of Simão de Miranda or Pedro de Ataíde after the storm, and he returned either with Cabral or Simão de Miranda. He seems to have been present when Cabral met the Zamorin and was on shore at the time of the massacre and was among those saved. Since Cabral was on board his ship during the uprising, he could not have been the author. Only Frei Henrique, Nuno Leitao da Cunha, and a sailor are mentioned, of the twenty who escaped. It may have been the work of some nobleman who went with the fleet, but it seems more probable, from the careful manner with which it was written, that it was composed by some one whose duty it was to make this record, possibly one of the writers. The only one holding this position whose name is known and who might have been the author is Joao de Sa, who had gone with Vasco da Gama as a writer and undoubtedly held a position of trust under Cabral. His duties would take him ashore at Calicut, and he returned with the fleet. Since Ravenstein considers that de Sa may have been the author of the so-called Roteiro of the voyage of Vasco da Gama, he may have had a similar duty to perform with Cabral's fleet.

The supplement to the narrative of the voyage shows an exactness in weights and values that indicates that it was made by one of the commercial men in the fleet, probably by either a factor or a writer, but not necessarily by the author of the Anonymous Narrative.

Some version of this account was known to the Portuguese historians who wrote at a later date, but no contemporary copy can now be found in Portugal. It seems to have reached Italy soon after the fleet returned. Because of the interest taken in Cabral's voyage, this narrative was well known in Venice, for at least four early manuscripts still exist in the Venetian dialect, and it was included in the first edition of Paesi.

****

"Wherein King Manuel in person consigned the royal standard to the captain.

In the year 1500 the Most Serene King of Portugal, called Don Manuel by name, sent his armada of ships, large and small, to the parts of India, in which armada there were twelve large and small ships. The captain-general of this armada was Pedro Aliares Cabrile, a fidalgo. These ships departed, both well equipped and in good order, with everything that they might need for a year and a half. Of these twelve ships, he ordered that ten should proceed to Calichut [Calicut] and the other two to Arabia, directing their course so that they might make a place called Zaffalle [Sofala] because they wished to establish trade with merchants in the said place, which place, Zaffalle, is found to be on the way to Calichut. In like manner the other ten ships carried merchandise that they might need for the said voyage. And on the 8th of the month of March of the said year they were ready, and on that day, which was Sunday, they went a distance of two miles from this city to a place called Rastello, where there is a church called Sancta Maria de Baller [Belem]. To this place the Most Serene King went in person to consign to the captain the royal standard for the said armada.

Monday, which was the 9th day of March, the said armada departed on its voyage with good weather.

On the 14th day of the said month the said armada passed the Island of Chanaria [Gran Canaria].

On the 22nd day it passed the Island of Capo Verde.

On the 23rd day one ship became separated from the said armada, so that no news of it has been heard from that day to this, nor can anything be learned of it.

How the ships ran because of the storm

On the 24th of April [actually the 22nd April], which was Wednesday of the octave of Easter, the aforesaid armada came in sight of land, with which they had great pleasure; and they went to it to see what land it was. They found it a land very abundant in trees, and there were people who were going there along the shore of the sea. And they cast anchor at the mouth of a small river. And after the said anchors were cast, the captain ordered a boat to be launched in the sea, in which he sent to see what people they were. And they found that they were people of dark colour, between white and black, and well built, with long hair. And they go nude as they were born, without any shame whatever, and each one of them carried his bow with arrows, as men who were in defence of the said river. On the aforesaid armada there was no one who understood their language. And having seen this, those in the boat returned to the captain; and then night came on. During that night there was a great storm.

On the morning of the following day we raised anchor, and in a great storm we skirted the coast towards the north (the wind was the sirocco) to see whether we might find some port where the aforesaid armada might stay. Finally we found a port where we cast anchor. There we found some natives who were fishing in their little barks. One of our boats went to where these men were and took two of them and these they brought to the captain to learn what people they were, and, as has been said, they did not understand one another either in speech or by signs. And that night the captain kept them with him. On the following day he ordered them to be dressed in shirts and coats and red caps. They were very content with this attire and marvelled at the things that were shown them. He afterwards ordered them to be put on shore.

A root from which they make bread, and their other customs

Likewise on that same day, which was the octave of Easter, the 26th day of April, the chief captain determined to hear mass, and he directed a tent to be set up in a place where he ordered an altar to be erected. And all those of the said armada went to hear mass and a sermon; whereupon many of those men joined them, dancing and singing, with their horns. And immediately after mass had been said they all left for their ships. The men of the land entered the sea as far as their armpits, singing and making merry and festivity. And then, after the captain had dined, the people of the said armada returned to land, taking solace and pleasure with those men of the land, and they began to trade with the men of the armada, and gave their bows and arrows for little bells and leaves of paper and pieces of cloth. Thus all that day our men took pleasure with them. And we found in that place a river of sweet water, and we returned late to the ships.

On the following day the chief captain decided to take in water and wood, and all those of the said armada went on shore. And the men of that place came to help them with the aforesaid wood and water, and some of our men went to the place where these men dwell, which was three miles away from the coast of the sea; and they bartered for parrots and a root called igname, which is their bread, which the Arabs eat. Those of the armada gave them bells and pieces of paper in payment for the said things. In this place we remained five or six days. In appearance these people are dark, and they go nude without shame, and their hair is long, and they pluck their beards. And their eyelids and over their eyebrows are painted with figures of white and black and blue and red. They have the lip of the mouth, that is, the lower lip, pierced. In the opening, they put a bone as large as a nail, and others wear there a long blue stone or a green one, and they hang from their lips. Women likewise go nude without shame and they are beautiful of body, with long hair. And their houses are of wood, covered with leaves and branches of trees, with many wooden columns. In the middle of the said houses and from the said columns to the wall they hang a net of cotton, that holds a man. And between the nets they make a fire. Thus in a single house there may be forty or fifty beds set up like looms.

Parrots in the newly discovered land

In this land we saw no iron nor any other metal. They cut wood with stone. And they have many birds of many sorts, especially parrots, of many colours; among them are some as large as hens; and there are other very beautiful birds. Of the feathers of the said birds they make the hats and caps that they wear. The land abounds with many kinds of trees and much and excellent water and ignames and cotton. In this place we did not see any animals. The land is large, and we do not know whether it is an island or mainland, but on account of its size we believe that it is terra firma. Its climate is very good. And these men have nets and are great fishermen and fish for various kinds of fish. Among these we saw a fish that they caught. It must have been as large as a barrel and longer and round, and it had a head like that of a pig and small eyes, and it had no teeth and had ears the length of an arm and the width of half an arm. Below its body it had two holes and the tail was an arm's length long and equally wide. It had no feet anywhere. It had hair like a pig and the hide was as thick as a finger, and its meat was white and fat like that of a pig. [This was undoubtedly a Manatee]. During these days that we stayed there, the captain determined to inform our Most Serene King of the finding of this land, and to leave in it two men, exiles, condemned to death, who were in the said armada for this purpose. And the said captain promptly dispatched a small supply ship that they had with them, in addition to the twelve ships aforesaid. This small ship carried the letters to the king. In these were contained what we had seen and discovered. After the said small ship was dispatched, the captain went on shore and ordered a very large cross to be made of wood, and he ordered it to be set up on the shore, and also, as has been said, left two convicts in the said place. They began to weep and the men of the land comforted them and showed that they pitied them.

A storm so great that four ships perished

The following day, which was the 2nd of May of the said year, the armada made sail on its way to go round the Cape of Good Hope. This voyage would be across the gulf of the sea, more than 1,200 leagues, that is, four miles to a league. On the 12th day of the said month, while on our course, there appeared a comet with a very long tail in the direction of Arabia. It was in view continuously for eight or ten nights.

On Sunday, which was the 24th day of the said month of May, as all the armada was sailing together with a favourable wind, with the sails half set and without bonnets because of a rain that we had the day before, while we were thus sailing, there came on us a head wind so strong and so sudden that we knew nothing of it until the sails were across the masts. And at that moment four ships were lost with all on board, without our being able to give them aid in any way. The other seven ships that escaped were also almost lost. And thus we took the wind astern with the masts and sails broken. And we were at the mercy of God; and thus we went all that day. The sea was so swollen that it seemed that we were mounting up to the heavens. The wind changed suddenly, although the storm was still so great that we had no desire to set sails to the wind. And going thus with this storm, without sails, we lost sight of one another, so that the ship of the captain with two others took a different route. And another ship called Il Re with two others took another route, and the other one, alone, took still another. And thus we went twenty days through this storm without setting a sail to the wind.

Concerning Zaffalle, a gold-mine

On the 16th day of June [actually the 16th of July], we came in sight of the land of Arabia and cast anchor close to the shore. There we had much sickness and no one went on shore. This land is thickly populated, and in it we saw many people; and then we raised anchor and went along the shore with good weather, and we saw great rivers and many animals, so that every place was inhabited.

Somewhat before Zaffalle, which is a gold-mine, we found people near two islands who were in two Moorish ships that were coming from this gold-mine, and they were going to Malindi. And when those of the said two ships caught sight of our ships, they began to flee. They headed for the shore and all cast themselves into the sea in order to reach land, and they threw all that they had into the sea so that our people might not take it away from them. Our captain ordered him, to come before him, after the aforesaid two ships had already been captured by our men, and he asked first whence they came. He replied that he was a Moor, a cousin of the King of Malindi, and that the ships were his, and that he was coming from Zaffalle with gold, and that he was bringing his wife with him. She and also one of his sons, while trying to flee to land, were drowned. When the captain of our armada learned that he was the cousin of the King of Malindi, which king he considered a very good friend of ours, he was very sorry and did him much honour. He ordered that his ships with all their goods, that he had taken, should be returned. The Moorish captain asked our chief captain whether he had with him any enchanter who might recover the gold that they had cast into the sea. Our captain replied that we were Christians and that among us such things were not the custom. Then our captain inquired concerning Zaffalle, which was not yet discovered except by reputation. This Moor gave him the information that Zaffalle was a mine of much gold and that a Moorish king possessed it, that this king lived on an island that is called Chiloa [Kilwa], and that it was on the route we were to take, and that Zaffalle was behind us. The captain took leave of him and we went on our way.

On the 20th day of the month of June [actually the 20th of July], we reached a small island that belongs to the same King of Zaffalle, Mozonbige [Mozambique]. It has a small population and in it there are rich merchants. From this island we took supplies and a pilot who would conduct us to Chiloa. This island has a very good port and is near the mainland. From here we departed for Chiloa, along the coast, where we found many inhabited islands that belong to this same king.

We reached Chiloa on the 26th day of the said month, and in that place six sails joined; the other one was never found. This island is small, near the mainland, and is a beautiful country. The houses are high like those of Spain. In this land there are rich merchants, and there is much gold and silver and amber and musk and pearls. Those of the land wear clothes of fine cotton and of silk and many fine things, and they are black men.

How the Captain, having received the safe conduct, talked with the King

As soon as we arrived there, the captain sent to ask a safe conduct from the king, and the king ordered that it be given to him immediately. As soon as the captain received the safe conduct, he sent Alfonso Furtado on shore with seven or eight well-dressed men as an embassy. He instructed them to say that they were ships of the King of Portugal, and that they came there from him to make a treaty with him and that they had much merchandise of kinds that he would like. And, moreover, he ordered them to say that it would give him pleasure to meet him. The said king replied to him that he was very content and that the following day he would meet him if he would be willing to go on shore. Alfonso Furtado replied that the captain had orders from his king not to go on shore, and that if he wished they might talk in their boats. And this they agreed to do the following day. And the next day the captain made ready with all his people, and the ships and the boats with all their banners raised and his heralds and the artillery in order. The king of the said land also ordered his almache, that is, boats, to be put in order, with much festivity and noise, according to their custom. The captain proceeded with his trumpeters and pipers. And they came within sight of each other. And as they were approaching each other, the bombards were ready with their matches and were fired. The noise was so great from this discharge that the said king with all his people was stupefied and frightened. And at once they held a consultation, and having talked they hurriedly took leave of each other. The captain returned to his ship, and on the following day again sent Alfonso Furtado ashore to begin to negotiate. He found the king very differently disposed toward the captain than he had been at first, excusing himself by saying that they had no need of our merchandise and that it seemed to him, the said king, that we were corsairs. And so Alfonso Furtado returned to the captain with this message. And thus we remained for two or three days, for we could accomplish nothing. And while we were there they did nothing but send men from the mainland to the island, for they feared that we might take the aforesaid island by force. And when the captain saw this, he determined to leave, and ordered the sails to be set for the voyage to Malindi. And along the coast we found many islands inhabited by Moors. There is another city there, that is called Mombaza [Mombasa]. The king is a Moor.

All this coast of Arabia is inhabited by Moors. Both on the island and on the mainland there are said to be Christians who wage many wars. We did not see any of them.

How the gift and the letter from the King of Portugal were presented to the King of Malindi.

We arrived at Malindi on the 2nd day of the month of August of the said year. In that place three ships of Gombaia [Cambay] were lying at anchor, and each one of these ships must have had a capacity of 200 botte. Their hulls are well built of good wood, tied together with cord (for they have no nails), and they are covered with a mixture in which there is much incense. They have no castles except in the stern. These ships come to trade from parts of India. When we arrived there, the king sent those to visit us with many sheep, hens and geese, and lemons and oranges, the best that there are in the world. In our ships there were some men sick with the scurvy, whom the oranges made well. As soon as we had cast anchor near the land, the captain ordered all the bombards to be fired and the ships to be decked with banners, and he sent on shore two factors of the king, one of whom could speak Moorish, that is, Arabic, to learn how the king was and to inform why we came, and that on another day he would send his embassy with the letter that the King of Portugal sent him. The king had great pleasure in our coming; and at the request of the king the factor who knew how to speak Arabic remained on shore. The next day the king sent two Moors of high rank who spoke Arabic to the ships to visit the captain. He instructed them to say that he had great pleasure at his coming, and he begged him to request anything that he might need from this land just as he would do in Portugal, for he and all of his kingdom were at the command of the King of Portugal. The captain at once ordered that the letter with the present that the King of Portugal sent him should be sent on shore. The present was this : a rich saddle, a pair of enamelled bridles for a horse, a pair of stirrups and their spurs, all of silver, enamelled and gilded, abreast strap and cords of the proper kind for the said saddle, and furnishings of very rich crimson, and a halter worked in gold thread for the aforesaid horse, and two cushions of brocade and two other cushions of crimson velvet, and a fine carpet, and a piece of tapestry, and two pieces of scarlet cloth (this present was worth more than a thousand ducats in Portugal), and also a length of crimson satin and a piece of crimson taffeta. They agreed in council that Areschorea [Ayres Correia], who went as chief factor, should take this present. This Areschorea went on shore with the letters and the said present, and there went with him many principal men and trumpets. And similarly the said king sent all his important men to receive the said factor. And the house of the said king was on the shore of the port. Before they arrived at the house of the king many women came to meet them with vases filled with fire, in which were placed so many perfumes that the odours pervaded the land; and thus they entered the house of the said king, who was seated on a throne, and many of the principal Moors with him. The king was greatly pleased, and they gave him the present and the letter, which in one part was written in Arabic, and in another in Portuguese. As soon as the king had read the said letter he talked with the said Moors, and they had great pleasure among themselves. All gathered in the middle of the room uttered a cry, rendering thanks to God that they had for a friend so great a king and lord as the King of Portugal. Immediately he ordered arms and lengths of silk cloth to be brought, and he ordered them to be given to those who had brought the present. And he told Areschorea that he wished him to remain on land until the ships left, because he had much pleasure in talking with him. Areschorea replied that he could not do so without permission from the chief captain. The king sent his brother-in-law bearing his ring to the captain, requesting that he should allow Areschorea to remain on shore, and that he might send on shore for all the things that he needed, and that he might take in water. The captain was satisfied with this. At once the king ordered that Areschorea be given a very honourable lodging, and that he be supplied with everything that he needed, that is, sheep and chickens and rice and milk and butter and dates and honey and fruit of every kind, save bread, which they do not eat. And thus the said Areschorea remained three days on land, the king talking continually with him of the affairs of the king, our lord, and of the affairs of Portugal, telling him that he would be very glad to see the captain again. Areschorea told him that the captain had no authority to disembark on land, but that they could see him in a boat, as the King of Chilloa had done. The said king refused this, but Areschorea persuaded him to do so, and immediately he sent word to the captain, who made ready with his boats, leaving the ship in good care. The boat in which he went had its canopy spread, and its people were armed under their garments, which were of very fine scarlet. And the king ordered two boats of the land similarly prepared with their canopies, and he also ordered a horse harnessed in the manner of Portugal; and his men on land did not know how to do this, so our men had to arrange it. The king descended some steps, and at the foot of the steps all the richest and most honourable people were awaiting him. These had a sheep, and when the king mounted the horse they slaughtered the said sheep, and the king rode over it on horseback. And all the people shouted very loudly with very high voices. This they did for ceremony and enchantment, and the custom is thus in Zambochob [Zanzibar]. Then he had a talk with the captain, who finally told him that he wished to leave but that he needed a pilot who would conduct him to Calichut. The king told him that he would order one to be given to him, and thus they separated one from the other. When the said king went on shore he at once sent Areschorea to the ships with much meat and fruits for the captain, and he also sent him a Guzerati pilot from the ships of Chombaia that were in the port. The captain also left two Portuguese convicts, one of them to remain in Melinde, and the other to go with the ships to Chombaia. The following day, which was the 7th day of August, they departed and began to cross the gulf to Calichut.

Concerning the Red Sea and Persian Seas and the island of Agradida

In this crossing, that took us along all the coast of Melinde, we left a very rich and beautiful Moorish city that is called Magadasio [Mogadishu]. And beyond this there is a large island with another very beautiful walled city. The island has a bridge, in the land that is called Zognotorre. And farther along the coast is the mouth of the strait of Mecca, which must be a league and a half wide, that is, the said strait. And there within is the Red Sea, and thus the House of Mecca and Saint Catherine of Mount Sinai. And from there are carried spices and precious stones to Caiero and to Alexandria across a desert by means of dromedaries, which are a special kind of camel. And concerning this sea there are many great things to relate. And passing the mouth of the strait on the other side, is the sea of Persia, in which are great provinces and many kingdoms that belong to the Grand Sultan of Babilonia. In the middle of this Persian Sea there is a small island that is called Gulfal [Julfar] where there are many pearls. And in the mouth of this Persian Sea is a large island that is called Agremus [Ormuz]. This belongs to the Moors, also the king who is the lord of Gulfal. And in this Agremus there are many horses that they take to all parts of India to sell and they bring a great price. And in all these lands there is great traffic of ships. And passing this Sea of Persia there is a province that is called Combaia, whose king is great and powerful. And this land is the most productive and rich in the world. In it there is much wheat and other grain and rice and wax and sugar, and here is produced all the incense of the world, and many cloths of silk and of cotton. And there are many horses and elephants. The king was an idolater, and recently a Moor was crowned because of the influential Moors who are in his kingdom. And there are still many idolaters among them. These people are great merchants, who on the one hand trade with Arabia, and on the other with India, which begins where they are. And thus they go along this coast as far as the kingdom of Calichut. On this coast are great provinces and kingdoms of Moors and of idolaters. And all that which is in this chapter was not seen by us.

We came in sight of India on the 22nd day of August. This was a land in the kingdom of Goga. And as soon as we recognized it we went along it until we arrived at a small island that is called Angradida [Anjediva] that belongs to a Moor. In the middle of it is a large lake of sweet water. It is uninhabited and a desert. From there to the mainland is a distance of two miles. This was once inhabited by Gentiles. And because it is on the route of the Moors of Mecca to Calichut they stop there because they require water and wood. And as soon as we arrived there we cast anchor in the sea; and we went on shore and spent nearly fifteen days taking on water and wood, and watched to see whether the Meccan ships would come; we wished to capture them, if we could do so. And thus the people of the land came to speak with us, and told us of many things. Our captain ordered us to show them great honour. And on this island there is a small chapel, in which, during these days when we were there, many masses were said by the clergy, whom he had to remain with the factor in Calichut. And thus we all confessed and partook of communion. And we took on the said water and wood. Since the ships of the said Moors of Mecca did not come, we departed for Calichut, which is seventy leagues distant from this island.

How the Captain went to the King of Calichut

We reached Calichut the 13th day of September of the said year. And at one league from the city a fleet of boats came out to receive us. In it came the Chunal [governor of the port] of the said city and a very wealthy merchant of Guzerate and the chief residents of this city of Calichut. They came on board the flagship, saying that the king was greatly pleased at our coming. And thus we cast our anchors into the sea before the city and loudly began to fire off our artillery, at which the Indians marvelled greatly, saying that no one had power against us except God. And thus we remained that night. The morning of the following day the captain determined to send the Indians ashore whom we carried from Portugal in our ships. These were five; that is, one Moor who had become a Christian among us and four Gentile fishermen, all of whom spoke very good Portuguese. The aforesaid captain sent these on shore very well dressed, that they might speak with the king and that they might tell him why we came, so that he might order a safe conduct given us so that we might go on land. This they did. The Moor spoke with the king because the others, who are fishermen, did not dare to approach the king, nor could they look upon him, because the king considers this the custom for his rank and magnanimity, as will be explained later on. The king ordered that the said safe conduct be given and that any of us who wished might go on land. And seeing this, the captain at once sent Alfonso Furtado with an interpreter who knew how to speak Arabic. He was to tell the king that these ships belonged to the King of Portugal, who had sent them to this city to make a treaty of commerce and of good peace with them; and for this it was necessary for the captain to go on shore; that he carried instructions from our King of Portugal that no one should go on shore without having others as a hostage for his person; and that His Highness, the said King of Calichut, should send to the said ships those men of the city whom the said Alfonso Furtado had in mind. The said king, having heard the said embassy, refused firmly, saying that those men whom they asked of him were very old and venerable men who could not go on the sea and that he would give him others. Alfonso Furtado told him that he could not take any except those, because they were given in the instructions of the captain from his King of Portugal. The king marvelled greatly at this; and they continued in this difference for two or three days. Finally the king agreed to send them, and it was told to the captain at once. And the captain made ready to go on shore and to remain two or three days, and he took with him twenty or thirty of the most honourable men and those in good standing, with his officials, as was fitting for the service of a prince. And he carried all the silver that was in all of the ships. He left as chief captain in his place Sancto de Trovar, to whom he gave instructions to do honour to those men of the land who had been given as hostages for the captain. The following day the king came to a house that he had near the sea shore to receive the captain, and from there he sent the aforesaid men of the land to the ships. They were five men, very honourable, and they carried with them a hundred men with swords and bucklers. With those men were fifteen or twenty drummers. And the captain departed from the ship with his boats; he had already sent on shore all the things that he needed. And as soon as the captain had embarked, the aforesaid five men set forth from the city. These did not wish to enter the ships until the captain came on shore. And over this they were in disagreement for a long time. Thereupon Areschorea entered one of their sambucos, that is, a boat, and persuaded them to enter the ship, the captain already being on his way to the land. And as the captain landed, many noblemen came to receive him. They carried him in their arms and all those who came with him, so that they did not set foot on the ground until in this manner they arrived at the place where the king was.

The apparel of the King of Calichut in his residence

The king was in a high house, placed within a canopy with twenty cushions of silk tapestry. And the covering of the canopy was of cloth of silk, which looked like purple. And he was nude above and below the waist. And he had around him a cloth of very fine white cotton, which was wound many times around him and worked in gold. He had on his head a cap of brocade made like a long and very high helmet, and he had his ears pierced. In them he had large pieces of gold with rubies of great price and likewise diamonds, and two pearls, very large, one round and the other pear shaped, larger than a large filbert. And he had on his arms bracelets of gold from the elbow down, full of rich stones, with jewels and pearls of great value. And on his legs he had great riches, and on one toe of his feet he had a ring in which was a carbuncle ruby of great brilliance and value. Likewise on the fingers of his hands he had many rings full of jewels with rubies, emeralds, and diamonds. Among them was one the size of a large bean. And he had two belts of gold full of rubies belted over the cloth. And the riches that he had on him were priceless. And he had near him a large silver chair, the arms and back of which were of gold and full of stones, that is, of jewels. He had in his house a litter with which he had come from the larger house. In this litter he enjoyed remaining continually, and it was carried by two men. It was rich beyond description. And he had also as many as fifteen or twenty trumpets of silver and three of gold. One of these was of such size and weight that two men had enough to do to carry it. The mouths of these three trumpets were full of rubies. And nearer to him he had four silver vases and many of gilded bronze, large candlesticks of brass, and others full of oil and small wicks. These were burning in the house, which was not necessary; he had them there for grandeur. And his father was there, standing five or six steps away, and also two of his brothers, all like himself with great riches upon them. And there were also many other honourable gentlemen who stood at a greater distance and also had great wealth upon them, in the same manner as the king. And when the captain entered he wished to go to the king to kiss his hand, but they made a sign to him that he desist, for it was not the custom among them that any one should approach the king; and thus he remained where he was. The king made him sit down, to do him honour. And he began to give his embassy. He read the letter of the King of Portugal, which was written in the Arabic language, and immediately he sent to his house for the present of the things that we shall mention below.

The present that was given to the King with the disorder that followed

To begin with, a basin of silver for washing the hands, made with figures in relief, all gilded and very large; a dish of gilded silver with its lid similarly worked, with figures in relief; two silver maces with silver chains for the mace bearers, and four large cushions, that is, two of brocade, and two of crimson, and a large carpet and two fine tapestries, very rich, one with figures and the other with foliage, and also a bronze vessel for washing the hands of the same work as the basin. And when the king had received this present and the letter and the embassy, he showed great pleasure. And he told the captain that he should send for the men whom he had put in his hands as hostages, for they were gentlemen and could not eat, drink, or sleep on the sea, and that if for any reason he wished to return to the ships, that the next day he would return them to him, and that he could come on shore to do all that he might find necessary. The captain withdrew to his ship and left Alfonso Furtado with seven or eight men with him to wait at his house. When the captain left the shore a zambuco with men of Calichut went ahead of him to the ship to inform those who were hostages that the captain was returning thither. And straightaway they threw themselves into the sea. Areschorea, the chief factor, quickly entered a boat and took two of the honourable men and two or three servants; and the others escaped by swimming to shore. And at this moment the captain reached the ship and ordered the two worthies put below deck. And then he sent word to the king that upon his arrival he had found this annoyance, that one of his clerks had brought about; that he had thereupon ordered the two worthies to be retained because many of his own men were on shore as well as much property, and that His Serenity should send these to him; and that he would send his men in return, whom he was treating very well. With this embassy there went to the king two of those men who had been taken with the ambassadors. And all that night the captain awaited the reply. And the next day the king came to the seashore with more than ten or twelve thousand men, and our people who were on land were seized for the purpose of sending them in his almache to make an exchange for those whom the captain had held; and while matters were thus, twenty or thirty almache came, and our boats set out with the aforesaid men who were hostages. And the almache did not have the courage to come alongside our boats, nor ours to their almache. And thus that entire day was spent without doing anything. And when they returned to land with our men they began to show them great discourtesy, frightening them by saying that they wished to kill them. That night our men were in great tribulation. The following day the king again sent word to the captain that he was sending him his men and his goods with the almache without carrying any arms and that he should thus send his boats. He immediately ordered it, and with them Sancto de Tovar, his captain, who reached the place where the almache were, and they began to receive all the silver and all the other things that they had on land; so that nothing remained but one almofresse, that is, a sack containing a bed and its furnishings. And while nearly all the men were thus, one of those gentlemen, who was in our boats that Sancto de Tovar had, took it in his arm and threw

it into the sea; and when our men who were in the almache saw this
they became so indignant and angry that they threw all the men of the
almache into the sea, and there only remained in the almache and in our
boats one old man, who was one of the principal men and a hostage of
ours, and two boys of our number remained in the almache, for they
could not escape. And the next day the captain, taking pity on the old
man who was a hostage and who had had no food for three days, sent
him ashore and gave him all the arms that had remained in the ships
belonging to those who had thrown themselves into the sea, and he sent
to ask the king to return these two youths. The king sent them. After
two or three days passed in this manner and no one went to land or
from land to us, the captain and the others conferred. The chief factor
said that if the King of Calichut would send two men for security he
himself would go ashore. The captain and the others were satisfied with
what the factor had said, but it was not known whether there was any
one who dared to go on shore; and immediately a cavalier named
Francescho Chorea said that he would go on land to talk with the king,
and this he did. He told him how Areschorea was preparing to come on
shore to make a treaty with his serenity and that he should send them
two merchants as hostages, one of them a very rich merchant from
Guzerat. The aforesaid Moor, called a Guzerate, replied to the king that
he would send him two of his nephews, whereat the king was very
content. The following day Francescho Chorea sent the reply to the
captain, and Areschorea quickly made himself ready; and the king sent
the hostages to the ship, and Areschorea went ashore; and in his
company eight or ten men. And late that day Areschorea returned to the
ship to sleep. And the following day he returned to shore to carry out
all that had been agreed on. The hostages, however, remained on the
ship. The king ordered him to be given the best house, which belonged
to a Guzerate merchant, and gave this merchant the task of teaching the
factor the customs and manners of the country. And thus Areschorea
began to negotiate and carry on trade. The language that our men spoke
was Arabic, so that no one could converse with the king except through
Moors as intermediaries. These are bad people and were much opposed
to us, so that they were at all times deceitful and prevented us from
sending anyone to the ships. And when the captain saw that every day
we were sending men to shore and no one was returning with reply, he
determined to leave and ordered sails set. We were thus captive on

shore in a house well guarded by many people. We saw that the ships were leaving. The Guzerate, for consideration of his nephews, who were on the ship, told Areschorea that he should send a youth in an almache to the ships. This youth was conducted to the captain, and the captain, heeding the protest of Areschorea, returned to port, and thus Areschorea began to deal with the aforesaid king; and he drew up the treaty, obtaining little by little what he wished. And since this Guzerate urged this on account of his men who were given as hostages on the ships, the king charged a Turk, an important merchant, to attend to our affairs, and quickly he had us leave that house for another, nearer the house of the said Moor, and soon we began to see some of our merchandise, of which we bought part.

And we remained thus for two months and a half until the aforesaid treaty was finally completed and agreed to. This was accomplished with much effort on the part of Areschorea and those who were with him. When the treaty was completed, which was done by much bargaining, the aforesaid king gave him a house near the sea, which had a garden. In the said house Areschorea set up a banner with the arms of the king. And as for the treaty, the said king gave him two letters signed in his hand, one of which was of copper with his signature engraved in brass. This was to remain in the house of the factor, and the other one of silver with its signature engraved in gold, which we were to carry with us to our King of Portugal. When these letters were finished, Areschorea went immediately to the ship and delivered this letter of silver to the captain, and took ashore the men who were on board as hostages. And from that day on they began to show confidence in us so that it seemed as though we were in our own land. And one day, while things were thus, a ship came there that was going from one kingdom to another. That ship was carrying five elephants; among them was a very large one of great price because it was trained for war. The ship that carried it was very large and had many well-armed people. And when the king learned of the coming of the aforesaid ship, he sent to tell the captain that he begged him to capture that ship, which was carrying the elephant; he said he had offered much money for it, but they did not want to give it up. The captain sent word that he would do so, but that he would have to kill if they did not wish to surrender. The king was content with this and sent a Moor with them to see how he took the ship and to tell them what was intended. At once the captain sent a caravel with a large bombard and well armed, with sixty or seventy men. They pursued the ship for two nights without being able to capture it. The next day they caught up with it and asked them if they wished to surrender. The Moors began to laugh because they were numerous, and their ship was very large, and they began to shoot arrows. And when the captain of the caravel saw this, he ordered the artillery fired so that they struck the said ship, and it surrendered at once. Thus they took it to Calichut with all its people. The king came forth to the shore to see it. And the captain of the caravel went at once to deliver the ship's captain and likewise the ship to the king. The king marvelled greatly that so small a caravel and with so few people could take so large a ship in which were three hundred men at arms. The king received the ship and the elephants with great pleasure and solace, and the caravel returned to the ships.

Customs and manners of Calichut

The city is large and has no wall around it, and in certain places of the land there are many empty spaces and the houses are distant one from the other. They are of stone and lime and carved within. On top they are covered with palms, and the doors are large and well worked, and around the houses there is a wall within which they have many trees and lakes of water in which they bathe and wells of water from which they drink.

And throughout the city there are other large lakes of water to which the people go frequently to bathe, and this because every day they bathe their entire bodies two, three, or four times. The king is an idolater, although others have believed that they are Christians. These have not learned so much about their customs as we who have had considerable trade relations in Calichut. This king they call Gnaffer. Almost all his nobles and the people who serve him are men dark as Moors. And they are well built men, and go nude above and below the waist. They wear fine white clothes of cotton and of other colours girded around them. They go barefoot, without caps, save the great lords, who wear caps of velvet and brocade, some of which are very high. Their ears are pierced, with many jewels in the openings. They wear gold bracelets on their arms. These nobles carry sword and buckler in their hands, and the swords are bare and wider at the point than elsewhere. Their bucklers are round like the rotelle of Italy. These are black and red. Thus they are the greatest jugglers with sword and buckler in the world, and have no other occupation. There are at the court numberless people who do these things. They marry one wife or five or six women, and those who are their best friends gratify them by sleeping with their wives, so that among them there is neither chastity nor shame. And when the girls are eight years old they begin to secure gain by this means. These women go nude almost like the men and wear great riches. They have their hair marvellously arranged and are very beautiful, and they entreat the men to deprive them of their virginity, for as long as they are virgins they cannot procure a husband. These people eat twice a day. They do not eat bread, nor do they drink wine or eat meat or fish, but only rice, butter, milk, sugar, or fruits. Before they eat they wash, and if, after they have washed, any one who has not washed touches them they do not eat until they have again washed, so that in this they make great ceremony. All day long both men and women go about eating a leaf that is called betella, which makes the mouth red and the teeth black, and those who do not do this are men of low degree. When some one dies, because they must wear black, they polish their teeth and do not eat it for several months. The king has two wives, and each one of them is attended by ten priests and each one of them sleeps with her carnally to honour the king, and for this reason the sons do not inherit the kingdom, but only the nephews, sons of the sister of the king. And, moreover, there dwell in the house a thousand or fifteen hundred women, to give greater magnificence to the state. These have no other duty save to clean and sprinkle the house before the said king wherever he wishes to go, and they sprinkle with water mixed with cow's dung. The houses of the said king are very large, and in these houses there are many fountains of water in which the king bathes. And when the king goes forth he goes in a very rich litter. Two men carry this, and thus they go with many players of instruments and many gentlemen with swords and bucklers, and many archers and guards before him, and porters and a canopy above him. Thus they do him more honour than any other king in the world, because no one dares to approach within three or four paces of him. And when they give him anything they give it to him on a branch, for they must not touch him. And thus when they speak to him they speak with the head lowered and the hand before the mouth, and no gentleman appears before him without sword and shield. And when they do reverence they place the hand above the head as one who gives thanks to Our Lord, and no official or man of low quality may see the king or speak with him, and especially fishermen. If a gentleman goes along a street and two fishermen should come towards him along the said way, the said fishermen either flee or receive many blows. When the king dies, these gentlemen and his wives burn the king with sandalwood to honour him (the people of low rank bury), and they sprinkle their heads and shoulders with ashes. They wear their beards full. They are great story tellers and writers. They write on a palm leaf with an iron pen without ink. And regarding the other class of men : there are great merchants who are called Guzerates who are from a province that is called Combaia. These and the natives are idolaters and adore the sun and the moon and cows, and should any one kill a cow, he is killed for it. These Guzerate merchants eat nothing that receives death, nor do they eat bread or drink wine, and if some youth should eat meat in error they send him out to seek the will of God on this earth, even though he be of the highest descent and a son of a great lord or merchant. These believe in enchantments and diviners. They are whiter men than the natives of Calichut. They wear their hair very long and also their beards. They go clothed in cloth of fine cotton; they wear veils and their hair wrapped about as the women do, and they wear sandals. They woo and marry one woman as we do. They are very jealous and hold to their wives, who are very beautiful and chaste. They are merchants of cloth and of adornments and of jewels.

Concerning the merchants and the voyage of spices to Cairo and Alexandria

There are other merchants who are called Zetieties and they are from another province. They are idolaters, and great merchants of jewels and of pearls and of gold and silver. They are blacker men. They go nude and wear small head-dresses, and under the head-dress they wear hair like the tail of an ox or a horse. These people are the greatest enchanters that there are in the world, for every day they talk with the devil invisibly. The wives of these men are very corrupt in wantonness, like the natives of the land. In this city there are Moors from Mecca and from Turkey and Babylonia and Persia and from many other provinces. They are great merchants and rich men, and they have all the merchandise that comes to this city of Calichut, that is, jewels of many sorts and very rich things : musk, amber, benzoin, incense, aloe-wood, rhubarb, porcelain, cloves, cinnamon, brazil-wood, sandalwood, lac, nutmegs, mace. All of these come from a distance, save ginger, pepper, tamarind, myrobalan, and cassia-fistula and also wild cinnamon, which all grow in the land of Calichut. These Moors are so powerful and rich that they command all the land of Calichut, and in the mountains of this kingdom there is a very great and powerful king who is called Naremega [Narasimha], and they are idolaters. The king has two or three hundred wives. The day he dies they burn him and all of his wives with him. And this custom prevails for nearly all the others who are married when they die. A ditch is made in which they burn him, and then his wife, dressed as richly as possible, attended by all her relatives, with many instruments and festivity, is led to the trench, and she goes dancing backwards. The trench has a fire burning in it and into this she lets herself fall. Her relatives are provided and ready with pots of oil and butter, and as soon as she has fallen into it they throw the said pots over her so that she may burn more quickly.

In this kingdom there are many horses and elephants because they wage war, and they have them so taught and trained that the only thing that they lack is speech, and they understand everything like human beings. And this we ourselves have seen in Calichut. The elephants that the king has, on which he rides, are the strongest and most ferocious animals in the world, for two of them draw a ship to land. The ships of this land navigate only from October or November until the end of March. Their summer is in these months, and the other months are winter, and in them they do not navigate their ships and they keep them on land. In the month of November the ships of Mecca leave Calichut with the spices and carry them to Vida [Jidda], which is the port of Mecca. And from there they carry them to Cairo overland and to Alexandria.

The great slaughter of the Moors and Christians in Calichut

After we had been in the land about three months and the treaty had been signed and two of our ships loaded with spices, the captain one day sent on shore to tell the king that he had been in his land for three months and had loaded only two ships, and that the Moors were concealing the merchandise from them and the ships of Mecca were secretly loading and were thus departing, and that the said captain would be greatly obliged to him if he would have this attended to with dispatch, because the time of his departure was already approaching. The king replied to him that he would be given all the merchandise he wished, and that no Moorish ship would be allowed to load until our ships were loaded, and if any Moorish ship should leave that the captain might take it to see whether the ship had any merchandise, and that he would have it given to them at the price that the said Moors had paid for it.

On the 16th day of December of the said year, as Areschorea was settling accounts with two factors and writers of two of our ships that were already loaded for departure, a Moorish ship left with much merchandise. The captain took it, and the captain of that Moorish ship, and the most honourable of his men among them disembarked and made great lamentation and uproar, so that all the Moors assembled and went to talk with the king, telling how we had on land more riches than we had carried to his kingdom, and that we were the worst robbers and thieves in the world, that as we had taken their ship in his port so would we do from that day onward, and that they were obliged to kill all and that His Highness should rob the house of the factor. The king, as a seditious man, agreed that this should be done. And we, not knowing anything of this, allowed some of our men to go on shore to do their trading throughout the city. We saw all the people come against our men, slaughtering them and wounding them; and the rest of us went to give them aid; so that on that shore we slew seven or eight of them, and they two or three of us. And we were about seventy men with swords and helmets, and they were innumerable, with lances and swords and shields and bows and arrows. And they so pressed us that it was necessary to retreat to the house; and during the retreat they wounded five or six men. And thus we closed the door with much effort, and they fought against the house even though it was surrounded by a wall as high as a man on horseback. We had seven or eight crossbows with which we killed a mountain of people. More than three thousand of their warriors assembled. And we raised a banner so that those on the ships might send us aid. The boats drew near the shore, and from there they fired their bombards and did no damage. Then the Moors began to break down the wall of the house so that in the space of an hour they razed it entirely. They sounded trumpets and drums with great shouts and pleasure, so that it seemed as though the king were with them because we saw one of his attendants. And Areschorea saw that we had no remedy whatever, and because we had been fighting for two hours so fiercely that our men could hold out no longer, he determined that we should sally forth to the shore, breaking through them to see whether the boats might not save us. We did this. And thus the greater part of our men arrived near enough to enter the water, and the boats did not dare to approach to receive us. And thus, because of little assistance, Areschorea was slain and with him fifty and more men. And we escaped by swimming, to the number of twenty persons, all severely wounded. Among these a son of the aforesaid Areschorea escaped; he must have been about eleven years old. Thus we entered the boats, almost drowned. The captain of the said boats was Sancho de Tovar, because the chief captain was sick. And thus they took us to the ship. And when the chief captain saw this dissension and bad treatment, he ordered ten Moorish ships that were in the port to be taken, and all the people whom we found in the said ships to be killed. And thus we slew to the number of five hundred or six hundred men, and captured twenty or thirty who were hiding in the holds of the ships and also merchandise; and thus we robbed the ships and took what they had within them. One had in it three elephants that we killed and ate; and we burned all nine of the unloaded ships; and the following day our ships drew nearer to land and bombarded the city, so that we slew an endless number of people and did them much damage, and they fired from on shore with very weak bombards. And while things were thus, two ships passed at sea and went to Pandarada [Pandarani], which is five leagues from here. And the ships went towards land where there were seven other large ships, in shallow water, and loaded with many people. We could not capture them because they were in very shallow water, and the captain quickly decided that we should go to Chochino [Cochin], where we might load the ships.

How the ships were loaded at Cucchino

And we departed for Cucchino, which is thirty leagues from Calichut, and is a kingdom of itself. They are idolaters of the same language as Calichut. And thus going on our way we found two ships of Calichut loaded with rice, and we went straight to them, and the people fled to shore in their boats and we took the ships. The captain, seeing that they did not carry merchandise, ordered them to be burned. And we reached Cucchino the 24th day of December, and cast anchor in the mouth of a river. The captain sent on shore a poor man of the Guzerate nation who voluntarily left Calichut to come to Portugal. And he was to tell the king, what had happened to the rest of us in Calichut and that the captain had sent him to say that he wished to load his ships in his kingdom, and for payment he carried money and merchandise. The king replied that he was grieved that so much injury had been done him, and that he had great pleasure in our coming to his land, for he knew what good people we were, and all that we wished for would be done. The Guzerate who went ashore told the said king that there was need for some security, which was obtained by exchanging man for man, and that he might send him as hostage any one of his men, and that immediately the men of our ships would go ashore. The king at once sent two of his principal men with other merchants, and samples of merchandise and hostages, who should go to the ships and should tell the captain that he would do all that he wished. The captain immediately sent the factor with four or five men ashore with orders to buy merchandise, keeping with him, however, the men who were hostages, treating them very honourably. Every day they were exchanged because the gentlemen of those parts do not eat on the sea; if by chance they did eat, they could not see their king again. And thus we were twelve or fifteen days loading the ships a distance from Cucchin, at a place called Carangallo [Cranganore]. In this place there are Christians, Jews, Moors, and infidels [Zafaras]. Here we found a Jewess of Seville who came by way of Cairo and Mecca, and from there two other Christians came with us; they said that they wished to go to Rome and to Jerusalem. The captain had great pleasure with these two men. When the ships were nearly loaded, there came an armada from Calichut in which there were from eighty to eighty-five sails, among which were twenty-five very large ones. When the king had news of the arrival of this armada he sent word to the captain that if he wished to combat with them he would send him ships and men. The captain replied that it was not necessary. The said armada, because it was already night, proceeded a league and a half beyond us. At nightfall the captain ordered full sail set, taking with him the men whom he had as hostages in exchange for those who remained on land, who were seven men. It appeared to the captain that he could defeat it without other help. And that night a wind did not arise; so that he could go against the armada of Calichut. The following day, which was the 10th of January 1501, we went near them and they came to us, so that we drew very near, one to the other. The captain determined to fight with them, since they were so close that we were within a bombard shot from them. Sancho de Tovar, a captain, with his ship and one small ship remained behind in such a manner that the captain saw that order could not be established among them, and decided to take his course to Portugal, since he had the wind astern. Nevertheless, the fleet from Calichut followed us all that day until one o'clock at night. And thus that night we lost them from sight. And thus the captain decided to continue to Portugal, leaving his men there with the factor on land, and taking the two men of Chochino with us. He began to cajole them, begging them to consent to eat, for now they had not eaten for three days and then they ate with great grief and sorrow, and we continued on our way.

The Kingdom of Chanonon, friend of our ships

On the 15th of January we reached a kingdom on this side of Calichut, which is called Chanonon [Cananore]. It belongs to the Caferis, whose language is like that of Calichut. As we were passing by the aforesaid kingdom the king sent word to tell the captain that he was greatly displeased that he had not come to his kingdom, and he begged him to cast anchor, and said that if our ships were not loaded, he would load them. When the captain learned this, he anchored and sent a Guzerate on shore to tell the king that the ships were already loaded and that they needed only a hundred barchara of cinnamon, which is four hundred chantaras. And immediately the king sent the said cinnamon to the ships with great diligence, trusting greatly in us, and the captain sent to pay for it in so many cruzados. And then much cinnamon came to the ship and there was no place in which to put it. The king sent word to the captain that, if it were for lack of money, we should not fail to load on as much as we wished on this account, that we could pay him on the return voyage, for he had well learned how the King of Calichut had robbed us and what good and truthful people we were. The captain thanked him very much, and showed the messenger, that is, the ambassador, the three or four thousand cruzados that remained, and then the king sent to inquire whether he wished anything more. The captain told him no, except that His Highness might send a man to visit Portugal. The king immediately sent a gentleman who was to come to Portugal with us. And the men of Chuchino, who had remained on the ship, wrote to their king that they were going to Portugal; and the captain also wrote similarly to the factor who remained there. In this place we did not remain longer than a day; and then we left to cross the gulf of Melinde. On the last day of January, when we were in the middle of the gulf, we found a ship from Combaia that was coming from Melinde; and without inquiry it appeared that it was a ship from Mecca, and we took it. It came very richly laden and it had more than two hundred men and women on board. And when the captain learned that they were from Combaia he allowed them to continue their voyage, except for a pilot whom he took from them; and thus they left, and we went on our way.

A shipwreck in the Gulf of Melindi

On the 12th of February, as night came on, when all the pilots as well as all the others who had charts believed themselves near land, Sancto di Tovar, who was captain of a large ship, said that he wished to go ahead with his ship. And he ordered all the sails to be set and thus he placed himself before the others. And when it was the hour of midnight he ran ashore and the ship began to burn. And when the captain saw this, he sent aid to him, but the wind increased so much during the night that they could not get it off, as everything was unfavourable. The captain immediately sent the boats to the ship to see whether the people might come from it. The ship was already open and so situated that it could not be dislodged. The wind increased so much that the other ships were in great danger, so that it was necessary to operate them by hand. Nothing was saved from it except the people in their shirts.

The ship was of two hundred tons [tonelli] and laden with spices. And from there we departed with the ships and passed by Melinde, where we could not enter. And thus we came to Monsabiche [Mozambique], where we took water and wood. Here we put the ships on dry land. And from there the chief captain sent Sancto di Tovar in a small caravel [charavellina] with a pilot to conduct them to the island of Zaffalle so that they might know about it, and we remained there to repair the ships. And from there four of us departed and went to a point where there was good fishing for parni. And when we left there a storm struck us that made us turn back, and one ship became separated so that we remained three ships.

The ships that returned to Lisbon

We arrived at the Cape of Good Hope on Palm Sunday, and from there we had good weather, with which we made the crossing and came to the first land near Cabo Verde at Bestenicha [Beseguiche], and there we found ourselves with three small ships that our King of Portugal sent to discover the new lands and one ship that we lost from sight when we went there. That went to the mouth of the strait of Mecca and stopped at a city where they took the boat with all the people who were in it. And thus the ship came with only six men, most of them ill, and they had nothing to drink but water that they collected in the ship when it rained. And thus we came and arrived in this city of Lisbon at the end of July. One day later there came the ship that we lost from sight when we turned, and Sancto di Tovar with the caravel that went to Zafalle, who said that Zaffalle is a small island at the mouth of a river, inhabited by Moors, and gold comes from the mountain. It comes from another people who are not Moors. And they exchange in the said island gold for other merchandise. And when Sancto di Tovar arrived at this place he found there many Moorish ships, and he took a Moor as his security for a Christian of Arabia whom he sent on shore. And there he stayed two or three days. And the Christian did not come, nor did they recover him. And thus he came away with the Moor to Portugal, leaving the Christian there. Thus from the armada that went to Calichut six ships returned; and all the others were lost.

The weights and money that they use

This is the price that spices and drugs are worth in Calichut and also the method of weighing and the money.

A baar of nutmeg, weighing four cantaras, is worth 450 favos.

One ducat is worth 20 favos.

A baar of cinnamon is worth 390 favos.

A faracola of dry ginger is worth 6 favos; 20 faracolas make a bacar.

Ginger preserved in sugar is worth 28 favos a faracola.

A bacar of tamarind is worth 30 favos.
A bacar of zerumbet is worth 40 favos.
A bacar of zedoary is worth 30 favos.
A bacar of lac is worth 260 favos.
A bacar of mace is worth 430 favos.
A bacar of pepper is worth 360 favos.
A bacar of long pepper is worth 400 favos.
A bacar of preserved sebuli myrobalans is worth 560 favos.
A bacar of red sandalwood is worth 80 favos.
A bacar of brazil-wood (verzin)is worth 160 favos.
A faracola of camphor is worth 160 favos.
A faracola of incense is worth 5 favos.
A faracola of benzoin is worth 6 favos.
A faracola of cassia-fistula is worth 2 favos.
A baar of cloves is worth 6oo favos.
A baar of white sandalwood is worth 700 favos.
A faracola of aloe-wood is worth 400 favos.
A faracola of rhubarb is worth 400 favos.
A faracola of opium is worth 400 favos.
A faracola of spikenard is worth 800 favos.
A peso of musk is worth 400 favos.
A mitricale of amber is worth 2 favos
(An ounce is six and one-fourth mitricali.)

A baar weighs about twenty faracolas, and a faracola twentyfour and three-fourths aratole of Portugal, which aratole are of from thirty-two to thirty-three libre in Venice, according to custom.

The ducat is worth twenty favos.

These are the prices of merchandise that are carried from here to Calichut, namely :

A faracola of copper is worth 45 favos.
A faracola of lead is worth 18 favos.
A faracola of silver is worth 54 favos.
A faracola of alum is worth 20 favos.
A faracola of white coral is worth 1000 favos.
A faracola of branched coral is worth 700 favos.
A faracola of bastard coral is worth 300 favos.

An almeno is another weight, that, in Portugal, is two arates and a half, and would be about three and one-eighth libre, a little more or less, according to Venetian usage. With this weight they weigh saffron, which is worth eighty favos.

Mention of the places spices come

Hereafter mention will be made of the places from which the spices and drugs come to Calichut.

Pepper comes from a land that is called Chorunchel [probably Cranganore]. This is 50 leagues beyond Calichut on the sea-coast.

Cinnamon comes from Zallon [Sri Lanka]; and cinnamon is found only in this place, 260 leagues beyond Calichut.

Cloves come from Meluza [Molucca], 740 leagues beyond Calichut.

Ginger is grown in Calichut, and some comes from Cananor to Calichut; it is 12 leagues according to this part of Portugal.

Nutmeg and mace come from Melucha [Molucca], 740 leagues farther beyond Calichut.

Musk comes from a land called Pego [Pegu], 500 leagues beyond Calichut.

Large pearls come from Armuzo [Ormuz], 700 leagues this side of Calichut.

Spikenard and myrobalans come from Combaia, 600 leagues this side of Calichut.

Cassia-fistula grows in Calichut.

Incense is obtained more than 800 leagues this side of Calichut.

Myrrh grows in Farticho [Fartak], and more than 700 leagues this side of Calichut.

Aloe-wood and rhubarb and camphor and galingal come from Chini [China] beyond Calichut 2,000 leagues.

Zerumbet grows in Calichut.

Very large cardamons come from Cananore, more than 12 leagues this side of Calichut.

Long pepper grows in Samoter [Sumatra].

Benzoin comes from Zana [Siam], 700 leagues beyond Calichut.

Tamarinds in Calichut.

Zedoary in Calichut.

Lac comes from a land called Samatore, beyond Calichut, 400 leagues.

Brazil-wood [brazili] comes from Tanazaar [Tenasserim], 500 leagues beyond Calichut.

Opium comes from Ade [Aden], this side of Calichut more than 700 leagues.

These are the weights and money that are used in Calichut, with the locations of spices.

Finis"

CHAPTER 20

BARTOLOMEO MARCHIONI'S ACCOUNT OF THE VOYAGE

Bartolomeo Marchioni was the head of the most prominent Florentine family in Lisbon. He was probably the richest man in Lisbon. He financed, in part, one small ship, the Anunciada, on Cabral's voyage, which was the first to return, and it is probable that Marchioni also furnished money to the king. When the first of Cabral's ships reached Lisbon, Bartolomeo Marchioni sent letters to Florence, the first dated the 27th of June 1501, announcing the return of the Anunciada, and a second written in July 1501, after the arrival of Cabral. These letters are of particular interest because they were written by an Italian resident in Lisbon who had a financial interest in the expedition.

****

The letter of 27th June 1501 :-

On the 23rd day of this month there arrived in Lisbon a small ship named the Anunziata that came from Calichut, and this related how the other caravels that came with it remained behind a few leagues, each league being 3½ of our miles; which ship gave an infinite amount of news, and here, by this, I give you that which is most important.

It is said that it is four months since the fleet left a land in the confines of Calichut, all loaded with spicery, and that five ships of their command were lost in this going. They went to the new gold-mine and to Calichut. There were eight when they arrived at Calichut. Great honour and good reception were given them; and they held mass on shore. Their merchants and factor then began to trade with them. And there in that part were thirty Moorish ships to load and carry spices over an ocean sea on this same voyage, whence they later went to Domascho. And wishing to load first, the Portuguese came to such a difference that the Moors raised a great tumult and killed all the Portuguese who were on land, including their factor. And when those in the Portuguese ships saw this, they withdrew the ships and began to burn the Moorish ships and to bombard the land; and they destroyed thus many houses and killed many people and burned fifteen of those Moorish ships. And through the counsel of an Indian they departed from there and went to another land where they found a king hostile to that of Calichut. And there they were made great honour and much and perfect reception. And there they traded all their merchandise and filled the ships with spices and other things. This king wished to give them much spicery and credit on their return, on their word. They did not wish to load because they had abundant cargo for their ships. And from there they departed friends, and he begged them that on their return they should not make any other port. And the said king sent an ambassador to our king with infinite presents; and promising that they would return to the said place, they departed. The Moors of Calichut had armed 150 sails with 15,000 Moors and came to attack our ships. And because our ships were laden and would have to fight, this was not to be considered, and putting themselves in order, they lost sight of them with the wind astern. And on their coming they found many kings and lords, and of all they had good reception and presents. And they have found the body of Saint Thomas, the Apostle, whose land they were not able to see, and many relics that they have brought here in quantity to the king. And with these ships come four ambassadors with two Christian gentlemen. And all wish to submit themselves to our king. And many other things they related which pages are not sufficient to write on, nor is there time; and this is the cargo carried :

> 300 chantara of fine pepper
> 160 chantara of cinnamon
> 60 chantara of lac
> 14 chantara of benzoin

These are the things to make mention of, and many other small spices. And what each of the other seven ships that are behind is loaded with, will be learned on their arrival.

They brought back two parrots of different colours that are an arm and a half long which are more than an arm and a half of ours. They are marvellous things. And they gave notice of many other and various birds and animals, so that where Pliny told untruths, these prove his history.

Bartolomeo Marchionni,
From Lisbon.

The letter of July 1501 :-

It was told in our last letter how only one of the caravels that went on
the voyage to Calichut had returned, and in that is seen the cargo that it
carried. Later, of the other five ships that were behind, three have
returned. The others are lost. And these have brought 3,000 cantara of
pepper, 1,000 cantara of cinnamon, and ginger, and cloves and other
spicery, so that from here they will be able to furnish by this route all
the West, and also Italy, in time. They must give great trouble to the
Venetians, and on the route more to the Sultan who enjoys the traffic
from there, because by this route they come at rather small expense and
more easily. This king is putting twenty ships in order, to depart from
this port the middle of November, or at latest next December. May it
please God to conduct them safely. They will derive great treasure in
this manner, and of it make great riches and all good and necessary
things.

The above-mentioned caravels went to the new goldmine and have
brought some back from the said mine, and this king puts ships in order
to send to that place, so that he may see the merchandise recently found
there, and of what nature it is, and what assortment, and how much is
given for it. This king has newly discovered in this a new world, but it
is dangerous to navigate over the expanse of these seas.

They have brought back many kinds of birds and animals unknown to
us, and more often such as are described by Pliny in his history. They
were held as falsehoods, but in these days what he relates is seen to be
true.

The two ships that went to the new gold-mine are believed to be lost
because there has been no news of them, and they say that the gold has
not before been known. They believe that at other times these seas have
been navigated, but later abandoned because they are so large. They

were unknown to us in our times. This king believes that such a voyage is a beautiful thing.

They say that they have some news of the island of Taprobana and hope in a short time to go there. May God permit them to go and return in safety, because each year new and beautiful things are known.

They say that they found a very large city that they say has silk-shops that belong to the king, with a hundred looms, and its work is of as many kinds as in the city of Strava, whence comes the Strava silk, which is understood to come from the East. The said city is called Zanzura and is within the Red Sea, and they tell of an incredible thing when they say that for 40 reals, which are 40 of our quatrini, an arm's length of crimson silk may be had, which may be found in abundance.

The Moors are white and resemble men of the Sultan of Babilonia. They say that they have sold Paternoster beads of amber at a silver mark and a half a string, which are six or eight [beads] each, at their place, equal to ten to twelve of ours, a string, and that such have resold for 2,000 silver marks, which is a good way to make great riches.

CHAPTER 21

KING MANUEL'S ACCOUNT OF THE VOYAGE

Letter from King Manuel of Portugal to the Catholic Sovereigns giving them an account of all that happened during the voyage of Pedro Alvarez Cabral along the coast of Africa even to the Erythraean Sea.

Source : Navarrete, "Coleccion de los viages y descubrimentos," tomo III. pp. 94-101.

****

Most exalted, excellent and puissant Sovereigns, my father and my mother : hitherto, since the first news arrived from India, I have not written to Your Majesties concerning Indian affairs because Pedro Alvarez Cabral, my Chief Captain of the Fleet that I had sent there, had not also arrived and after his arrival I postponed the matter because two of his ships had not also arrived; of these two, one had been sent to Sofala, (which is a gold mine recently discovered) not with the object of purchasing gold but only in order to obtain accurate information regarding affairs there; of the two ships that were to go there, one was lost at sea and the other was separated from the fleet in stormy weather and did not go there. And after the aforesaid ships had arrived and when I was about to notify everything to Your Majesties, Pero Lopez de Padilla told me that you would be glad to receive news as to the manner in which events had transpired there and that which follows is a summary of everything that happened.

My aforesaid Captain sailed from Lisbon with thirteen ships on the ninth day of March of last year. During the octave of the Easter following he arrived at a country that he first discovered and on which he bestowed the name of Santa Cruz; in it he found the people naked as in the days of primal innocence, mild and peaceable and it would appear that our Lord intended that that country should be miraculously discovered for it lies most conveniently and is indeed necessary to the voyage to India for the repair and watering of ships and, because the voyage that he had to make was long, he did not delay for the purpose

of obtaining information regarding the country but he sent back a ship
thence to me to inform me that he had discovered it and continued his
voyage by way of the Cape of Good Hope and in that ocean, before
arriving at the Cape, he experienced great storms owing to which on
one day four ships foundered together before his eyes and not a single
person on board these ships escaped [drowning] and at the same time
another ship disappeared regarding which we have as yet no news and
the ship in which he continued the voyage and also the other remaining
ships passed through great danger and thus he went on his way in order
to touch at Quiloa, a Moorish port, under the lordship of which place is
Sofala for he carried my letters and messages for the king of it in order
that he might establish peace with him and he negotiated with the king
regarding trade and purchases at the aforesaid gold mine. And before
he arrived at the aforesaid kingdom he met two ships carrying a great
quantity of gold and he captured them but, seeing that they belonged to
the aforesaid King of Quiloa, he allowed them to proceed after paying
them much honour. He was very well received by the king who came in
person to meet my Captain on the sea and the Captain entered his boat
with him and sent presents to him and after he had seen my letters and,
[received] my messages he agreed to the treaty [of peace] and since the
ships that had been destined for the aforesaid gold mine were amongst
those that had been lost no traffic [in gold] was begun there at that time
because the merchandise that the other ships carried was not such as
was suitable for that country. And he departed thence and sailed to
Malindi, another kingdom, for he carried my letters and messages for
the king of that place also who, is also a Moor [Mahometan] and who
had acted well towards D. Vasco who was the first to go there to make
the discovery of it and the aforesaid king came to him on the sea, and
also sent him presents and confirmed and established a treaty of amity
and peace with him and gave him the pilots that he required for his
voyage. These kingdoms are on the Erythraean Sea; they join a country
of heathen people on the landward side, and these heathen join the
country of Prester John; those of the former country call the people of
Prester John "Coavixi" which means "marked with an iron" in their
language as in fact they are and they mark themselves with an iron as a
sign that they are baptized in water. And he departed thence for Calicut,
which is more than seven hundred leagues distant thence, which city, as
we believe that you already know, is a city of heathen who adore many

things and believe that there is only one God and it is very populous and there are many Moors in it who until now have always traded there in spicery for it is a place like Bruges in Flanders. Thither come the chief products of India for in it there is only canna fistula and ginger, and my Captain arrived there five months after his departure from Lisbon and was very honourably received by the king who came to talk with him in a house by the sea with all his grandees and many others and there my Captain gave him my messages and established peace and concluded an agreement and the aforesaid king ordered a copy of the agreement to be made in writing on a sheet of silver with his seal of inlaid gold as is the custom in his country in matters of great importance and also to be written on leaves of some trees that appear to be palms on which they always write and of these trees and their fruit are made these things following : sugar, honey, vinegar, fuel and cordage for ships and for all other purposes. And there are others from which are made some of the sails of ships and they make use of those trees for every purpose for which it is possible to use them and the aforesaid fruit, besides providing those articles that are made from it, is also their principal nutriment especially when they are at sea. And, after the agreement had been thus concluded. with the aforesaid king, my factor landed with the whole household, which I sent for the aforesaid factory and he began immediately to deal with his merchandise and to load the ships with spicery. And meanwhile the King of Calicut sent to tell my Captain that a large and well-armed ship belonging to another king who was his enemy had sent to tell him that it was passing before his harbour without any fear of him and that it had annoyed him previously on other occasions and he begged my Captain to give orders to capture it, dwelling upon the matter as something gravely concerning his high estate and his honour. And my aforesaid Captain, taking into consideration the agreement that he and the aforesaid factor had just received from the aforesaid king and in order to confirm peace and amity, agreed to do this and, in order to show him the strength of our people in ships and artillery, he only sent the smallest ship he had with one lombarda and overtook it in the port of a neighbouring king and before his eyes and those of all his people the ship was captured and brought to Calicut with four hundred men and some artillery and with seven elephants in it trained to fight that were worth thirty thousand cruzados there for they gave five thousand cruzados for one of them alone and with other merchandise, namely, spicery and my Captain sent it to him as a present and gave it to him with all that it contained and he came to the beach to see it for it was a great surprise to them that so small a ship with so few men should capture so large a one with so many men and to receive the message that the aforesaid Captain sent him concerning it and he came with all his retinue and in gala attire. And when this amity had been established and agreement made concerning the ships trading in spicery, the Arabs, chiefly those of Mecca who were there, seeing the great loss that would result to them, tried in every possible manner to stir up strife between my factor and the king and stirred up a tumult in order to interrupt the trade and, as all the merchandise was in the hands of the Arabs, they concealed it and, sent it away privily to other places. And, when the aforesaid Captain knew this, he sent to tell the King of Calicut of it, complaining to him and asking him to fulfil what he had agreed to, namely, that within twenty days merchandise would be given to him wherewith to load the aforesaid ships and that, until they were loaded, no permission would be given to other ships to load and the king replied that he would give orders that all the merchandise in the country should be given to him at once and that, if any one took in cargo in his port without the knowledge of his officers, he would give my Captain opportunity and authority to detain the ship until he should send his aforesaid officers in order that they might take steps to have it delivered up to them. And when the Arabs knew this, they agreed amongst themselves to load one of their ships openly with great diligence but nevertheless to conceal merchandise with even greater diligence than they had previously exercised and they did this in order to give occasion for the commencement of the outbreak for they are powerful and the city contains people of many nationalities and has a large population and the king can with difficulty prevent popular tumults. And when my factor saw that the ship was being loaded he asked the Captain to detain it as had been agreed upon with the king and the aforesaid Captain, fearing an outbreak, hesitated to do this and the factor again asked him to detain it notwithstanding this [risk] and told him that the principal Arabs and also some of the heathen people said that if the ship was not detained he would not be able to load his ships at all and from that which followed it would appear that the ship was loaded in order to give an occasion for the outbreak. And my

Captain, after hesitating many times, fearing that which followed, sent to tell the people of that ship, in virtue of the authority that had been granted to him for this purpose, that it was not to sail but they would not agree to this and it was then necessary to give orders to detain it and the Captain ordered his boats to bring it inside the harbour whence it would not be able to depart without his permission. And as soon as the Arabs saw this and this being the opportunity that they desired at that very moment they came quickly with all the other people whom they had previously incited to attack the aforesaid factor and his house. And he and the few people whom he had with him defended themselves for a short time and they then sallied forth from the house and came to the seashore to rally there. And my Captain, who was sick at that time, sent all his boats to assist him and although the sea was very rough yet he collected some of the people; they killed the factor and fifty others with him were either killed or taken prisoners and, when this had been done and the aforesaid Captain saw that the king had not interfered and had sent him no message but on the contrary that he was providing himself with certain equipment that signified war and that he himself had seized my property that had remained on shore, after waiting for a day to see if he had repented of this affair, when he saw that still no message was sent and feared lest the king should arm himself powerfully, as he afterwards did, in order to prevent the revenge that might be taken upon him, he then consented to take the matter in hand at once, and took possession of ten strong ships that lay in the harbour and gave orders to put to the sword all the people in them, save a few who hid themselves, whom afterwards he resolved not to kill but brought them to me as prisoners and he gave orders to burn the aforesaid ships before the harbour and that caused great alarm to the king and to the people of the country and there were in the ships three elephants that died and in this manner he spent all that day and as soon as it was night he went with all the ships and placed himself as near the land as possible along the front of the city and at dawn of day began to bombard it with artillery and bombarded it till night and chiefly the houses of the king to which he did much damage and he killed many of his people as he afterwards learned and he killed one of his principal men who was with the king, upon which the king immediately left the city as it was evident that he was not safe in any part of it. [My Captain] sailed thence and went to another of his ports called

Fandarene [sic] which he also damaged with artillery and killed some of his people and thence he sailed for Cochin which is the place from which the spicery comes and it is thirty leagues beyond Calicut and on the voyage he found some other ships of Calicut that he also captured and ordered that they should be burned. And when he had arrived at Cochin and had informed the king of that which had taken place at Calicut, he was very well received by him and concluded an agreement with him in the same manner as he had done at Calicut and he put my factor on land and some men with him for which purpose hostages who were honourable men were given him whom they brought to him. And they loaded the ships in sixteen days and they fetched the merchandise in their boats to the ships with so much friendliness and with such care that it appeared as if our Lord had permitted that outrage at Calicut in order that this arrangement might be concluded that is much more profitable and safer than the other one because [Cochin] is a much better port and has a much larger trade, for much of almost all the kinds of merchandise that go to Calicut is to be found in that country and the other kinds go there before going to Calicut and at that city of Cochin there are many ships and he learned that only fifty ships belonged to the merchants. In that kingdom there are many faithful Christians, followers of Saint Thomas, and their priests follow the apostolic manner of living with much strictness, only keeping for themselves what is given to them as alms and they practice celibacy and have churches in which they say mass and they consecrate buckwheat bread and wine that they make from raisins and water for they can make no other; they have no images in the churches but only the cross and all the Christians wear apostolic vestments and have their beards and hair uncut. And there he obtained certain information regarding the place of burial of Saint Thomas which is one and fifty leagues distant thence on the sea-coast in a city called Mailapur with a small population and he brought me earth from his sepulchre and all the Christians and also the Arabs and the pagans go to his house in pilgrimage on account of the great miracles that are done there and [my Captain] also brought some of the Christians who came of their own free will and by the permission of their primate in order that we might send them to Rome and Jerusalem and that they might see the condition of the Church in those places for they are of opinion that they would be better governed if they were ruled by Saint Peter whom they believe to have been the chief of the apostles for they were so informed by them. And he had also certain information regarding great Christian peoples who live beyond that kingdom of Cochin and who come in pilgrimage to the aforesaid house of Saint Thomas and they have very powerful kings who obey one only and they are white men with their hair in plaits and are clothed like warriors and their country is called Malchima whence come porcelain ware and anil and amber and aloes-wood that they bring from the river Ganges, which is in their direction and there are vases of porcelain so delicate that one vase is worth one hundred cruzados there. And when he was in that kingdom of Cochin and when the treaty had been concluded and the ships loaded, there came a message to him from the King of Cananor and one from the King of Colum [sic] that adjoin it inviting him to come to them because he would find a more profitable market there but, as he had already made an agreement, he asked them to excuse him. At this time when he was on the point of leaving Cochin, the same king sent one to tell him that a strong fleet was coming against him from Calicut and that fifteen thousand men were in it and my Captain did not consider it desirable to fight against it because his ships were laden and he had but few people and it did not appear to him to be the right time nor to be necessary to risk [the combat] in case some [men] of the fleet should be killed or wounded and [having regard to] the length of the voyage which is one of four thousand leagues from here; therefore he set sail and they did not hinder him and did not venture to put out to sea but turned back fearing to go after him and thence he made his way to the kingdom of Cananor, to one of the kings who had sent to ask him [to come], and as he was passing along, when they saw him from the land, [the king] sent him another message begging him to call there for he wished to send me his envoy with him and him he brought to me and during the one day he was there [the king] ordered so much spicery to be delivered to the ships that there was sufficient for a cargo if the ships had been empty and it was given in order that he might bring it without payment as a present to me in order to obtain my friendship and all his grandees also came to my Captain and told him on behalf of the king that he would see there that he would be treated in a different manner from that in which he had been treated at Calicut, that they would assist him and that he would land in person with all his fleet on the water and, after he had thanked them much in my name, he took his leave, saying that in the other fleet which was to be sent soon he would send my reply to everything. And he continued his journey and at the middle of that crossing he captured a very large ship laden with merchandise and he supposed that it was one of those of Mecca that at that season have to leave Calicut and, when he found that the aforesaid ship belonged to the King of Cobaia [sic], he let it go on and sent a message by it to the aforesaid king that he had left it alone because he was not there in order to make war on any one and he had only made war upon those who had not observed the treaty of peace that they had concluded with him in my name. And, when he had proceeded further, one of the ships, that had a cargo, was lost for it ran aground during the night and the ship's company was saved and he ordered that the ship should be burned because it could not be saved. And from this port.....he sent the ship to obtain information regarding the gold mine of Sofala as has already been mentioned and this ship has already arrived here and has brought me authentic information concerning that place and also concerning the trade and the merchandise of the country and the great quantity of gold that is there and there he heard that among the men who carry gold to the coast there are many who have four eyes, two in front and two behind, and they are little men and red and they say that they are cruel and that they eat men with whom they are at war and that the cows of the king wear heavy collars of gold round their necks. And near this gold mine are two islands where they collect many seed-pearls and much amber. And my aforesaid Captain sailed thence and arrived at Lisbon sixteen months after he had quitted it and, thanks be to God, not more than three men died of sickness in this voyage and all the others returned in health and good bodily condition. Then there came a reliable message to the effect that one of the ships, that had sailed for Sofala and that had been supposed to be lost, was returning and would arrive here one of those days and they say that it entered within the [inner] Erythraean Sea and that it is bringing silver thence and also some information regarding matters there although indeed we were well informed by my aforesaid Captain regarding the aforesaid Erythraean Sea and he was made acquainted with it in many ways. I leave the other details concerning this matter to Pero Lopez who was present at all. Most exalted and most excellent and most puissant sovereigns, Father and Mother, may our Lord have your lives and your royal estate in His holy keeping.

Written at Santarem this nine-and-twentieth day of July. EL REY.

CHAPTER 22

THE VENETIAN LETTERS

The anxiety of the Venetians to retain the sole monopoly of the European trade in spices and drugs made them view with apprehension the growing power of the Osmanli in the East. To protect her threatened commerce, Venice sought the aid of the Christian states of Europe. Spain, too, had reason to fear the Moslems because of the expulsion of the Moors. There was thus a common bond between the two nations. Domenico Pisani was appointed ambassador to Spain by the Venetian Senate on the 7th of September 1500. Because of the friendly relations between Spain and Portugal and their proximity, he represented Venice in Portugal as well. His chief duties were to remind Ferdinand and Isabella of promised aid, and to seek the assistance of the Portuguese fleets against the Turks. At this time the Venetian diarist Marino Sanuto proposed that someone should be sent to Portugal to offer condolence to Dom Manuel because of the death of his infant son, and also to endeavour to obtain the naval aid that the Venetians desired. The name of Il Cretico was suggested. He was Giovanni Camerino, who is also called Giovanni Matteo Cretico, who was a reader of Greek rhetoric at Padua. Because he had spent seven years on the island of Crete, he was usually called "Il Cretico" He was "a person of great learning in Latin and Greek", and it was agreed that he be sent as a secretary to Pisani because of his suitability and because in this capacity less expense would be incurred. Henceforward Il Cretico was usually in attendance at one court while Pisani was with the other, but early in 1501 they were both in Lisbon. Through their efforts Dom Manuel was induced to send an armada under João de Menezes to assist Venice against the Turks. This left Belem on the 15th of June 1501. We know that Pisani was in Lisbon in March 1501, because he wrote a letter from there on the 13th of that month addressed to Granada. He then returned to Spain leaving Il Cretico in his place. Il Cretico remained in Lisbon until September, and was therefore present when the Anunciada returned and also at the arrival of the flagship towards the end of July. When the first of Cabral's ships arrived from India on the 23rd of June 1501, he wrote a letter to Venice, telling briefly what he could learn regarding the voyage. This letter sheds some additional light on the voyage of Cabral and the cargo that it brought back. It shows also the participation of Bartolomeo Marchioni in the expedition and the elation of Dom Manuel upon the return of the fleet. It was the first news that the Venetians received telling of the return of Cabral's expedition and of what had occurred in India, although they had heard vaguely through Egyptian sources of its arrival there. The dismay that this report caused in Venice is vividly told by the diarist Priuli. The letter of Il Cretico was also the first account of Cabral's voyage printed in Venice, and may have been the first one printed, but no copy is now in existence. According to Girolamo Priuli, it was published in 1501. The statement made by Il Cretico that the fleet proceeded for two thousand miles along the coast of Brazil after leaving Porto Seguro has caused discussion among some historians of this voyage. In considering this statement, it may be well to remember that the letter was written largely from hearsay and is inaccurate in many particulars. If we accept what Il Cretico states we must deny that of other authorities generally considered more trustworthy, who definitely affirm the contrary.

Il Cretico seems to have sent his letter to the Doge at Venice, then Agostino Barbarigo. A copy was evidently also sent to the Doge through Pietro Pasqualigo and a second copy through Pisani. The introduction to the letter sent by Pisani as given by Sanuto is as follows : "Most Serene Prince, I believe that Your Serenity has learned through letters of the Magnificent Ambassador, Domino Piero Pasqualigo, Doctor, the chapter of the letter of Missier Cretico, Doctor, who is with the kingdom of Portugal, of the 27th of July in Lisbon.", Then follows the letter that Il Cretico sent to Venice as given in Paesi. The letter as sent by Pisani, however, is dated the 27th of July 1501, instead of the 27th of June, as given in the version of Cretico's letter printed in Paesi. The former date is evidently an error.

It is given in the diaries of Marino Sanuto and Girolamo Priuli. It was included among the letters in book vi of the first edition of Paesi novamente retrovati, and in subsequent editions and translations.

Another secretary who accompanied Pisani to Spain was Angelo Trevisan di Bernardino. Trevisan had been secretary of Domenico

Malipiero, the Venetian annalist, in 1489 and in 1498 when the latter was purveyor to the Venetian armadas. Malipiero was interested in the recent Spanish and Portuguese voyages, and, taking advantage of this opportunity, he requested his former secretary to secure for him such information as he could regarding them. Trevisan used every effort to do so. He became personally acquainted with Columbus and with Peter Martyr, who had by this time accumulated many notes for his Decades. While Peter Martyr was in Egypt in 1501, obtaining a treaty from the Mameluke for the protection of the Holy Land, Trevisan had access to his papers, and sent to Italy a portion of his first Decade, which was published in Venice in 1504 and known as the Libretto. Trevisan asked Il Cretico, when he was in Lisbon, to obtain for him information concerning the Portuguese voyages, and particularly regarding the fleet of Cabral, which was then expected. Trevisan wrote several letters to Malipiero telling of what progress Il Cretico was making in response to his request. Upon his return to Spain, Il Cretico brought back with him information regarding the voyage of Cabral. In one letter written from Exigia in September Trevisan states that Il Cretico had come well informed in regard to the voyage to Calicut and was at work composing a treatise that would be very fine and acceptable to those who are pleased with such things. This is the basis for the belief that Il Cretico compiled or at least translated a portion of the anonymous Portuguese narrative, which was sent to Malipiero and possibly also to others in Venice, and which was printed in the Paesi in 1507. The letters of Trevisan, a text of the narrative of Cabral's voyage generally called that of "The Anonymous Pilot", a translation of a letter written by Dom Manuel to the Spanish sovereigns in 1501, and others relating to the Spanish voyages have been preserved in Malipiero's papers. They were presented to the Venetian Senate, and then passed into the possession of the patrician Jacopo Soranzo, whose library was later dispersed. Part of it passed into the hands of a priest, the Abbé Canonici, and part into the library of Amadeo Sviger. The Canonici library, at the beginning of the last century, went to England, and was incorporated in the Bodleian Library. The Sviger library was divided between the Marciana Library and the Archivio di Stato in Venice, the library of the Counts Mannin in Passeriano, and that of the Reverend Walter Sneyd of London. It is in this last collection that the letters of Trevisan relating to the voyage of Cabral were later to be found. When Guglielmo Berchet was compiling his monumental work on Columbus he located these letters and published them together with the first part of the Anonymous Narrative. The portions of the Trevisan letters referring to the voyage of Cabral or to Il Cretico translated in this volume are from the texts as given by Berchet.

Another letter was sent to Venice at this time, written by Giovanni Francesco de Affaitadi. The Affaitadi family had for many years held a high position in Cremona as bankers and merchants. At some time before the discovery of America they established a branch at Lisbon, as did other Italians, to secure a portion of the trade that the Portuguese were developing in their African and island possessions. Here the Affaitadi engaged at first in the sugar trade with Madeira, but with the return of Cabral's fleet they became interested in that of spices. Giovanni Francesco de Affaitadi, the head of the house at Lisbon, held a position as a Venetian merchant similar to that of the Florentines, Bartolomeo Marchioni and Girolamo Sernigi. Affaitadi, because of his wealth and his commercial and banking connections, occupied almost a diplomatic position at Lisbon, so that on the return of Cabral's fleet he wrote a letter to the Signoria concerning it. He was asked by Pietro Pasqualigo, the Venetian oratore, upon his leaving Lisbon, to keep the Venetian Republic informed of the results of later voyages to India.

****

Il Cretico's letter

Copy of one chapter of the letter of D.Cretico, Nuncio of the most illustrious Signoria of Venice in Portugal

Dated the 27th of June 1501

Most Serene Prince, etc., I believe that Your Serenity has learned through letters of the Magnificent Ambassador that this Most Serene King has sent ships on the voyage to India. These have now returned, but of thirteen that went, seven were lost on the voyage. In the first place, Most Serene Prince, along the coast of Mauritania and Getulia towards the south as far as Cape Verde, which in ancient times was called Hesperia, where the Islands of the Hesperides are; here begins Ethiopia, and from here on it was unknown to the ancients; from here the shore of Ethiopia runs towards the east, so much so that it corresponds to the line of Sicily. From the said coast there are nine degrees, five or six of them this side of the equinoctial line. And in the middle of the said coast is la mina of this Most Serene King, and from there on a cape, extending nine degrees beyond the tropic of Capricorn, stretches towards the south. This cape is called that of Good Hope. Then comes the breadth of Barbary. From this place more than five thousand miles of shore stretch inward towards us. From this cape it extends again towards a cape called Prasim Promontorio by the ancients. The other side thus far was known to the ancients. From here again it runs almost directly east to the Trogloditia, where there is another vein of gold that they call Zaffala. There the ancients affirm is a greater quantity of gold than anywhere else. From here they enter the mar Barbarico, and then into that of India and then arrive at Colochut [Calicut]. This is their voyage and it is more than fifteen thousand miles but, by cutting across, they shorten it somewhat. Above the Cape of Good Hope towards the west they have discovered a new land. They call it that of the parrots, because some are found there that are an arm and a half in length, of various colours. We saw two of these. They judged that this was mainland because they ran along the coast more than two thousand miles but did not find the end. It is inhabited by nude and handsome men. On their voyage they lost four ships. Two, they sent to the new mine; they judge that these are lost. Seven went to Colochut, where at first they were well received; and a house was given them by that lord. Some of the ships remained; the others went to other places near by. And afterward came the Sultan's merchants, who were angry because they had interfered with them and wanted to load first. The factor of this Most Serene King complained to the lord (of Colochut), who was of the opinion that he should come to an understanding with the Moors, and said that if they took on a cargo he should take the spices away from them. As a result of this they came to blows, and all the land favoured the Moors. They ran to the house assigned to the Portuguese, and they cut to pieces all who were (within and) on the land. Those were about forty. Among them was the factor who had thrown himself into the water to escape. When the other ships, which were ten, learned this, they came and destroyed the people of the

sultan, and with their artillery they did great damage to the land and
burned a number of houses, because they were covered with straw. On
account of this uproar they departed from Colochut and were conducted
by their guide, who was a baptized Jew, to another land about forty
miles farther on, called Cuzin [Cochin], belonging to another king,
enemy of the King of Colochut. He made good company with them and
has a greater supply of spices than there is at Colochut. They took on a
heavy cargo (they loaded seven ships with spices) at a price I fear to
tell, because they declare they have obtained a cantara of cinnamon for
a ducat and less. This lord of Cuzin sent his ambassadors with these
ships to this Most Serene King and also two hostages, who returned in
safety. On their return the Moors and people of Colochut made plans to
capture them and armed more than one hundred and fifty small ships
with more than fifteen thousand men. However, since they had cargoes,
they did not wish to fight. Those could not attack them because these
sailed with a side wind that they could not use. In coming they reached
an island where is the body of Saint Thomas, the Apostle. The lord of
this treated them very kindly, and, having given them relics of the
aforesaid saint, asked them to take spices from him on credit until the
return voyage. They were laden and could not take more. They have
been fourteen months on the voyage but only four on the return, and
they say that in the future they can make it in eight months or ten at the
most. On the return voyage six of the seven ships came back safely; the
other ran upon a shoal. Its people were saved. This one was of six
hundred botte (and richly laden). Up to this time there has arrived only
one of three hundred botte; the others, are near, it is said. This one
arrived on the eve of Saint John. I was with the Most Serene King, who
called me and told me that I might congratulate him because his ships
had arrived from India, loaded with spices; and so I rejoiced in due
form with him. He had a feast held in the palace that evening and a
ringing of bells throughout the land (city), and on the following day he
had solemn procession made throughout the land. Afterward, when I
found myself with His Majesty, he referred again to his ships and he
told me that I should write to Your Serenity that from now on you
should send your ships to carry spices from here. He would make them
welcome and they could feel that they were at home. And he would
forbid the Sultan to go for spices. He wishes to put forty ships in this
trade, some going, some returning. In short, he feels that he has India at

his command. This ship that has returned belongs to Bartholomio, a Florentine, together with the cargo, that consists of : pepper, about three hundred cantaras; cinnamon, one hundred and twenty cantaras; lac, fifty or sixty cantaras; benzoin, fifteen cantaras; of cloves they have none because the Moors had carried it away, nor ginger either because it does not grow in the place where they took their cargo, but only at Colochut. There are no small spices of any sort. They say that they lost many jewels during the disturbance at Colochut. Also, this should not be omitted : that the ambassadors of a king of Ethiopia, named King of Ubenam, came here. He has sent a present to this Most Serene King, of slaves and ivory teeth, although such things have been coming here for some time. Near there also grows pepper, but it cannot be compared with the other. Moreover, this ship, on its return, met two very large ships that had left the new mine and were going towards India. They had a great amount of gold, and because they feared that our men desired to capture them they immediately offered fifteen thousand dobras. Each (ship) was worth more than five hundred thousand. But our men did not wish to seize anything; instead, they offered them presents and good will, for they wished to be allowed to navigate those seas.

Angelo Trevisan's letter

Extracts from the letters of Angelo Trevisan to Domenico Malipiero

From Granada, the 21st of August 1501 :

Furthermore : We are daily expecting our doctor from Lisbon, who left our magnificent ambassador there : who at my request has written a short account of the voyage from Calicut, of which I will make a copy for Your Magnificence. It is impossible to procure the map of that voyage because the king has placed a death penalty on any one who gives it out. This is as much as I can do now for the service of Your Magnificence, and if it seems possible to do more, command me.

From Granada (without date, but probably in September 1501) :

In regard to the desire of your magnificence to learn of the voyage to Calicut, I have written you at other times that from day to day I am expecting Messer Cretico, who writes me that he has composed a small work. As soon as he arrives, I will see that Your Magnificence has part of it.

From Exigia, the 3rd of December 1501 :

Messer Cretico, also a loyal servitor of Your Magnificence, renders thanks that you have deigned to salute him so kindly in your letters, and commends himself to you greatly, congratulating you from his inmost heart on your good fortune. He comes from Portugal at the end of this September, well informed concerning the voyage to Calicut, and is continually working on a treatise that will be very fine and acceptable to those who are pleased with such things.

If we return to Venice alive, Your Magnificence will see maps both as far as Calicut and beyond there less than twice the distance from here to Flanders. I promise you that everything has come in order; but this, Your Magnificence may not care to divulge. One thing is certain, that you will learn upon our arrival as many particulars as though you had been at Calicut and farther, and Your Magnificence will be made a participant in everything, as perhaps others will not.

Letter of Giovanni Francesco de Affaitadi

Letter of Giovanni Francesco de Affaitadi to Domenico Pisani

Lisbon, the 26th of June 1501,

Magnificent Orator, etc.

Several days ago I wrote through Zuan Vesiga, but today we have yours in which you instruct that we give an account of the expedition of the armada of this Most Serene King. Although Missier Cretico will have written also, I wish to give news of the departure of this armada, that left here the 17th of June, and on the 18th was at Lacus [Lagos] in the land of Algarius [Algarve], which is forty leagues from here. From that place, Lacus, we are advised that on Monday last the said armada was increased by many ships and many men, and as I was advised through a letter of last Sunday, more than two thousand men were added from the Kingdom of Algarius in addition to those who went from here with the ships that departed. The reason that this king sends this armada to this place of the Moors, is to capture it. And this was done on Saint John's Day, by an assault on land. This is as much as is known of the aforesaid armada to the present day. It is expected that they will then pursue the route to which they were assigned. May God grant them victory.

Your Magnificence will know that in the afternoon there came one of the small ships that in January arrived at Colocut, which place is that whence spices are expected. And because I know that you will be pleased to hear the news that they bring, I shall advise how this Most Serene King sent to the said Coloqut twelve ships, large and small, of which ten were his own, one of Signor don Alvaro in partnership with Bortolo, a Florentine, and Hironimo and a Genoese, and the other of Conte de Porta Alegra and also certain other merchants.

In all there were twelve ships, large and small, of which, at the beginning, when at a distance of eighty leagues, one of the ships of this king was lost, of which there has never been any news. The other eleven pursued their voyage, arriving at a place called Cavo de Bona Speranza. One day in July, after dinner, there arose a great wind so that by this accident there were lost three other ships belonging to the king and the small ship of the Conte di Porta Alegra. Thus there remained only seven. These continued until they arrived at Coloqut. I may also say that before they arrived at Coloqut, they went along the coast a distance of one hundred leagues, arriving at a place where the king did them great honour and sent them supplies of meat, lambs, and other presents. They then went to Coloqut. The captain had a talk with the king of that place, and in the name of this Most Serene King, made him presents of many things, so that they became great friends. And the captain returned to the ship and he instructed the chief factor, with the other designated officials, that they were to remain on land; and they began to contract and to exchange their merchandise. At that time there was to be found in the said place of Coloqut a fleet of ships of the Moors of Mecha, who were there to load spices. One day the Moors and the factor of the king came to a misunderstanding, one saying that he wished to load before the other, and the Moors killed twenty-five or thirty of the principal Portuguese, among whom were the chief factor and writers and certain frati de observantia whom the king sent in the said armada. Some of those who were on land threw themselves into the sea. They swam to the ships and gave notice of what had happened to the captain, who ordered all ships ready to sail. And he began to bombard the Moorish ships, resulting in sending about twelve ships to the bottoms and killing more than three hundred Moors. This done, he began to fire the bombards towards the shore and killed many people, burning many houses. And the next day they captured many of the men of Coloqut and took them to their ships. The captain deliberated as to returning here. A Jew, whom the other captain brought when the first voyage to Coloqut was made by this king, who was sent in this armada, but who all this time was never permitted to go on shore, told the captain not to return, but to go some seventy or eighty leagues farther, which would bring him to the proper place where spices grew. This place belongs to another king. The captain, after considering the proposal of the Jew, determined to do what he said, and he ordered them to sail towards this place which this man told him of, so that he arrived at this land, which is called Chuchi [Cochin], where the captain sent men on shore to talk to the king of this land and to relate to him what had happened in Coloqut. The king of this land is a great enemy of the King of Coloqut, and on learning this he sent four of his most important men to the ships, in exchange for four others whom the captain sent on shore. And they began to trade, so that in nine days all seven of the ships were loaded with spices, namely, cloves, cinnamon, nutmegs, pepper, and other kinds of spices. And after the ships were entirely laden, the king sent another fourteen small boats of spices, and they returned them because they could not carry them. This the king sent them as a gift, without money or anything else in exchange. The King of Coloqut, while this armada went to load at this place, because he was an enemy of that other king and doubting if the traffic of Coloqut would be of sufficient importance, ordered a large armada to be sent to capture the ships of Portugal. In this armada went more than fifteen thousand men. The King of Chuchi, who learned the news of this armada, informed the Portuguese captain, making him a great offer to save him as much as he could. And the latter took his departure, while the four men from the ships who were on land remained there, and the four others of the land who were in the ships came here with the said ships. And this they did with great friendship. One day while the said ships were ready to leave, to start on their return voyage, the armada of Coloqut appeared, and those of the ships spread sail and, having a favourable wind, left behind the armada of Coloqut because those ships did not sail unless they had the wind astern.

In Coloqut were gathered together a great value of things that had already been purchased. There always existed on the voyage thither a great sum in these ships of the king. The fame of the riches of this king is so great that a third part is a large thing. After they had left Chuchi, as has been said before, when a distance from the said place of two hundred leagues, they found another land called Lichinocho [Cananore], and there lived a very rich king, who sent presents to the captain and sent him two ambassadors who came to the King of Portugal. Leaving this king, they departed on their voyage and came to Zofala. In this place they say there is a great trade in gold. And of the twelve ships, the king ordered that two should go to this land. But when the four ships were lost they were obliged to go to this land of Zofala. They continued and one day there was a great wind, so that one of the seven ships went aground; and the people were saved. The captain ordered the said ship to be burned with the merchandise. When they arrived at the Cape of Good Hope, the captain ordered all the other ships to join together and they went together for three or four days. He then ordered that this one that has come, because it was the best sailor, should leave the others and should come to give news of those ships to this King of Portugal. And so it was done. This ship that has come is the smallest of all, and it belongs to Signor Alvaro and the three other merchants named above. It is the poorest of all the others; it carries three hundred cantara of pepper and two hundred of cinnamon, nutmegs, lac, and benzoin; and bears news of these things, namely, that all come laden.

This discourse I have made to advise Your Magnificence of the success of this matter of Coloqut. The above news was obtained from a mariner of the small ship that has arrived, which ship is still at Restello and is daily expected here. It is understood that another is expected who is advised of everything in particular, etc.

This letter arrived in Venice the middle of the month of July 1501

CHAPTER 23

THE VENETIAN DIARIES

Four Venetians, Domenico Malipiero, Marcantonio Michieli, Girolamo Priuli, and Marino Sanuto have left a record in the form of diaries that give us an intimate knowledge of what appeared to them of interest in their city, almost day by day, from 1457 to 1535. It is in two of them, those of Girolamo Priuli (1476-1547) and Marino Sanuto (1466-1533), that is found, to a large extent, the information that reached Venice regarding the voyage of Cabral. The portions of the diaries of Malipiero and Michieli that now exist contain no references of importance to the Portuguese voyages.

****

Extracts from the diary of Girolamo Priuli 1501- July

Previous to the 24th of this month letters had come from Portugal from a nuncio of the Venetian Signoria, sent to that place on purpose to learn minutely the truth of the voyage to India begun by that king.....which event was of greater importance to the Venetian state than the Turkish war, or any other wars that might have affected her. This nuncio wrote to the Venetian state by his letter of the 6th of June last as follows. This letter was printed, which is the same as that herewith.

[Here follows in the text of Priuli the letter of Il Cretico. This is also given in Paesi and in the diary of Sanuto.]

At this point is finished the copy written to the Venetian state as is stated above, from a person worthy of belief. However, I leave it to the most intelligent readers as to how it appears to them, for in this letter are many things of great wonder in our times and almost incredible, that give me something very instructive to consider; but time will better enable us to understand the truth. But if God will lend me life, I shall endeavour to note the result so far as it can be understood, for already so much has been found out that nothing more can be learned now than infinite time desires should be known. It is understood, further, how the

above-mentioned King of Portugal sent with the aforesaid ships coral
and cloths of every kind, and money to the value of 60,000 ducats
[provided] by the aforesaid king and other merchants for this voyage to
India. And how much profit was derived from it, it is not possible to
judge, because the spices have been taken to Portugal. It is true that
seven ships were lost; nevertheless the other six which have arrived
home have carried so much spicery for so much value of treasure, that
it is almost difficult to judge it. I can say for the profit, that from one
ducat they can make more than one hundred. But every intelligent
person should know there was not so much profit as is written, but at
any event it was great. And if this voyage should continue, since it now
seems to me easy to accomplish, the King of Portugal could call
himself the King of Money because all would convene to that country
to obtain spices, and the money would accumulate greatly in Portugal
with such profit as would follow each year from similar voyages. When
this news was truly learned in Venice, the whole city was much stirred
by it, and every one was stupefied that in this our time there should
have been found a new voyage that was never heard of or seen in the
times of the ancients or of our ancestors. And this news was held by the
learned to be the worst news that the Venetian Republic could have
had, to lose the liberty abroad. And the wars and the travails that we
now have and for some time may have, are of the smallest moment in
comparison with this news. And for this reason I wish to tell the truth
and not to deceive. There is no doubt whatever that the city of Venice
came to such reputation and fame as it now enjoys only through the
sea, namely by the continual traffic and navigations that it has made by
the voyages, because they carry each year a large quantity of spices
with their galleys and ships, so that very great damage would be done
to deprive them of it. And as is said, the whole world flocked to Venice
with ducats to buy spices and other needs, and also placed their goods
there. Whence through the arrival of foreigners and through the traffic
of selling and buying each year and in every trading season, the city of
Venice has come to this excellence that it has attained, and only
through these voyages and this maritime traffic. And this they have
gained by the sea, and with this they have also been able to sustain the
war and acquire the state on the mainland as is seen. The reason why
the profit from the terra firma is very bad, as well in war as in forced
service, is that they consume as much as they raise.

Therefore, now that this new voyage of Portugal is found, this King of Portugal will bring all the spices to Lisbon. And there is no doubt that the Hungarians, Germans, Flemish and French, and those beyond the mountains, who formerly came to Venice to buy spices with their money, will all turn towards Lisbon, for it is nearer to all the countries, and easier to reach. And for this reason they will have a better market because all of this is of importance. And this is because the spices that come to Venice pass through all of Syria and through all of the countries of the Sultan. And in each place they pay very large duties and similarly in the Venetian state they pay unsufferable duties, presents and excises. Therefore, through the countries of the Sultan, extending to the city of Venice, the presents, duties, and excises are so great that I might say this, that whatever costs a ducat would be multiplied in price by these to the amount of sixty or one hundred ducats. That is, I say, that which costs a ducat in Calicut with the duty, presents, and excises mounts as above said. Therefore, the King of Portugal, having found this voyage the other way round, would alone have the spices of the caravels, which they would import for much less in comparison with the other spices mentioned above, and for this reason they could give the spices a much better market than can the Venetian merchants; furthermore, it is shorter to conduct the spices to Flanders, Hungary, England, France, and other places from Portugal than to carry them from Venice. It may be said in conclusion, that assuming this voyage from Lisbon to Calicut has begun, the spices in the Venetian galleys must lessen and also the merchants. And when this traffic in merchandise is lessened in Venice, it can be considered that the milk and nutriment of Venice are lessened to a putino. And because of this I see clearly the ruin of the Venetian city, because as the traffic lessens, so lessens the money that has produced the Venetian glory and reputation. Many still believe that this news cannot be true; others say that the King of Portugal could not continue this navigation to Calicut because of the thirteen caravels sent on the voyage to India only six returned in safety, and that the loss is greater than the gain; and that furthermore he will not find people who, for fear of life, will wish to go. Others comfort themselves, saying that the Sultan will provide for all this, because when the spices do not arrive in Syria and Alexandria, that he will lose the great treasure and profit that flowed from this, and because of this he will be incited to make all provisions regarding it.

Others, furthermore, say to their profit, that always in places and large cities both ingenious persons always find something to say in favour of their belief and ill-wishers have things to say about things that may do harm. This is the only thing that matters, and it is of greatest importance, because with this news spices of all sorts will descend in price greatly in Venice, for the usual customer on learning this news will be restrained and obstinate in buying, as would the prudent ones. I know I have said and written too long regarding this matter. I beg the reader that he excuse me, and chiefly because I have written in a confused and poorly adapted manner. For of the new matter and its great importance to our country, I have made what little transport to the pen as was appropriate. I am tired.

1501-August

On the 23rd of this month there departed from Venice three large galleys on the voyage to Flanders. The Captain was Sier Alvixe di Prioli. These galleys had about 150 bales of spices : namely, 33 bales of pepper, beledi ginger 100 bales, cloves 12 bales, and other kinds of spices to complete the amount; still they had little spices. And this was because the Venetian merchants, hearing this news of the Portuguese caravels coming from India, judged that the spices that arrived in Lisbon must go to Flanders, as seems reasonable, and everything would be lower in the West, because of this news. And this was the reason why very little spices went with the present galleys, compared with similar galleys. From many sources it is learned in Venice how the caravels coming from Calicut to Portugal have not arrived, save one, as is related before, and that the others, not being with it, are believed to be lost. And the above-mentioned caravel, which has arrived, has not as much spices as is said. And much comment is made regarding this, particularly by those who would desire that this voyage should not be found. And it is said further, that the King of Portugal was poorly satisfied with this voyage, and through the loss of these caravels he will lose this year, with these caravels on this voyage, 50,000 ducats, and that he does not wish to send this voyage again. And every one has his own opinion. And they retain similar hopes which are all vain, because this voyage to Calicut, which the King of Portugal will make every year, will become frequent and cause the ruin of the Venetian state.

1501-September

On the 9th of this month letters came from Lisbon of the 1st of August. And through letters from Genoa and Lyons and other parts, it is learned that the caravels that were expected loaded with spices are in Portugal.

Three of the said caravels came from Calicut and one from the gold-mine which had a large quantity of gold. And the above mentioned caravels had such a quantity of spices as is related above. Still it is variously reported, some say more, and some less. One report is that there was a very great quantity of spices, chiefly pepper and cinnamon, and a little beledi ginger; others say that there were 3,000 cantara of spices in all. And one cantara is 150 lire in weight. Nevertheless, it matters little now what the quantity of spices is; but the importance is the finding of the voyage and the trade, which each year will carry a large quantity of spices. This news, as has been said above, was considered very bad news for the city of Venice, and some very wise people are inclined to believe that this thing may be the beginning of the ruin of the Venetian state, because there is no doubt that the traffic of the voyage and the merchandise and the navigation that the city of Venice made each year thence, are the nutriment and milk through which the said Republic sustained itself. And without doubt, from this traffic and voyages, because of the profit that each year is derived from them, the Venetian senators have risen to such honour and glory and fame and exaltation to which they find themselves. Whence it is that the King of Portugal has found this new voyage, and that the spices which should come from Calicut, Cochin, and other places in India to Alexandria or Beyrout, and later come to Venice, and in this place become monopolized, whence all the world comes to buy such spicery and carry gold, silver, and every other merchandise, with which money the war is sustained; today, with this new voyage by the King of Portugal, all the spices that came by way of Cairo will be controlled in Portugal, because of the caravels which will go to India, to Calicut, and other places to take them. And in this way the Venetians will not be

Page 219

able to take spices either in Alexandria or Beyrout. And when the spices lessen to the Venetians, then will also lessen the profit and the money. And, in consequence, when the money is less, they will not be able to do things that would be good; and little by little it will be consumed until it is exhausted. Still, this is a presumptuous prognostication, since the heavens may dispose otherwise. And truly the Venetian merchants are in a bad way, believing that the voyages should make them very poor, doubting whether spices would be obtainable in Syria because they would be taken in India. And later the German merchants and other nations who are accustomed to come to buy the spices in Venice, because they can have cheaper and better merchandise, will go to Portugal to secure the spices because each one seeks his own profit. At all events the results of this matter will demonstrate the effects.

1501-September

On the 14th of the said month, letters came from Portugal, from Lisbon, from the Venetian secretary, of the 4th of last month, regarding the caravels come from India; through which confirmation is learned of the arrival of four caravels loaded with spices that have returned from Calicut with 3,000 cantara of spices : namely, 2,000 cantara of pepper, which is, in our method of loading, 800; 600 cantara of cinnamon; the rest to the total between ginger, sandalwood, and benzoin; and with one cantara equal to 150 of our lire. The King of Portugal did not, in truth, show much contentment with this voyage; and this because of the caravels that were lost and shipwrecked, and the death and drowning of the men; and he said that because of this voyage, he would lose 80,000 ducats. Still, the said king is preparing 24 caravels to send on the said Indian voyage anew, and he says that he wishes the said caravels to go farther beyond Calicut than on the past voyage; and this is because the King of Calicut did not make good company with his people who went with the ships. From which it can truly be held as certain that this King of Portugal should become a great lord of money discovered through this voyage, because he will find all the spices of India in such quantity that spices will no longer come into the hands of the Moors, either in Cairo, or in Syria; and the course of merchandise will become diverted to Lisbon, where the spices will be, and every one will go there to purchase, and all merchandise of all parts of the world, with the money, will flow to Lisbon to buy like spicery, because it is easy to go from Flanders and other places, as well as to have there a better market. The before mentioned Venetian secretary also wrote how, in the equipment of the said caravels, there was no difficulty in finding men who wished to go on the voyage. And this, although they might perish, since last year, as appears above, many caravels were lost; still such was the great gain, that people put themselves in danger of life because of the gain. In fact, the king from Lisbon, to repair the loss received in the past voyage, as appears above, has made a requirement that on all the spices which with other things that should come with the aforesaid caravels in the Indian voyage, there should be paid, or rather given to the king, 29 per cent, and the remainder the merchants of the caravels could sell at his command. How much damage this voyage made to the Venetian city has been related above; nothing further need be said.

1501 - September.

On the 19th day of the said month through letters of the Venetian orator, who arrived at Lisbon, in Portugal, to that Most Serene King, seen and honoured and accepted with all demonstrations and with very large words of that king of friendship and goodwill for the Venetian state, etc., all pro orma, it is learned of the arrival of the Portuguese caravels come from Calicut in India, regarding which so much has been said above. And many merchants and others in Venice in the past have not wished to believe it; until now that they see the letters of the orator, they are enlightened with the quantity of spices above mentioned. And on this day, also in consonance with this news, through letters from Bruges in Flanders, there is learned that two caravels have arrived in that part, come from Portugal with spices brought from Calicut, and that they have begun to sell. The pepper is somewhat green and small, but still good; the cinnamon is somewhat large. So that this can be considered the beginning of the damage that the Venetian state can receive from the voyage found by the King of Portugal.

Extracts from the diary of Marino Sanuto

On the 22nd of February 1501 Dom Manuel wrote a letter in Latin to the Venetian Doge, Agostino Barbarigo, in which he offered an armada to aid the Venetians against the Turks. In this he uses his new title, which was confirmed by the Pope in 1502, 'King of Portugal and of the Algarves on this side and beyond the sea in Africa, Lord of Guinea, and of the Conquest, Navigation and Commerce of Ethiopia, Arabia and India'. This letter was sent to the Doge by Domenico Pisani, with a letter written from Lisbon on the 13th of March. In it he tells of the ancient friendship between the two states and refers to the congratulations that the Doge had sent to Dom Manuel regarding the marriage of his majesty. On the 23rd of March he again writes of the preparations being made for the fleet of João de Menezes and makes the following reference to that of Cabral.

The 23rd of March 1501. He writes further that a year ago the King of Portugal sent thirteen caravels to Calicut for spices, and they say that they are expected shortly; and he is jubilant to have found the way to the spices. And the king told them that as a consequence of this he would derive great benefit. And there are now in port four other caravels with merchandise for Calicut, and they will depart in three or four days. The way is very long; it is four thousand leagues, sixteen thousand of our miles; and he has talked with men who returned with the caravels that went as above.

From Spain, from Sier Domenego Pixani, the cavalier, our orator [without date, but placed in July 1501]

He writes of the progress of the armada of the King of Portugal that went to Calicut and of the caravels that returned with spices; and he sent the copy of a letter received from Lisbon of the 26th day of June of Zuan Francesco Afaitado which, because it is very long, will be noted later. And this news of the arrival in Portugal of spices from Coloqut gives to those of this land much to think of : especially considering that the other six ships that were in convoy with this caravel are daily expected, and the merchants are fearful of their ruin.

August 1501. From Alexandria, through letters of June in those of the Bragadini, of San Sovero and Sier Beneto Cabriel.

The news of the spices of India arrived in Portugal is verified : and that the Moors in Cairo have learned that ships and caravels have arrived in Coloqut and loaded with spices : and the Moors wishing to disperse them, forty Franks are dead.

On the 30th of September [1501] there arrived here a royal orator of Spain going to the Sultan of Cairo who embarked on our Alexandria galleys. It is said that he goes to pray the Sultan to release the brothers of Monte Syon and to treat them well; and that thirty thousand Moors of Granada are baptized of their own wish, and not by compulsion.

Copy of a letter of Sier Filippo Contarini to Sier Vetor Querini, dated in Alexandria the 4th day of September 1501.

[This letter begins with a list of commodities both for import and export at Cairo with the current prices. It then gives a description of the disordered rule of the Mamelukes, which necessitated the closing of the Moorish shops, and of the large sums of money given to the eleven thousand or twelve thousand slaves in Egypt who belonged to that class.]

Regarding the things of India and Calicut. In the first place : we have word of the arrival safely there of eight Portuguese caravels, with merchandise and money. And while engaged in buying and selling, Moorish merchants overcame them and drove them from there. And they told the said lord that these were corsairs and men of bad character and that he should not sell anything to them, and if they continued to come it would be the total ruin of his country. In this manner they convinced him with many other reasons. And they so knew how to say such things that the people became excited, and they gave them arms, and forty of those Portuguese who were on shore are dead, and in this manner they put them to flight. The boats took sail and all are departed. And according to what they write, they have loaded eight hundred schibe of spices in their ships. And they almost departed without paying the said Indians or giving them anything in exchange. On the contrary. This is as much as I have been able to learn through a Moorish letter written by the nephew of Amath Bubacho who had gone to India, as a canzelier.

From Spain, from the Orator, given at Saragossa, the 12th day of October [1502].

How the princes had not yet arrived; and the Queen is in Castile, where it is said she will be to provide for the war against France. And through another letter of the 12th this orator writes that he has had letters from Lisbon, from Zuan Francesco Ascaitato, of Cremona, of the 10th of September. He advises that the four ships expected from India that left eighteen months ago have not arrived; and the caravels sent last year to discover la terra di Papagá or rather of Santa Croce, returned on the 22nd day of July; and the captain referred to having discovered more than 2,500 miles of new coast and never having found an end of the said coast. And the said caravels have come laden with brazil-wood and cassia, and they have brought other spices, etc.. I note that as to the news from Calicut, on the 13th day there arrived at Lisbon the caravels with spices, which news is in the hands of Sier Alvise de Molin.

CHAPTER 24

CA' MASSER'S ACCOUNT OF THE VOYAGE

Under the pretext of engaging in business in Lisbon, a Venetian named Leonardo Massari, better known as Ca' Masser, arrived there on the 3rd October 1504. According to Heyd, Ca' Masser is the abbreviation for della casa dei Massari. Ca' Masser was actually sent to Portugal by the Venetian senate to secure information regarding the fleets that were being sent to India, and to make a report concerning their cargoes and other matters of interest to that Republic. Venetians, were suspected at this time in Lisbon, perhaps because so much information regarding the Portuguese voyages had been sent to other places. In spite of the secrecy that Ca' Masser maintained, his true mission was known to Dom Manuel through a Florentine, Benetto Londa, a nephew of Bartolomeo Marchioni. On the arrival of Ca' Masser in Lisbon, he was immediately called to the royal palace. Here the king questioned him at length, and as a result had him sent to prison. Later, when he was able to convince the king that the story he had first told him was true, Ca' Masser was released and had no further difficulties. Ca' Masser remained in Portugal for two years, and upon his return to Venice made a report concerning the first nine voyages to the East, in which he gave much information regarding the cargoes and trade conditions, as well as an interesting description of the court of Dom Manuel. The following is a translation of his account of Cabral's voyage.

****

On the 9th of March of the year 1500, His Highness sent 13 ships, large and small. The captain was Pedralloro and one Ali Scorer as his factor, with the said Gaspar. And he went on the voyage around the Cape of Good Hope. On the way there overcame him a sudden storm, through which seven ships were lost and there only remained six ships, which continued their voyage to India. The first stop where they had commerce was in Chuchim, and there they treated with that king, who showed that he was glad that they navigated in that part, and he became a good friend of this Most Serene King. And he put on shore the said factor, Ali Scorer. And thus for his security, the Portuguese made a fortress there on a point of the Chuchim river as a habitation for the said factor and security for his merchandise, so that the Portuguese enjoyed some security. And there he contracted with the King of Chuchim copper and other small merchandise and money, and took in exchange spices, strong pepper K 2,000 [K is the abbreviation used by the Venetian for cantara, about one hundred pounds]. And he returned thence to Lisbon in 1501 on the 29th of July with six ships, which were on the voyage about 18 months. On this same voyage in returning from Chuchim, the said captain with the said factor, Ali Scorer, went to Colocut and had a talk with that king, and the factor went on shore with certain merchandise. And the King of Colocut made him a certain factory where the Portuguese could live and place their merchandise securely on land. And there being good harmony between the factor and the King of Colocut, the king showed a desire to trade with them in his land, and this was agreed to by the factor with about 47 men. After some days, three or four Portuguese came to words with certain Moors, of which many live in this land. And this was because certain Portuguese had done some violence to a certain Moor, so that the said Portuguese were wounded. These suddenly ran to their factory, and many of them came out armed against the Moors. And all the Moors who were found there committed many outrages. And because the captain took, the day before, a sambuco of 300 Moors, all the Moors united with great fury to go against the said Portuguese and entered within their factory and cut to pieces all the 47 men with the factor. And from this there grew a war between the King of Colocut and this Most Serene King of Portugal. And the King of Colocut had three Portuguese hostages in his house for security, who made the king understand how they had been inconvenienced by the Moors. It is certain the said king had the greatest displeasure at such inconvenience, and was very sorry for it, and tried to find some provision so that he might punish those who were malefactors. But there was such a large number (it was said there were 5,000 Moors), and all was turmoil in the land, that the king could not follow it farther. When the chief captain of the ship learned what had occurred on shore, he suddenly commenced to bombard the land and ruined many houses on the face of the shore. With this there was born the war with the King of Portugal.

CHAPTER 25

CABRAL'S LATER YEARS

On Pedro Cabral's return preparations were immediately made for another and larger fleet that was being assembled as quickly as possible to sail to India in 1502. Pedro Cabral was appointed by Dom Manuel to command the new fleet. For eight months Cabral worked to complete these preparations, but adverse circumstances prevented him from profiting by this appointment, because at the last moment he was superseded by Vasco da Gama.

Various reasons for this change have been given by the historians. Castanheda states that on Cabral's return the king determined to send a large armada to Calicut to avenge the massacre. Vasco da Gama, with whom the desire for revenge was always a strong motive, told the Rajah of Cochin that his reason for wishing to come to India a second time in command of a fleet was that he might take vengeance upon the Rajah of Calicut because of insults put upon himself.

Cabral was at first selected to command this fleet, but "for some just reasons it was given to Vasco da Gama". De Goes states that Cabral was offended and refused the position because the five ships of Vicente Sodré were excluded from his command. Barros also alleges that Cabral was dissatisfied because Vincent Sodré was to have command of a section of the fleet independently of the Capitão-mór and that he begged to be relieved of the command. Even should the view of the matter taken by Barros be the right one, there would still be no question of disgrace nor even of royal disfavour.

Corrêa asserts that Vasco da Gama interposed and produced a letter from Dom Manuel that authorized him to claim the chief command in any fleet destined for India even if it were anchored at Restello and ready to sail and that he desired to exercise this right on that occasion. The king, who had been greatly moved by the news of the various disasters to the ships of the fleet commanded by Cabral and of the massacre of Portuguese at Calicut, listened to the request of Vasco da Gama, expressed his desire that Cabral should not proceed to India and promised that he should have command of the next Indian fleet. Corrêa tells us that it was the queen who insisted that Vasco da Gama be given the chief captaincy. We know that there was an active feud between the partisans of Vasco da Gama and those of Pedro Cabral, and that Cabral left the court never to return. Whether Pedro Cabral committed some act that offended the king, or whether da Gama finally persuaded Dom Manuel to live up to his agreement and thus caused the enmity of Cabral, we do not know; but there certainly existed a hostility between the two captains that so annoyed the king that on one occasion, when it was discussed in his presence, a partisan of Vasco da Gama was banished to Arzila for life.

Cabral did not again participate in public affairs but retired to his small estate at Jardim, near Santarem. The annual allowance of 13,000 reals, confirmed in 1497, was still paid and a further grant made. There exists a mandate to pay 13,000 reals to Pedraluarez and the agent's receipt for that amount dated 4th of April, 1502, and another mandate to pay him 30,000 reals with the agent's receipt of the same date. In these documents Cabral is styled 'Fidalgo da nossa Casa,' but a higher honour awaited him.

About two years after his return from India Cabral married Dona Izabel de Castro, who was related to some of the best families in Portugal, and through her received some addition to his income. She was descended from Dom Fernando of Portugal and Henry of Castile. Her father was Dom Fernando de Noronha, and her mother, Dona Constança de Castro, was a sister of Afonso de Albuquerque. Prior to her departure from court with her husband, she was a lady-in-waiting to Queen Maria, and she continued to retain her standing at court while in seclusion. Cabral had six children : Antonio Cabral, Fernão Álvares Cabral, Constança de Castro e Noronha; Guiomar de Castro, Izabel and Leonor.

Cabral merely seems to have spent his time quietly at the royal city of Santarem or in the immediate neighbourhood of that picturesque town. He had landed property there and there is extant a royal letter - too lengthy, verbose, and involved in its composition to be reproduced here - in which Cabral is authorized to submit to ecclesiastical arbitration a dispute with a certain Antão Gonçalves regarding the exchange of certain property belonging to Cabral at the place called "O Logo do Pereiro" for the Quinta do Recio belonging to a Chapel in the Monastery of São Francisco at Santarem. The document is dated 17th of December, 1509. In the same year another royal letter confers certain privileges, the nature of which is not defined, in consideration of military service to be rendered by Pedraluarez, who was also to furnish horses, men and arms whenever the king should require him to do so :

"Dom Manuel etc. To all judges and Magistrates of our Kingdoms and officers and inhabitants of the comarca and judicial district of Estremadura and to all other officers and persons whom the knowledge hereof concerns in any degree whatsoever and unto whom these our letters patent or an extract thereof shall be publicly shown by authority and by command of the justiciary, Greeting : Know ye that, desiring to show grace and favour to Pedro Aluares Cabrall, resident in the town of Santarem, fidalgo of our household, etc., and having seen letters of approval signed by us by virtue of which it pleases us to grant him the benefit of the privilege hereafter following in consideration of his being prepared to serve us in war with his horses, arms and men whenever for our service we command him, we hold it to be right and we command, etc. Given in due form at Evora on the 18th day of February by the king's command to the Bishop of Guarda, etc. Joham Aluarez drafted this in the year 1509."

The source of this document is Torre do Tombo - Chancellaria de D. Manuel, liv. 44 °, fl. 62. (Frey Gonçalo Velho, I. p. 300).

In 1518, or perhaps prior to that date, Pedro Cabral was appointed a Cavalleiro do Conselho and as such he enjoyed a monthly allowance of 2,437 reals in addition to his other emoluments. However, Pedraluarez was not destined to enjoy his honour for long nor did he live to see his nephew Governor of India.

In the same year his eldest son, Fernão Alvarez, was in receipt of a moradia as a "moço fidalgo". This son married Margarida Coutinha, daughter of Dom Gonçalo Coutinho, and was made a Commander of the Banho in the Order of Christ. It is through Fernão Álvares Cabral whom the family line descended. The second son Antonio subsequently died in 1521 unmarried. One daughter, Constança de Castro, was married to Nuno Furtado, Commander of Cardiga. Another daughter, Guiomar de Castro became a Dominican at the Convent of Santa Maria da Rosa in Lisbon, and subsequently died whilst prioress. Pedro Cabral's other daughters, Izabel and Leonor, became nuns.

There existed three documents of the year 1520 (3rd of November, 3rd of November, and 5th of November) that were registered in the Chancellaria of Dom Manuel, bestowing annual pensions of 30,000 reals upon Izabel de Castro and of 20,000 reals upon Antonio and upon Fernão Alvarez Cabral :

"Dom Manuel, etc. To all to whom this our letter shall come we make known that, having regard to the many services that we have received and in future expect to receive from Fernã dAlurz Cabrall, our young noble, son of P° dAllrz Cabrall, whom may God forgive, and desiring to show him grace and favour, we hold it well and it is our good pleasure that he receive and hold from us a pension from the first day of January next of the year fifteen hundred and twenty-one thenceforward and for as long as it shall be our good pleasure of twenty thousand reals annually, wherefore we command the Comptrollers of our Exchequer to have this letter registered in our books of the Exchequer and to give notice in writing each year of the place where he may have due payment and for his protection and to keep us in remembrance hereof we command this our letter, signed by us and sealed with our pendant seal, to be given to him. Given in our city, the city of Evora, this fifth day of the month of November - Jorge Frz drafted this - in the year fifteen hundred and twenty."

The source of this document is Torre do Tombo - Chancellaria de Dom Manuel, L° 39, fl. 6o. (Trabalhos Nauticos, II. p. 140.)

It is possible to determine the date of Pedro Cabral's death with approximate accuracy. He was alive, as we have seen in 1518 and there existed three documents of the year 1520. In these, the name of

Pedraluarez occurs followed by the words 'quem Deus perdoe,' signifying that he was dead.

He died therefore in 1518, 1519 or 1520, most probably in 1520, for the pensions would probably be bestowed very soon after his decease. He was buried at Santarem in the Chapel of Saint John the Baptist in the Church of the Convent of Santa Maria da Graça, later converted into the Hospital of São Antonio. An inscription in Gothic letters upon a stone in the pavement of the Chapel marked the position of the place of burial of the family. The inscription was as follows :- "Aquy Jai pedraluarez cabral e dona Jsabel de Castro sua molher cuja he esta capella he de todos seus erdeyros aquall depois da morte de seu marydo fui camareyra môr da infanta dona marya fyllia de el rey dõ João nosso sñor hu terceiro deste nome." (Here lie Pedraluarez Cabral and Dona Isabel de Castro his wife whose chapel this is and that of all their heirs; she, after the death of her husband, was First Lady of the Bedchamber to the Infanta Dona Maria, daughter of Dam João our Sovereign Lord, the third of that name.)

A vignette of Cabral in armour engraved by Abrantes after a portrait by Cunha was to be seen in 'Elogios e Retratos'. It is there said to correspond with the portrait in the palace of the Velho family which, as has been already stated, was connected with the Cabraes by marriage.

Pedro Cabral's grave was opened in 1882 to verify the remains. The resting place of the discoverer of Brazil had no adequate memorial, nor could it be readily seen by the public.

It would not perhaps be unjust to describe Pedraluarez Cabral in the language of the stage as the under-study of Vasco da Gama. And yet his contribution to the knowledge of the geography of the southern hemisphere, however blindly made and as it were by haphazard, is of scarcely less importance than that made by Vasco da Gama himself. If it was a great achievement to cross the South Atlantic for the first time and for the first time to lead a fleet from America to Asia, Cabral must be placed amongst those who have achieved great things. And the importance of his expedition is enhanced by the fact that in the course of the voyages made by captains engaged in it, Madagascar was visited for the first time by Europeans and Sofala and the Gulf of Aden for the first time by the southern route.

Undeterred by the unprecedented losses that he had sustained, Cabral, when he reached the East African coast, pressed forward to the accomplishment of the task that had been assigned to him and was able to inspire the surviving officers and men with like courage. "India must be won" had been the king's command and all the Portuguese of that day, as well those who of necessity stayed at home as those who ventured abroad, appear to have been prompted by the ambition that inspired that command. In India, Cabral faithfully carried out the king's instructions and succeeded in opening a factory at an Indian port and in establishing permanent friendly relations with two petty sovereigns on the Malabar Coast.

The voyage met with many disasters and losses in men and ships; yet no Portuguese historian places any blame on Cabral. He was certainly not responsible for the loss of the ship of Vasco de Ataíde near the Cape Verde Islands, nor for the sinking of the four ships during the storms in the South Atlantic; neither can he be blamed for the straying of the ship of Diogo Dias, nor, according to the accounts of the later chronicles, for the insubordination of Sancho de Tovar, which caused the loss of his ship and cargo.

The voyage of Cabral added amazingly to man's knowledge of the Atlantic Ocean and especially to his knowledge of the climate of the South Atlantic and enabled the right season for sailing to India to be selected. This knowledge was bought at a stupendous cost but Cabral cannot be blamed for that nor for the fact that an insight into the true character of the Moplahs and of the vacillating Rajah of Calicut had to be bought at great cost also.

Cabral's position in the history of Portuguese conquest and discovery is inexpugnable despite the supremacy of greater or more fortunate men. He will always be remembered in history as the chief, if not the first discoverer of Brazil. It will perhaps never be known to what extent that discovery was fortuitous and to what extent it was deliberately planned.

Pedro Álvares Cabral appeared in history only for a few months and there are few discoverers about whom we know so little. From a position of comparative unimportance at the Portuguese court he was selected to fill one of the greatest moments in the history of his country. Since the Portuguese people had expected too much from it, the voyage was not regarded as a success, and this view has perhaps been adopted by historians. In the light of its results, however, it stands out as one of the greatest of Portuguese voyages.

BIBLIOGRAPHY

The following are the principle English language sources of information concerning Pedro Cabral. They also contain references to the original sources of information :

Pedro Cabral (James MacClymont, William Brooks Greenlee, Pero Vaz de Caminha) [2009] - Biography of Pedro Cabral, documents concerning him, the discovery of Brazil, the discovery of Madagascar, documents concerning Pedro Cabral and the voyage, and all of the known contemporary accounts of the voyage.

Pedraluarez Cabral (Pedro Alluarez de Gouvea) : his progenitors, his life, and his voyage to America and India (James Roxburgh McClymont) [1914] - Biography of Pedro Cabral, and documents concerning him.

The Voyage of Pedro Alvares Cabral to Brazil and India [1937] (translator and introduction - William Brooks Greenlee) - Brief biography of Pedro Cabral, the discovery of Brazil, the discovery of Madagascar, documents concerning Pedro Cabral and the voyage, and all of the known contemporary accounts of the voyage.

http://viartis.net/publishers

FOR MORE BOOKS BY VIARTIS